Political Bargaining

Political Bargaining

Theory, Practice and Process

Gideon Doron
and
Itai Sened

SAGE Publications
London • Thousand Oaks • New Delhi

© Gideon Doron and Itai Sened 2001

First published 2001

 SAGE Publications Ltd
6 Bonhill Street
London EC2A 4PU

SAGE Publications Inc.
2455 Teller Road
Thousand Oaks, California 91320

SAGE Publications India Pvt Ltd
32, M-Block Market
Greater Kailash - I
New Delhi 110 048

British Library Cataloguing in Publication data

A catalogue record for this book is available from the British Library

ISBN 0 7619 5250 0
ISBN 0 7619 5251 9 (pbk)

Library of Congress catalog card number available

Printed in Great Britain by Athenaeum Press, Gateshead

Contents

List of Figures and Tables

Figures

Tables

List of Commonly Used Symbols

N	The set of all relevant players or agents in a game
O	The set of all possible Outcomes
i, j	Generic members of the set N of all relevant agents
a,b	Generic elements in the set O of all possible Outcomes
$\in$	An element of or a member in
$i \in N$	i is a member of the set N of relevant players in the game
$a, b \in O$	'a' and 'b' are elements of the set O of all possible Outcomes
$\forall$	For every member or for all members in a set
$\forall i \in N$	For every member i of the set N of relevant agents in the game
σ	The Strategy Space specifying all possible combinations of strategy choices by all the relevant players in the game
σ_i	The Strategy Choice Set of player i
σ_i	A particular strategy of player i
$\sigma_i \in \sigma_i$	A Strategy of player i is an element of i's Strategy Choice Set
$\sigma = (\sigma_1,...,\sigma_n) \in \sigma$	A Strategy Vector specifying a particular combination of strategy choices for all the relevant players in a game
$\sigma \in \sigma$	A Strategy Vector is an element in the Strategy Space of the game
$\sigma = \sigma_1 X...X\sigma_n$	The Strategy Space is often expressed as the Cartesian product of the choice sets of all individuals involved in the game
$\subseteq$	Subset
$\subset$	Proper Subset

$C \subseteq N$	A Coalition C of relevant agents is a Subset of the set N of all the relevant agents in the game
$bR_i a$	Outcome 'b' is weakly preferred by agent i to outcome 'a' or 'b' is at least as good for agent i as outcome 'a'
$bP_i a$ $\equiv$ $bR_i a$ but not $aR_i b$	Outcome 'b' is strictly preferred by agent i to outcome 'a' which is logically ($\equiv$) equivalent of saying that 'b' is at least as good for agent i as outcome 'a' but outcome 'a' is not as good for agent i as outcome 'b'
$bI_i a$ $\equiv$ $bR_i a$ and $aR_i b$	Agent i is indifferent between outcome 'a' and outcome 'b' which is logically ($\equiv$) equivalent of saying that Outcome 'b' is at least as good for agent i as outcome 'a' and outcome 'a' is at least as good for agent i as outcome 'b'
$\Pi: \sigma \Rightarrow U \subseteq \Re^n$	The pay-off function Π is a mapping from the strategy space σ to the utility space U. Each individual assigns a utility $u_i(\sigma)$ to any strategy vector $\sigma=(\sigma_1,...,\sigma_n) \in \sigma$. This utility may vary from $-\infty$ to ∞. The uni-dimensional line, $\Re$, represents this range. Therefore U, the utility space of all agents involved in the game is a subset of this the n-dimensional $\Re^n$ space
$u_i(\sigma)$	The utility agent I gets when a vector σ of strategic choices is the strategic choice of the relevant agents in the game
$\Gamma = \{N, \sigma, \Pi\}$	A game is denoted by Γ and is defined by three primitives: The set of relevant agents, N, the strategy space σ that defines all possible combinations of strategic choices that individual agents can choose and Π, denoting the pay-off function
ρ_i or x_i	i's ideal, most preferred point
$0 < \delta_i \leq 1$	A fixed discount factor that denotes the extent to which the value of the 'pie' diminishes with every round of bargaining
$f(\beta)$	A common prior belief where $f(\beta)$ is a probability density function, that denotes the belief agents have about the probability that the number β, is any integer $k \in Z = \{0,1,...,n\}$
$\sigma_{-i} = (\sigma_1,..., \sigma_{(i-1)}, \sigma_{(i+1)},...,\sigma_n)$	A vector including the strategy choices of all the players relevant to the game except player i
$U \subseteq \Re^n$	The set of feasible utility n-tuples vectors, the utility space

$U=(u_1,...u_n)\in U$	A utility vector with u_i denoting the pay-off for $i\in N$
v	The characteristic function (or correspondence) that assigns to every subset of players a vector of pay-offs (or a set of vectors of pay-offs) that this subset of players (or 'coalition') can allocate to members of society
$v(C)$	A *characteristic function* of the coalition C, $v(C)$, is a collection of utility vectors, such that if C can guarantee u_i to any member, $i\in N$, then **u** is in $v(C)$
$\Gamma=(v,N,U)$,	*A game in characteristic function form* where v is the characteristic function, N is the set of all agents and $U \subseteq \Re^n$ is the utility space
R_i	A preference order of individual *i*. It is a *weak preference order* if it is complete, transitive and reflexive (see definitions in the text)
$\Re = \{R_1,...,R_n\}$	A set of preference orders of individuals in society, often referred to as the *preference profile* of individuals in society
R (without a subscript)	The preference order of society. We would like to be able to aggregate $\Re$, the *preference profile* of individuals in society, into **R**, a *weak social preference order*. The aggregation should take into account, at least to some minimal extent, the preference orders of the individual agents in society. We call such an aggregation scheme, a social preference function (SPF) denoted by $S(\Re,O)=R$
$S(\Re,O)=R$	A social preference function (SPF) that determines the social preference relation **R** between every pair of outcomes $a,b\in O$, given the preference profile, $\Re$, of agents in society, and the set of feasible outcomes **O**
D_s	The set of decisive coalitions. Formally, D_s is defined as: $D_s = \{ C \subseteq N: \forall\, a, b \in O,\ \text{if}\ \forall\, i \in C\ aP_ib,\ \text{then}\ S(\Re,\{a,b\}) = aPb\}$
$u_i(x) = \varphi_i(\lvert x-\rho_i\rvert)$	The utility $u_i(x)$ that agent *i* derives from an outcome $x\in\Re^m$ is assumed to be a function φ_i (that is specific to agent *i*) of the Euclidean distance between x and ρ_i, where ρ_i represents the most preferred outcome, or ideal point, of *i* in $\Re^m$
$y\sigma_{(U)}x$	Coalition $C_r\subseteq P$ is decisive by σ if for any utility function **U** and any pair $x,y\in\Re^m$, if all members of C_r prefer **y** to **x** – write $yP_ix\ \forall\ i\in C_r$ – **y** is preferred to **x** by σ, which we denote by $y\sigma_{(U)}x$. In this way a voting rule σ can define the set of decisive coalitions D_σ

$C(\sigma,U)$	The core in a weighted voting game σ, given U, is defined as: $$C(\sigma,U) = \{\, y \in X \mid x\sigma_{(U)}y \text{ for no } x \in \Re^m \,\}$$
Ψ	A common belief about the electoral responses to different vectors of party positions.
$C(x,y)$	A binary choice procedure between any pair of outcomes x and y
$\bigcap\limits_{y \in R^m} C_m(x,y)$	The intersection of all binary choices between x and any $y \in \Re^m$. The core includes any x such that x $$\in \bigcap\limits_{y \in R^m} C(x,y)$$
$x = C_m(x,y)$	Majority rule is a binary choice procedure where x = $C_m(x,y)$ if and only if the number of members who weakly prefer **x** to **y** is greater than the number of those who prefer **y** to **x**
$x \in$ $\bigcap\limits_{y \in R^m} C_m(x,y)$	**x** is in the majority core. If **x** is a binary majority winner against all other alternative outcomes, then **x** is in the majority core

Preface

The science of politics is the study of human interactions in what we call the 'political sphere.' The distinction, however, between the 'political' and other forms of human interaction is for the most part arbitrary. Political science is a distinct scientific discipline not because it deals with an autonomous domain of knowledge, but because a sufficient number of scholars are willing to address similar questions and problems, to conduct research by recognized methods, and to convey their ideas in a certain way. In other words, there exists a corpus of academics who are interested in producing and sharing ideas about what they define as the science of politics.

Political science is in many ways a parasitic discipline. Taking the observations and perceptions of the Greek philosophers as the foundation for its study of the legal aspects of society and its institutions, political science borrows ideas and tools from the entire scientific realm. Moving on from the essentially normative endeavor of defining good and bad and what ought to be, it now predicts and shapes what is and what will be. It is in the context of its current manifestation that our book must be read and understood.

Perceiving reality as composed of individuals who have to develop certain arrangements for living and working together is at the core of the discipline described here. These arrangements are either constructed voluntarily by individuals or they are imposed upon them. Politics then, deals with thought-guided arrangements arrived at by continuous struggle within real and perceived constraints. The specific human context often affects the kind of arrangements reached. In this sense, the United States or Canada are political arrangements that emerged on a national level and assumed a certain form. But so are the Polish government, the British parliament, the coalition of parties in Denmark, or the congressional lobby that was formed to shape legislation for equal rights. Arrangements are made at the local and regional level, between groups and nations, between individuals, and between individuals and various types of collectives. These arrangements may be explicit or implicit, building upon sets of ideas rooted in the minds of the individuals. Often, the products of human interactions translate into durable institutions. Guided by laws, regulations, and norms, these arrangements help individuals obtain their goals.

Underpinning this general view of politics is an understanding that individuals differ in age, sex, belief systems, tastes, preferences, interests, aspirations etc.

Despite these differences, they opt to live together and to subject themselves to a particular collective arrangement. In fact, it is often the political arrangement that serves as the principle means by which they bridge their differences. This bridge is constructed by finite or ongoing processes of bargaining.

The process of political bargaining is, then, the real stuff of politics. This book reviews various modalities of bargaining reflected in different forms of human interaction. From the hypothetical 'state of nature', we move up through higher manifestations of human aggregation until we reach the institutionalized political level. This book is concerned with the process: its setting, the interests of the players involved, the conditions and properties that affect their calculations and, consequently, their ability to obtain desired outcomes.

Surprisingly, very little systematic attention has been paid by political scientists to the theoretical study of political bargaining. Whilst many scholars of economics, game theory, organizational theory, international relations and psychology, view bargaining as an important tool in their fields, we have found no study that describes this phenomenon as central to the study of political science. In this respect, we present an innovative approach to the study of politics. Our goal is to present this approach and at the same time to introduce the basic methodological tools necessary for an understanding of this analytical framework. Following the example of our teacher, William H. Riker, in his *Liberalism against Populism*, we try to provide the reader with a tool box, whilst at the same time providing clear guidelines as to how it can be used. We also have to admit to sharing our fundamental world-view with the reader, for which we apologize in advance.

Of the many colleagues, friends and students who assisted us with comments and suggestions on various drafts of this manuscript, space and professional restraint enable us to credit only few. Much of the hard work in putting this book together was supported by NSF grants SBR 94-22548 and 96-17708, and Ben Gurion University in the Negev. Anat Shenker and John Ginkel carefully combed our manuscript. Gary Miller and Christina Fong made many helpful suggestions along the way. Steven Brams, Douglass C. North, Norman Schofield and Kenneth Shepsle continue to inspire us. But, to paraphrase Isaac Newton, if we saw a bit further it is because we stood on the shoulders of a giant, those of our beloved teacher, William H. Riker, to whom we dedicate this book.

On a personal note we want to thank Lucy Robinson, our editor at Sage Publication for her patience and support for this project and Susan Kennedy, our English editor, and Jonathan Nadav our technical editor. We thank our parents and children for keeping it all in humble perspective. Last but not least, Gideon Doron thanks Becky Kook and Itai Sened thanks Sarit Smila for the wisdom and kindness they exercised in the important role they played in our lives during the period we spent researching and writing this book.

Gideon Doron and Itai Sened
Tel Aviv and St. Louis

Introduction

This book reviews various modalities of political bargaining. Except for the introductory chapter, which provides an intuitive account of political bargaining, it is written in the tradition of formal political theory. That is, our arguments are carefully defined in the language of logic and mathematics. Hence, their validity may be examined in terms of their internal and external consistency. The untrained reader may skip the technical derivations and results presented, and concentrate on the essence of our arguments.

We start by demonstrating the prevalence of bargaining in social life. Then we define political bargaining in order to distinguish it from other forms of bargaining. We continue by explaining the logic differentiating the two main types of collective bargaining: economic and political, and discuss the principle factors affecting the process of political bargaining. The last section describes the logic behind selecting an organizing principle that moves from the abstract idea of human interaction to the concrete level of political bargaining.

1 The Prevalence of Bargaining

This book describes the different modes by which people interact with each other so that they can live comfortably together and obtain desired outcomes by an ongoing process of bargaining. This process takes many forms, some requiring action and choice, whilst others are passive and require acceptance of the status quo. Our book is based on the premise that society is a collection of more than one active individual. Since we define society as consisting of at least two interdependent people, this study is concerned more with understanding the nature of the interaction which takes place between individuals than with the internal processes of change which occur within the individual. Limiting the interest in bargaining to social interaction is not very helpful since 'society,' defined in such broad terms, consists of a variety of interdependencies among its members. Thus, to provide a general scientific explanation of the studied phenomenon, one must distinguish between social interaction that involves bargaining amongst the members, and that which does not. Once accomplished, political bargaining becomes a sub-set of social interaction within our intuitively defined 'bargaining space.' The task is now to define a border between relationships within the bargaining space and those human interactions outside that space.

Social interactions in general and bargaining in particular are forever taking place in the imperfect 'human set' and not in 'God's set' of perfect knowledge (Riker and Ordeshook, 1973). They involve an attempt at optimization within certain constraints, such as a lack of knowledge of some components that define the interaction. These include the exact goal of the people involved, the intensity of their desire to obtain it, and the many ways open to them to attain it. By simplifying complex problems, scientists often play God (Hempel, 1966); postulating perfect information in their theoretical models, they evaluate reality in the context of such assumptions. Indeed, 'perfect market competition,' wherein buyers and sellers maximize their utility, or 'frictionless surface,' where physicists test theories, are but two examples of situations that prevail in the realm of the Divine and not in the world we know. In the real world, people do not maximize. They forever optimize, or in Simon's terms, they *satisfice* (Simon, 1957, 1982). Bargaining, then, is a kind of interaction between real people in the real world, who more often than not are unable to reach the best possible outcomes on account of the real constraints within which they operate.

Essentially, bargaining is a process, often structured in a rigid legal form, which involves an exchange of some tangible or intangible valued item. Because of the presence of others, the people involved in the process must accept outcomes that are less than ideal for them, or trade one possible favored outcome for another.

Bargaining takes various forms. Some forms preserve prevailing arrangements and allow people to continue acting as they always have done. Other forms of bargaining ensue changes in these arrangements (Doron, 1996). The actual manifestation of bargaining in the empirical world depends on a multitude of factors: the number of people involved, the nature of their differences, the spectrum of possible outcomes, the varying aspirations regarding the durability of prevailing arrangements. Primary among these factors is the spatial distance and degree of intensity between these differences. At some point, differences among people cannot be bridged and no amount of bargaining, arbitrage or negotiation is effective. For example, when individuals opt for absolute truth as a resolution of their differences, no bridging arrangement can be applied. Protracted religious wars launched in the belief that 'God is on my side' are one such example. In such circumstances, singular or mutual destruction might be the outcome. Politics enters, and a bargained arrangement is found, when the 'absolute' stand is weakened, enabling constructive compromise. Indeed, the term 'politics' is often taken to mean engaging in activities involving tradeoffs, deals, and compromises between unlikely parties.

The need to bargain arises as the mutual desire of individuals to settle differences within explicitly or implicitly agreed upon boundaries. The more intense the prevailing differences, the greater the need for their resolution through bargaining. As explained below, however, such situations often lend themselves to easier solutions. Even the boundaries of familiar entities such as a 'nation,' or a 'state,' in as much as they are fabricated constructs, are products of bargaining (Anderson, 1983). People define the boundaries of these collective entities in different ways; some are willing to include groups inside these boundaries, while others may want to exclude these and others from entering (Kook, 1995). The ultimate outcome of this ongoing deliberation determines both the scope within which further bargaining can be conducted and the identity of the players involved.

From the perspective of bargaining as a channel for various sorts of agreements, one could perceive democracy as consisting of at least two layers of arrangements. One defines the 'rules of the game,' whilst the other determines the rules to be used to change the rules of the game. Non-democratic systems are also characterized by rules. However, these rules hinder or prohibit people from changing the rules in a non-violent manner. Hence, while bargaining is a common feature in all spheres of the democratic game, in non-democracies its scope is restricted to areas that do not affect the game itself. Later in this book we provide an analysis of the internal nature of the bargaining process that takes place within different types of democratic systems (Chapters 5 and 6 ahead).

How do politics and bargaining relate to each other? For the purposes of this book, politics serves both as the context in which bargaining takes place and as a means of bridging differences. The following illustration demonstrates how non-political human interactions evolve into what we intuitively refer to as political ones, and how these are subsequently resolved through bargaining.

Consider a group of unrelated individuals moving freely in a given space. As long as each moves to his or her destination without meeting or crossing the path of another, the inherent differences within the group are politically and economically irrelevant and no conflict of interest is recorded. Now add more people to this space, change their destinations or increase the frequency with which they cross paths. In short, limit the space considerably, or create a real scarcity of time, space or energy. By doing so, you introduce a potential for conflict among the individuals which necessitates some regulating arrangements.

Although we cannot be sure how people will behave under the new circumstances, we can build upon several reasonable assumptions concerning human behavior. Presumably, the individuals would initially attempt to regulate their behavior in a tacit manner so as to avoid unpleasantness. While walking they would watch how others walked, and while driving they would reduce their speed and watch for approaching cars. They would behave according to rational expectations. People know that recklessness may cause fatal accidents, and expect others to share that knowledge, make similar choices and behave accordingly. In other words, an intuitive personal benefit/cost calculation, in the context of risk, determines behavior. One can never be sure, however, that others will make equivalent calculations; and indeed, accidents do occur.

Thus, the field of unrestricted choice is voluntarily limited. Expectations are somehow internalized by the actors and manifest themselves in choices that take the form of regulated behavior, such as giving others the 'right of way.' Accordingly, all drivers going in one direction would drive on a given side of the road and allow others to do so too. A practice, a convention, or a social norm is thus established, and although no mechanism exists to penalize violators, most people follow suit because it is mutually beneficial. No outside intervention or interpersonal bargaining is necessary to develop this practice. It is adopted for convenience. The underlying logic leading people to adopt this framework may be banal: they have seen others doing the same or they are following the example of the car ahead. Even so, accidents continue to occur and further measures are called for to minimize their frequency. At this point some institutionalized coordination among the concerned individuals must be established. The tacit signals that previously shaped behavioral conventions have become insufficient. A more explicit arrangement must be devised, and political bargaining enters into the picture. The bargaining process becomes increasingly comprehensive as a function of the acceleration and escalation of the real or perceived conflict that emerges among the concerned individuals over the shared space. The solutions to this actual or potential conflict are designed in accordance with the intensity of the conflict. For example, if road signs were found to be an ineffective regulatory device, and accidents continued to occur, then additional devices would be required.

There are many questions that arise once the problem moves from the private to the public domain. For example, where and how should the regulatory device be installed? Who should finance its operation? Who should supervise the process of implementation and enforcement? What should happen to violators? Who should protect the drivers against arbitrary decisions made by the policing agency? The arrangement that has been reached must satisfy other important criteria, too. For example, if the operation is conducted with public resources – payments transferred by individuals to a joint pool for the financing of regulatory services – they must be seen as utilized efficiently. Enforcement must be consistent and unbiased so that all violators receive the same punitive treatment. The policing agency must have the necessary authority for people to obey its dictates. In short, many issues, conceptual and technical, directly or indirectly related to the specific issue in question, must be resolved one way or another.

Thus, in order to solve our traffic problem, we have to establish a government. In establishing a government, individuals continue to bargain over the scope and method of conducting their affairs. This process of political bargaining, which defines politics, is the central theme of this book.

2 Political Scarcity and Boundaries

Before demonstrating how political bargaining works, it is important to emphasize one element from the above illustration: that of scarcity. Introducing scarcity into the relevant space caused interdependence among individuals and moved them into the public domain. The science and practice of economics are based on the fundamental axiom of scarcity. Indeed, without that real world constraint and subsequent conceptual identification of scarcity as limiting the supply of a certain commodity, no demand schedules could be established and no price mechanism could exist to determine values and quantities.

Scarcity also shapes the science and practice of politics. The insufficient recognition of its importance in politics stems from the vagueness of the boundaries of the subject matter. Unlike economics, which reflects the empirically constrained world of resources, the study of politics deals with a much more broadly defined subject matter. It studies thoughts, symbols, myths, perceptions, beliefs and freely given statements and opinions. However, without some sort of limitation, real or imposed, on 'the realm of ideas,' it is difficult to compare, rank, measure or judge what is important or relevant for understanding the studied phenomenon. Scarcity defines politics, but does not serve, as it does in economics, as its first or even most basic building block. Scarcity manifests itself in state borders, in the size of public administrations, national budgets, representative bodies, and in the number of parties and size of ruling coalitions (Sened, 1996, 1997). All these factors are finite and can be measured in terms of 'more' or 'less.' It is possible to study and rank such items, and to effect quantitative change in them through a bargaining process. In cases involving, say, national budgets, effective bargaining could yield greater resources to certain groups and fewer to others. Hence, the 'politics of the budgetary process' (Wildavsky, 1974) becomes the prime example of Easton's definition of politics as the realm of 'authoritative distribution of values' (Easton, 1953). Of course, as illustrated above, when values, tangible or intangible, are not scarce, no distribution is required and consequently there is little need for politics. In other cases, such as those concerning the composition of the ruling government, coalition-builders bargain for fewer members, realizing that smaller structures generally provide greater benefit for each participant (Riker, 1962).

Scarcity and limitations on a given resource are somewhat less recognizable when one moves to the realm of ideas. How can one deal with ideas when they could, potentially, be generated by anyone at any given moment? But the reality is that they are not. In every society there are various screening mechanisms set up to decide what is important, essential, interesting and consequently durable. *A priori* prediction of what elements would be durable in the 'realm of ideas' is impossible. However, the various screens transform this intangible realm into a real 'market,' whose characteristics are similar to those associated with tangible markets of scarce resources. Within this bounded market a bargaining process can prevail.

Several human factors ignite the process of bargaining. These factors are related to people's attempts to minimize actual and potential uncertainties, and to maximize certain desires. For example, the search for individual and collective identity, a prevalent topic in recent scholarship on 'nation building,' is presumably a product of the need of individuals both to obtain and to transmit certain familiar signals to others in their immediate environment. Familiarity, then, may evolve into a joint pattern of behavior, interests, tastes or even political preferences (Simmel, 1955). Those who share similar identities, be they religion, ethnicity, or gender, at times self-defined as 'we,' position themselves next to or against the 'them,' often utilizing the political sphere to preserve and perpetuate these differentiated identities (Buber, 1966).

The struggle to contain uncertainties takes many forms. It manifested itself, for example, in the erection of defense mechanisms against potential threats to the group's survival. Such threats could come from internal or external sources. Solutions to external threats are usually military, whilst internal ones are the police and court systems (Epstein and Knight, 1997). To finance and maintain these mechanisms, people pay with their labor, material resources, or obedience.

They do so willingly, following the dictate of their governments, because the alternatives are perceived as less beneficial. This is essentially the origin of the notion of rights and obligations (Sened, 1997).

The questions to be asked then are: what is the scope and what are the kinds of uncertainties one is freely choosing to avoid, and what are the types of tradeoffs people willingly make between particular sets of rights and obligations. The answers to such questions become the essence of collective life. They are purely political. Indeed, people stay and submit themselves to governance by other people in organizations, churches, local communities, or in their nations because these institutions provide partial answers to their needs. In exchange they restrict and alter their behavior and/or pay other dues. The determining factors in how much and to what extent these tradeoffs are made is arrived at by a continuous process of bargaining between the individuals and these collectives.

Over time and in different places these tradeoffs may yield different outcomes. In all places they reflect the nature of the regime. In dictatorships people are willing (or coerced) to obey the directives of one person and in an oligarchy of several. This willingness persists as long as the exchange of desired values made between the rulers and their subjects maintains some equilibrium. As David Hume suggested, even a despotic regime must be sensitive to the desires of its subjects (MacIntyre, 1988; Sened, 1997). In democracies, the prevailing equilibrium is tentative, by definition, because citizens preserve the option to replace their rulers. Thus, the highest level of bargaining intensity between government and citizens takes place before election time. During this period, the bargaining relationship is reflected, for example, in the levels of government expenditure on the domestic budget.

But a government's performance is examined continuously. The quality of public policy-making and the adaptation of laws and regulations provide citizens with information with which to assess their government's performance. Governments are attuned to this constant assessment and decisions are adjusted accordingly. This book analyzes the nature of the bargaining process in terms of the relationship between governments as producers of public policy and the public as their consumers.

In democratic regimes, competition over the distribution of scarce resources is conducted between political entrepreneurs who articulate the messages of specific groups, bringing them to the public agenda and to the deciding bodies (Ainsworth and Sened, 1993). This in itself is a bargaining process conducted between individuals who opt for one or another form of distribution. This is also the essence of party politics, and viewed from the perspective of bargaining, it is one of the areas given careful consideration in this book.

In short, bargaining prevails in most aspects of the phenomenon we choose to define as 'political.' This is because, in order to move from the private to the public domain, from the singular to the plural, it is necessary to bridge prevailing differences among the individuals involved. The bridge is necessary because the elements, over which these differences exist, whether tangible or intangible, are scarce and somehow bounded by particular constraints. Individual choices are thus affected, and collective outcomes shaped, by this bargaining process.

3 Political Bargaining: A Non-Technical Definition

Bargaining in its broadest sense is a constant social phenomenon. The mere fact that a myriad of individuals is able to live together and interact implies that some explicit or implicit process of bargaining underlies collective interaction. It is our task here to reveal this process, in so far as it is relevant to our understanding of the political phenomenon.

Bargaining takes place when two or more players – individuals, organizations, parties, corporations or states – make a tangible effort to reach an agreement over the mode of allocation, distribution or redistribution of scarce resources. The process need not be structured or verbal. It takes many forms consisting of many elements. When the process is structured and verbal, commanding the presence of all involved parties, say, at a bargaining table, we usually refer to it as negotiation moving towards a formal or informal agreement.

Like the term bargaining, the adjunct term 'political' can also be defined in its broadest sense to include, for example, some elements of interaction occurring between husband and wife, or parents and children. In this book, however, we use the narrow and widely accepted definition of politics advanced by David Easton as the domain of 'authoritative allocation of scarce resources.' Combining this with our definition of the term 'bargaining,' we define 'political bargaining' as 'a tangible effort made by two or more agents with some conflict of interests to reach an agreement over an authoritative allocation of scarce resources.' Note that by introducing the notion of authoritative allocation of scarce resources, we get a clean distinction between political and economic bargaining. The equivalent definition of 'economic bargaining' may be: 'a tangible effort, made by two or more agents with some conflict of interests, to reach an agreement over allocation of scarce resources through the price mechanism.' These two definitions highlight the difference between the study of economics and the study of politics. Economics is the science of market allocations effected through the price mechanism. Political science studies allocations of scarce resources in the 'political sphere,' where price mechanisms are unlikely to succeed as reliable mechanisms for bargaining. Therefore, different mechanisms of hierarchical and coercive authority are introduced into a state to facilitate the bargaining process that would presumably fail if it relied solely on the free market and the price mechanism. We return to this point below, when we discuss the theme of this book.

4 Factors Affecting the Political Bargaining Process

All political bargaining situations are characterized by some common elements. The most important are: players, differences of interest, interdependency, time factors, rules of progress, agreed solutions and method of enforcement.

Players

The number of players varies from one situation of political bargaining to
another. To make a bargaining situation 'political,' at least two agents must be
involved. It is, of course, possible to consider a situation in which only one
person is involved. This is the area which Brams (1980) analyzes in 'Biblical
Games' and 'Super-being,' where God is an active player making strategic
decisions that affect the choices of the human player (Brams, 1980). Von
Neumann and Morgenstern (1944) began the construction of their seminal game
theory as applied to economic behavior with one person playing against nature.
The study of single individuals who position themselves against God, nature, a
lottery or some other non-human mechanism, belongs to the field of decision
theory and is not dealt with here.

At the other extreme, all members of a given society can be seen as involved in
a bargaining process, whether in theory or practice. In this respect, the process of
voting can be viewed as the manifestation of political bargaining. Likewise, a
government's distribution of public goods is affected by the policy makers'
perceptions of people's priorities, with the understanding that satisfying public
demand enhances political support (Sened, 1997). Bargaining in the various
policy areas occurs on a daily basis in the form of a continual feedback between
givers and receivers, intensifying and peaking, as noted before, as the day of the
election approaches (Tuftee, 1978).

Between these two extremes, political bargaining can involve two players – as
in the case of two states attempting to define their geographical borders – or a
few players who, for example, attempt to form a political coalition. It is of the
utmost importance to identify the number of players involved. When two players
bargain with each other, the solution they may reach is quite different from the
one that could be obtained when both bargain in the presence of a third player.
Additional players may provide honest arbitrage or impose constraints on the
process, guiding it in a direction that is not compatible with the interests of the
two players. Likewise, while cooperation may or may not occur in a bargaining
situation involving only two players, collaboration is almost always present in
cases involving more than two players. The temptation to build an alliance with
some against others is generated by the positive incentives to be obtained by
combining forces. The process of coalition building is a defining characteristic of
political bargaining (see Chapter 5 below).

Players need not just be individuals, whose preferences, desires and interests
require settlement through bargaining. Organizations of various forms can also
be engaged in the process of bargaining; states negotiate with other states,
governments with other governments and labor unions with their management.
Thus, for analytical convenience, we follow the so-called *as if* principle.
Accordingly, organizations or other types of human collectives are perceived *as
if* they behave like 'unified actors' (Bueno De Mesquita, 1981). Utilization of
this principle as a conceptual tool assigns to organizations attributes that one
usually ascribes to individual players. Hence, using 'players' or 'agents,' as the
prime unit of analysis provides wider theoretical possibility.

Differences of Interest

The process of political bargaining is aimed mainly at bridging existing differences between the agents involved. These agents may have differences of interest, taste, preferences, values, or belief systems.

Our intuition usually dictates that the smaller the difference between individuals over the same value or good, the easier it should be to bridge it through bargaining. But it is hard for an outsider to determine whether a difference is large or small. An objective assessment of the differences between individuals may not reflect the subjective perceptions of the people involved. It is thus impossible to conduct an interpersonal comparison of utilities, which is a measurement of the intensity of preference held towards a given value.

But the fact that it is not wise to engage in interpersonal comparison of utilities does not mean that we cannot distinguish between different situations by the intensity of the conflict of interests. Interestingly enough, extreme levels of conflict of interest do not necessarily lead to the breakdown of the bargaining process. It is often the case that through bargaining, radical differences lead to faster and more satisfying solutions. For example, consider a cake made of two layers, one chocolate and the other strawberry. Two people are to divide this cake. If both have a strong preference, say, for the chocolate, then they would have to bargain over the question of who gets what part of the cake, and arrive at a solution. This solution may not provide complete satisfaction for either party. If they had distinct preferences, then each would obtain one of the two layers with minimal negotiation and high satisfaction (Brams and Taylor, 1996).

When two or more players are involved in a bargaining situation, a range or set of possible solutions could be identified and the empirical outcome could fall at any point within this range. This range of solutions to a bargaining situation allows scope for the art of bargaining. Given the number of solutions possible, it would depend on the maneuvering skills of the players involved as to which prevailed. Interpretations of moves, threats, counter-threats, timing, trust, commitments, loyalty, experience, patience, creativity, the ability to misrepresent one's preferences or lie about future moves and intentions, are all components in the bargaining process.

Interdependency

To be able to bargain, the individuals involved need to have something in common that they all value even if their interests are diametrically opposed. Consider the Hegelian idea of the master and his slave. The master exploits the labor of his slave, who in turn values his freedom. Their interests, so it seems, are completely different. Yet, by definition, they are locked in an interdependent relationship. This is because, among other things, the identity of the master and his own welfare depend on the labor his slave provides. This mode of dependency provides some sound advantages and protection to the slave. For example, the master cannot disable the slave. It quickly becomes unclear who is more dependent on whom for sustenance (Edwards, 1967: 438-9).

This type of Hegelian interdependency prevails in human interactions more generally. Management may dismiss its strikers only to lose vital, experienced, labor. A winning party may eliminate future elections, only to face violent overthrow by an unsatisfied public. Similarly, a dictator who is insensitive to the desires of his subjects cannot wish to achieve a 'perpetual peace' in Kantian terms and prolong his reign, and must use means other than fear to pacify the people (Kant, 1963). Likewise states, even the most powerful, cannot violate at their own will the recognized sovereignty of other states. As Sadam Hussein discovered so vividly during the 1991 Gulf War, international order is often as important as personal ambition.

Thus, some basic level of interdependency is a necessary condition for bargaining. In some fundamental sense, all individuals are interdependent. The air above us is shared; its preservation constitutes a common interest. The fact that so many individuals, organizations, and states irreversibly pollute the air and destroy the environment presumably has to do with the human propensity to maximize benefits in the short-term while ignoring long-term effects.

Time Factor

Time is an important consideration in the bargaining process (Rubinstein, 1982). It may serve strategic as well as tactical considerations. Strategically, the time framework is usually decided prior to the initiation of the bargaining process. Tactically, within the said framework steps are taken to delay or speed up the process. In the event that involved parties agree to implement their solution at or before some fixed date, agreement must be reached as to when this will be. This point in time becomes the subject of bargaining. The following illustration may clarify the difference among varying concepts of time in bargaining processes.

Employers wishing to improve the welfare of their workers must assess whether their demands should be accepted or turned down. If they are turned down, the workers could strike to coerce management to change its mind. Before deciding to strike, workers' leaders must calculate the resources that management has at its disposal. If management sees the cost of the strike as more significant than the demands of the workers, then striking would be an effective weapon. In addition, workers' leaders must assess the level of support they can obtain from their own workers, from the families of the workers and from other workers in the same organization or in other organizations. They also have to assess the amount of support they can expect from the local and national unions, the media, their political representatives, and from the public at large. In addition, they have to evaluate the potential response of management. What is the likelihood that management will give in? Can management withstand a great loss in revenue and for how long? Can management mobilize other workers to cross the line and would they do that? Would they use the courts, media and the public to oppose the strikers? Of course, there are many other considerations on both sides, but those specified above are sufficient to construct two strategic choices for each of the parties. Figure 0.1 below is one possible representation of the conflict between the workers and management.

Players	Management		
	Strategies	No Compromise	Compromise
Workers' Union	No Compromise	1,1	4,2
	Compromise	2,4	3,3

Figure 0.1 The Management–Workers' Union Chicken Game

What mode of confrontation could one expect given the information in Figure 0.1? First, workers may initiate a strike without specifying a time limit and vow to continue striking until all their demands have been met. On the other side, management may decide, as a matter of principle, to ignore all their demands. The two sides would then dig into their position until everyone is bankrupt. This is situation (1,1). The outcome is clearly untenable and unstable. If management decides to dig in, the workers would be best off compromising; alternatively, if the workers decide on uncompromising strike, management would be advised to try to appease them. Second, workers and management may both decide to compromise at a certain point. This will lead to the (3,3) outcome. But this outcome cannot prevail either, because each side would rather defect from the compromise or raise its demands if it sees that the other side is willing to compromise. Thus, if workers decide on permanent strike, management is better off compromising (4,2) and if management takes the hard-nose approach, the workers would do best to cave in. This is the (4,2) outcome. These two results are stable because if the workers take the tough line, management is best off compromising and if the management is tough, the workers are best off compromising. We call such stable situations *Nash Equilibria*, which we define technically in Chapter 1. We may add that the game structure depicted in Figure 0.1 is usually referred to as *The Game of Chicken*.

Rules of Progress

In *The Theory of Moves*, Brams (1994) proposes a method of explaining and, hence, predicting, the outcomes of situations involving conflicting sides with several options facing them, to reach a solution on a time axis. The essence of a player's ability to move depends on his or her specific 'powers' (e.g. threat) and the set of constraints within which maneuvering is possible. In politics, a player is usually not free to move at will as there are other players whose 'powers' have to be taken into account. Also, a movement should be compatible with logic and rationality. One only moves to a better position, at least in the long-term view.

Whatever the case may be, to reach a solution some rules should guide the interaction. Many bargaining situations are ignited only after parties agree to follow certain ground rules. These rules may be products of creative endeavor, of previous bargaining phases, or they may be an integral part of the 'culture of negotiation' that exists in a given society. It seems that in western cultures, negotiations are more 'outcome oriented' than in eastern cultures. Hence, much of the energy invested in the interaction concentrates on obtaining specific outcomes. In the East, attention is given to the process, manner, behavioral codes, or to other features not directly related to outcome. Thus, bargaining in different cultures may lead to remarkably different outcomes, precisely because different rules or codes of conduct are followed (Cohen, 1990).

Rules of progress also mean that before bargaining takes place, it should first be ascertained which issues are on the agenda and which are not. Among those selected for negotiation, an order of priority should be established. Since it has been demonstrated that the order of business can be crucial in determining the outcome of the bargaining process, great attention has been given to the procedure and individuals that set the agenda or the order of the bargaining process. There are many more factors that affect bargaining: contextual, procedural, structural and cultural. Some of these, especially those that are relevant to the understanding of political phenomena, are addressed in this book.

5 Unifying Theme

The unifying theme of this book is that the most crucial aspect of politics is the bargaining process between central governments and different interests in society. This bargaining relates primarily to the allocation of scarce resources and to human and property rights that governments grant to their citizens. The defining characteristic that distinguishes *civil society* from the primitive *state of nature* is a bargained order (Sened, 1997).

First and foremost we bargain about individual rights that governments are willing or unwilling to protect for us. The Hobbesian *state of nature*, of war of all against all, stops when a powerful player imposes order. This newly imposed order is then negotiated and re-negotiated through a complex bargaining process between powerful government agencies and their constituents. When, for one reason or another, the bargaining process collapses, society returns to the Hobbesian state of nature of the war of all against all (Sened, 1997).

Sometimes the bargaining process takes place in, or through, representative legislative bodies of government. But this is only one mechanism of political bargaining. Representative bodies have advantages and disadvantages that we discuss at length below, but they are by no means the only mechanism through which social order evolves.

One famous bargaining mechanism is the price mechanism of markets. For decades, economists have been studying market mechanisms in general, and the price mechanism in particular. The *general equilibrium theory* has established that in a world with (1) well defined property rights, (2) enough buyers and sellers and (3) complete and perfect information, the price bargaining mechanism of competitive markets will lead to efficient allocations of resources. This result, at times referred to as the Arrow-DeBreu Theorem (1954), is one reason why economists favor market mechanisms over any type of government allocation.

The Arrow-DeBreu Theorem (1954), however, is mostly relevant for a world with zero transaction costs. Transaction costs are usually defined as 'the costs associated with the transfer, capture and protection of rights' (Barzel, 1989: 2). In the world in which we live, transaction costs are usually very high (Coase, 1981). When transaction costs are high, market mechanisms fail. It is when market mechanisms fail that other bargaining mechanisms are necessary to resolve social and economic disputes. One could think about the political process as an analogue to *market contestability*. The term *market contestability* refers to the idea that even if not enough producers are present at the market place, the fact that new producers could *contest* the market by entering into production is sufficient to keep prices of production down. Political structures serve as substitutes and complements for *market contestability* when *market contestability* is unlikely to be achieved by unconstrained market forces alone.

The Arrow-DeBreu Theorem (1954), as well as that of Coase (1960) demonstrate that if property rights are well-defined, then private goods will be used optimally in a competitive free market. Recently, more attention has been given to the study of the assumption of well-defined property rights or, its close relative, the assumption of zero transaction costs. Neither is very realistic in any society, but scholars have only recently begun to pay attention to the study of the consequences and cases in which these assumptions are unlikely to hold (Olson, 1993; Sened, 1997).

In this book, we start from the premise that securing low transaction costs and well-defined property rights requires central agencies that can rely on their monopoly over the use of force to protect the human and property rights of individuals in society (Umbeck, 1981; Sened, 1995a, 97). In modern society, as in more ancient societies, low transaction costs depend on a host of factors, such as reliable information, free and safe transportation, cheap and secure energy resources, central banks and other structural conditions. Some of these structures can only be produced by 'natural monopolies.'

In general, 'natural monopolies' will not create inefficient allocation of resources so long as they are *contestable*. This means that as long as opportunistic players can enter the market, provide the goods and exit without too many sunk costs, the fact that the average cost curve is declining in the relevant range – which is the condition for natural monopolies to emerge – is of little consequence. This is so because the threat of entry by opportunistic players keeps the monopoly at check and forces it to produce at the lowest possible cost of production. However, when entry and exit into and from the market involve the risk of losing considerable sunk costs, the market is not contestable and the product or service provided by a 'natural' monopolist will be provided at inefficient quantities and prices.

Governments and politics often enter the game in domains where markets tend not to be contestable. Governments that provide services that can be provided by a free market should, eventually, be driven out of the market by firms that, in a free market, should produce these goods and services more efficiently and at lower prices than inefficient governments (Weimer and Vining, 1989: 94-123). Therefore, sooner or later, governments will restrict themselves to the provision of goods and services that the free market is unlikely to provide efficiently due to *market failures* (Weimer and Vining, 1989: 79-93).

In general, we should expect governments to restrict themselves to the provision of structural conditions for economic activity, such as basic education, health care, infrastructures of energy, transportation and communication and, most importantly, law and order. In providing these crucial services, government agencies should be expected to charge monopolistic prices for their services. In such cases we expect inefficient provision, at high, monopolistic prices.

The question is, therefore: what keeps governments from charging monopolistic prices for the structural services they provide for their constituents? More fundamentally, what forces bring governments to provide and constantly extend the range of services they provide? We argue that the answer to this question can be found in the fact that constituents and special interest groups can bargain with political power-holders by threatening to unseat them, or by withholding economic and political support that can reduce their benefits (Riker and Sened, 1991; Sened, 1997). In this way competitive elections and other forms of checks and balances that characterize the 'game of politics' serve as analogues, at the political level, to market contestability at the market level (Wittman, 1989,1995). When market contestability is impossible to achieve at the market alone, political bargaining helps, through long bargaining processes, to keep powerful political and economic players from abusing their control over the provision of structural services.

We argued above that one could distinguish between political science and economics along these lines. Economics is a science that studies market mechanisms that operate mainly through the use of price mechanisms. Political science studies the world of bargaining over allocations that either cannot, or are not usually made, through free market, price bargaining mechanisms.

This book deals with politics. Whilst many books have been written on the general subject of coordination and bargaining in the market environment (e.g. Binmore and Dasgupta, 1987), we know of no other book that discusses, from a broad general perspective, the problem of 'out of market' bargaining processes.

Just like market mechanisms, 'out-of-market' mechanisms have common features. Usually such mechanisms operate in environments of high transaction costs. More importantly, they usually operate and achieve coordination through the use, or misuse, of coercion and authority.

Easton (1953) pointed out that the science of politics is the study of 'authoritative allocation of scarce resources.' We contrasted this notion of political science with the study of economics, which is the study of the allocation of scarce resources through the price mechanism. This book provides basic tools for learning about and participating in the world of politics. It is based on the premise that the world of politics is a world that is mostly preoccupied with authoritative allocations of scarce resources, and that such authoritative allocations are, in the end, the outcomes of complex bargaining processes between competing interests in society.

6 The Structure of the Book

The remainder of this book is organized into seven chapters, with a short concluding chapter. Chapter 1 introduces the main concepts of the book and elaborates the theme of the centrality of bargaining mechanisms in the art, practice and science of politics.

Chapter 2 presents the classical social problem. We present two analytical tools that scholars have used, in the last decades, to explore this problem. Social choice theory in general (section 2.2) and the spatial theory of electoral competition in particular (section 2.3), have clearly demonstrated the considerable difficulty involved in aggregating the preferences of individual members in society into social preferences and decisions (Riker, 1982). This implies that the traditional view of democratic regimes as mechanisms of aggregating individual preferences into social decisions is problematic.

This book proposes an alternative angle for the study of society and government using tools of bargaining theory. The central goal of this book is to provide analytical tools that enable us to study how governments and special interest groups reach bargained agreements and how these agreements are enforced. This view is a departure from the common tradition in the study of politics that emphasizes the study of governments as representing individual preferences and enforcing more or less 'just' compromises of these preferences.

Why do we need a bargained agreement and why do we need an enforcer to enforce it? This question leads us to the second major theme of Chapter 2, in which we present the social problem as a 'prisoners' dilemma game' (Taylor, 1987), where conflicting interests are bound to reach inefficient outcomes, because, as strategic players, they are unlikely to cooperate (section 2.4).

Chapter 2 presents a picture of society that is almost diametrically opposed to the picture normally presented by neo-classical economists. Neo-classical economics presents us with a very optimistic, not to say utopian, picture of a human society in which individual agents and interests reach optimal resource allocations through the use of the price bargaining mechanism in a competitive market environment driven by market forces. According to this picture, the only enemy of social order and prosperity is government intervention.

Contrary to this utopian view, we describe society, where unchecked by political institutions, as a Hobbesian *state of nature* that is bound to lead to the 'war of all against all.' As Hobbes described it three and a half centuries ago:

> Hereby it is manifest, that ...without a common Power to keep them all in awe, [humans] are in that condition which is called ...Warre, where every man is enemy to every man ...And the life of man, solitaery, poore, nasty, brutish, and short.

It is this *state of nature* that the *civil society* is constructed to avoid. What distinguish *civil society* from the *state of nature* are political norms, conventions and institutions. A competitive free market may emerge as part of this institutional structure. But even here, it is unlikely to be a 'natural result' of market forces, but an outcome of a long political bargaining process that rarely, though sometimes, yields pure forms of competitive free markets (section 2.5).

Institutions that protect and support competitive markets, like most other social, economic and political institutions, are constructed by powerful political entrepreneurs to enhance and maintain their own interests (Knight, 1992). Nevertheless, those who construct and control those institutions cannot totally ignore the rest of society. Almost without exception, those in power must seek the support of their constituents. The political and economic support of the constituents is, almost always, a necessary condition for the continuous stream of benefits that accrue to rulers and government officials. It is this dependence that allows the constituents gradually to bargain for property and other individual rights that they want the ruler to guarantee in return for their economic and political support (Sened, 1997).

In the following chapters we demonstrate and provide concrete examples of the usefulness of different bargaining models to the understanding of diverse political phenomena in various spheres of politics and political science. In Chapter 3 we follow a model proposed by Sened (1997) that explains how civil society emerges from an anarchic 'war of all against all' into the organized civil society, through a bargaining process.

In the following chapters we survey recent results that explain how various societies achieve different political and economic outcomes through political bargaining. In Chapter 4 we discuss recent results by Ainsworth and Sened (1993) and Olson (1995) that explain the role of political entrepreneurs in the bargaining process that produce the social contract and how the contract is constantly re-negotiated and modified. At the end of the chapter we discuss the deficiencies of a bargaining process that rely solely on the good will of government officials and powerful political entrepreneurs. We suggest that these inherent deficiencies may explain the emergence of representative, legislative bodies that have become such universal political institutions in the last three centuries. In the following two chapters we discuss bargaining mechanisms that have evolved in and around the basic political institution of representative governments in the last three centuries.

In Chapter 5 we present the electoral process as a bargaining process. Political entrepreneurs who run for office start by positioning themselves in an imaginary political space to appeal to the tastes and preferences of the electing constituents. Soon enough, candidates deadlock in positions that maximize their share of votes, such that, given the positions of the other candidates, they cannot increase their own share by moving in the political issue space. At this stage candidates begin a long bargaining process with competing interests in society in order to obtain endorsements from as many interest groups as they can, by promising special legislation and budget allocations once they are elected.

The discussion in Chapter 5 is based on recent research by Schofield and Sened (2000) and is relevant mostly to parliamentary systems. Presidential systems constitute a distinctively different political organization of democratic society. Parliamentary systems rely heavily on multiparty electoral competition and the coalition formation process by which a government is established in those systems. In bi-cameral presidential systems elections are held for each chamber separately and then the president is elected on yet another separate ballot. One feature that distinguishes presidential systems from parliamentary systems is the checks and balances provided by these different bodies of government elected separately. This is the subject matter of Chapter 6.

The bargaining process over the organization of social life and the allocation of scarce resources begins at a local level with political and economic organizations that help articulate and organize different interests into coherent groups and organizations. Local organizations, however, must bargain with central authorities for the allocation of scarce resources that require higher levels and magnitudes of organization like the common phenomenon of nation states with organized armies.

The institution of the state is needed in order to defend property rights and provide structures for the prosperity of individual citizens. The bargaining process through which local interests bargain with central governments over future legislation and resource allocation takes place, in modern western societies, in and around the legislative bodies of the state. In western democracies these legislative bodies are elected in general suffrage. The process of general election and social choice whereby individual preferences are aggregated into social choices is a fascinating bargaining process where candidates and voters negotiate the terms of the post-electoral deal.

But in their role of protectors of property rights and interests of their constituents, states often reach impasses when they deal with each other. The international arena discussed in Chapter 7 is different than the domestic arena as it is far less regulated. In this respect the international arena still reminds us of the Hobbesian *state of nature*. So in discussing this topic we revert back to the more basic modes of bargaining when institutional structures, international norms and conventions provide only little guidance and accommodation to the bargaining parties.

In this way the book starts and ends with the discussion of the *state of nature*. But in between we move from primitive modalities of bargaining to the complex game of politics that characterize modern democracies and then back to the less structured environment of international politics. We hope that in the process we make a convincing argument for the prevalence of bargaining in politics at all the different levels at which it is present. We also hope that in the process we provide the reader with a better understanding of the scientific study and the logic of practice of political bargaining in a wide variety of circumstances.

1 A Conceptual Framework for the Study of Political Bargaining

1.1 Introduction

The introductory chapter presented the theoretical context in which the phenomenon of political bargaining should be understood. It defined the phenomenon and explained how it evolved and its prevalence in our lives. Finally, it outlined several factors that are always present in the process of political bargaining. In this book we look at the various levels of political bargaining. To follow our argument, the reader needs to be familiar with some basic conceptual tools used in our theoretical analysis.

The theoretical approach we adopt is referred to as *rational choice theory*. This means that we adhere to two basic premises: *methodological individualism* and *purposeful action*. The first premise implies that political outcomes result from actions taken by rational individual agents in society. The second premise postulates that these rational agents have goals that they try to achieve within the framework of the physical environment in which they operate and in the context of their expectations of other agents.

The purpose of this book is to explain how strategic choices made by individual rational actors yield, through complex bargaining processes, the political outcomes that define the social orders in which we live.

It is appropriate to evaluate the merits of political outcomes in normative terms. Here, however, we are mainly concerned with a positive theory of the bargaining process through which social order emerges and evolves. We provide explanations for processes and outcomes, with little, if any, attempt to evaluate their ethical merits and demerits. Our purpose is to provide tools for understanding, not tools for normative evaluation. Some judge this approach as normatively objectionable because it restricts itself to the study of the rational aspect of human behavior as a foundation for explaining political outcomes. We find this objection out of place. If we are able to explain political phenomena we contribute to the science of human behavior. We have our normative values like everyone else, but we are not students of ethics, we are students of politics. We are not ignorant of or oblivious to normative evaluations. We simply leave it to others to study ethics while recognizing that the tools we use allow us to study only the positive side of human interactions in the political sphere.

1.2 The 'Hard Core' of Rational Choice Theory

In his *Methodology of Scientific Research Programmes* (1978), Lakatos explains that science advances through the evolution of research programs (p. 47-8):

> I have discussed the problem of objective appraisal of scientific growth in terms of progressive and degenerating problem shifts in series of scientific theories. The most important such series in the growth of science is characterized by a certain *continuity* which connects their members. This continuity evolves from a genuine research programme adumbrated at the start.

> All scientific research programmes may be characterized by their 'hard core.' The negative heuristic of the programme forbids us to direct the modus tollens at this 'hard core.' Instead, we must use our ingenuity to articulate or even invent 'auxiliary hypotheses,' which form a *protective belt* around this core, and we must redirect the *modus tollens* to these.

The hard core of a research program includes basic epistemological assumptions, methodological imperatives and definitions of what should be the focus of research. In this chapter we define the hard core of the rational choice research program. The following chapters survey a series of exemplary achievements that are part of the growing protective belt of this dominant research program within contemporary social sciences.

The protective belt of a research program is made up of its cumulative achievements. The greater the achievements are, the stronger the belt that protects the hard core of the program. A research program degenerates when its protective belt whither under attack, but the hard core never stands 'direct trial,' since the core consists of axioms, premises or assumptions that need not stand the test of either external verification or falsification. The program collapses only when its protective belt is so thin that it can no longer withstand systematic, scientific criticism.

Basic Assumptions

We now turn to a brief discussion of the hard core that defines the rational choice theory research program to which we adhere. Rational choice theory is based on two central assumptions: Methodological individualism and purposeful action.

1. Methodological individualism: Social outcomes result from actions taken by rational, individual social agents.

This assumption states that strategic choices made by individual players, as to how to get the most out of every situation in which they are involved as agents in society, ultimately determine the political outcomes. This assumption is straightforward and requires no further discussion, except perhaps to emphasize that the term 'social agent' pertains to theoretical units of analysis and not necessarily to private people. 'Individuals' are singular units with well-defined, coherent preferences and action sets that try to choose, in every given situation, an action or a strategy from their action or strategy set, to obtain the outcome that ranks highest on their preference order. Using this methodology to analyze social situations, we implicitly utilize the *as if* principle (Friedman, 1953). That is to say that we may move to various levels of social aggregation and analyze different organizations *as if* they possessed individual preferences and strategy sets, even though we know that they do not, and cannot, share such properties.

2. **Purposeful action:** Individual agents are rational in the sense that they have goals which, given the physical environment within which they operate and their expectations of other agents, they purposefully seek to fulfill.

Purposeful action requires further clarification because it lies at the heart of the rationality assumption on which this entire research program is founded. The assumption can be broken down into two distinct parts. First, agents are postulated to have well-defined goals. Second, agents are assumed to do whatever they can to achieve these goals, given their physical environment and expectations of other agents. These two parts are now described in further detail.

(2.1) Rational preferences: every agent understands what s/he wants to achieve. In more technical terms, we assume that every agent can order all possible outcomes in a binary ranking relation called a *weak order.*

To assume that an agent can order outcomes in a *weak order*, denoted by '**R**', implies that three conditions are met: completeness, transitivity and reflexivity.

(2.1.1) Completeness: $\forall\ i \in N,\ \forall\ a,b \in O,\ bR_ia$ or aR_ib

Read: for every ($\forall$) agent i, who is a member ($\in$) of the group of relevant agents N, and for any two possible outcomes a,b of the set of all possible outcomes O, either b is at least as good for i as a (bR_ia), or a is at least as good for i as b (aR_ib). This means that any agent can order any two outcomes and identify which of the two s/he weakly prefers. If bR_ia and aR_ib then bI_ia, denotes that agent i is indifferent between a and b. If bR_ia but not aR_ib, bP_ia denotes that agent i strictly prefers b to a.

(2.1.2) Transitivity: $\forall\ i \in N,\ \forall\ a,b,c \in O,$ if aR_ib and bR_ic then $aR_ic.$

Read: an agent who weakly prefers a to b and b to c, weakly prefers a to c.

This condition is the most fundamental assumption of rational choice theory. It assumes that agents are logical in their preferences in the sense that beyond their ability to order any pair of possible outcomes (completeness), they can order the entire set of outcomes transitively. We can appreciate how fundamental this assumption is by contemplating its failure. Preference orders that fail to meet the transitivity requirement are called *cyclical*.[1] Such preference orders can hardly serve anyone in making rational choices between outcomes. If aP_ib and bP_ic, but cP_ia, we get a cyclical preference order $aP_ibP_icP_ia$. But if $aP_ibP_icP_ia$, it is not clear how agent *i* may make a rational choice among **a**, **b**, and **c**. S/he would not choose **a** since s/he prefers **c** to **a**. S/he would not choose **c** since s/he prefers **b** to **c** and s/he would not choose **b** because s/he prefers **a** to **b**.

In the next chapter we discuss one of the most important achievements in the field of social choice theory known as 'Arrow's Impossibility Theorem' (Arrow, 1951). Assuming that rational agents can order all possible outcomes in weak orders and some basic restrictions on social choice mechanisms, Arrow proved that there exists no social choice mechanism that can aggregate any preference profile of rational individuals into a social preference weak order. Riker (1982: 136) concluded a discussion of this result noting that 'the unavoidable inference is ...that so long as a society preserves democratic institutions, its members can expect that some of their social choices be unordered or inconsistent. And when this is true, no meaningful choices can be made.' The inherent difficulty in aggregating individual preferences into social choices does not mean that complete arbitrariness guides social decisions. It means that social choices can be manipulated (Riker, 1986) and can lead to unintended or undesirable outcomes. Indeed, this is one of the reasons why political bargaining is so crucial in every aspect of our social lives.

To complete our definition of a weak order we define reflexivity as:

(2.1.3) Reflexivity: $\forall\ i \in N,\ \forall\ a \in O$, if aR_ia.

Reflexivity requires that any outcome in the set of feasible outcomes be weakly preferred to itself. This requirement is self-evident and we rarely refer to it.

2.2 Rational Actions: Every agent is assumed to do whatever is in his or her power to get the most out of every situation in which s/he is involved.

To explain this second part of the assumption of purposeful action, we present the main methodological tool that serves the hard core of rational choice theory: Game Theory.

Game Theory

Rational choice theory associates social events with games (Riker and Ordeshook, 1973: 119; Gardner and Ostrom, 1989). A game is defined as a set of rules (Von Neumann and Morgenstern, 1944). These rules characterize the set of relevant decision units, or agents, involved in the situation; the set of possible choices of action, sequences of actions or probabilities assigned to possible actions that we call strategies; and the pay-offs associated with every combination of strategic choices by the set of all the relevant agents involved in the game.

Definition 1.1: A game $\Gamma = \{N, \sigma, \Pi\}$ is an abstract representation of an event **E**:

1. $N = \{1, ..., n\}$ is the set of agents or analytical decision-making units. They may be citizens, officials, parties, political, social or economic organizations, or even entire states.
2. Each agent, $i \in N$, has a set of strategies, σ_i, from which s/he can choose a particular strategy: $\sigma_i \in \sigma_i$. The Cartesian product of the choice sets of all individuals involved in the game, $\sigma = \sigma_1 X ... X \sigma_n$, is called the strategy space. $\sigma = (\sigma_1, ..., \sigma_n) \in \sigma$ denotes a particular combination or a 'vector' of strategic choices, specifying a strategic choice for each and every agent $i \in N$.
3. A pay-off function $\Pi: \sigma \Rightarrow U \subseteq \mathfrak{R}^n$ is a mapping from a strategy space to a utility space. Each individual assigns a utility $u_i(\sigma)$ to any strategy vector $\sigma = (\sigma_1, ..., \sigma_n) \in \sigma$. This utility may vary from $-\infty$ to ∞. The uni-dimensional line, $\mathfrak{R}$, is used to represent this range and the n-dimensional $\mathfrak{R}^n$ to denote the utility space of all n agents involved in the game. The pay-off function Π, assigns a utility vector to every strategy vector. $\sigma_{-i} = (\sigma_1, ..., \sigma_{(i-1)}, \sigma_{(i+1)}, ..., \sigma_n)$ is conventionally used to denote the strategic choices of all agents except i.

Definition 1.2: The strategy vector σ^* is a Nash Equilibrium if and only if for every player $i \in N$, $u_i(\sigma^*) \geq u_i(\sigma^*_{-i}, \sigma_i)$, $\forall \sigma_i \in \sigma_i$.

Thus, a strategy vector is a Nash Equilibrium if no player 'would have obtained a larger pay-off if s/he had adopted an alternative strategy, given the strategies chosen by the other players' (Friedman, 1986: 3). In section 1.4 we discuss the Nash Equilibrium concept in further detail. Here, we only wish to clarify the idea of representing social events as abstract mathematical structures and using equilibrium solution concepts to predict the set of expected outcomes. Equilibria can also be understood as stable, self-fulfilling, expectations that agents have *vis-a-vis* each other. Each agent expects other agents to behave as they do because no agent can be better off by behaving in a different way than what s/he is expected to, because s/he cannot do any better by behaving in any other way, given how s/he expects all the other agents to behave.

We can now make better sense of the assumption of purposeful action. It states that rational agents are rational inasmuch as they make strategic choices that are best for them given the physical features of the situation in which they are involved, and the strategic choices they expect other agents to make in those circumstances. In other words, an action can be defined as rational if it is consistent with the logic of the Nash Equilibrium concept as explained above.

Social scientists use two game-theoretic frameworks to analyze the social bargaining situation: cooperative and non-cooperative game theory. The following two sections introduce the concepts on which these two respective theoretic frameworks are based. In section 1.5 we introduce the bargaining problem at its simplest form, as introduced by Rubinstein (1982, 1985).

1.3 Cooperative Game Theory in Political Bargaining Theory

The central concept in the cooperative, game theoretic, analytic approach is the concept of the *core*. The *core* of a cooperative game is the set of allocations that no winning coalition would over-ride in favor of (an)other allocation(s). We now turn to formally define this concept.

Let $u=(u_1,...u_n) \in U$ denote a utility vector with u_i denoting the pay-off that $i \in N$ receives. *A game in characteristic function form* is denoted by: $\Gamma=(V,N,U)$, where V is the characteristic function (or correspondence) that assigns to every subset of players a vector of pay-offs (or a set of vectors of pay-offs) that this subset of players (or 'coalition') can allocate to members of society. N is the set of all agents and $U \subseteq \Re^n$ is the set of all feasible utility n-tuples vectors or the utility space. Let C be a subset of N, called coalition. Using these notations we can define the solution concept of the *core*.

Definition 1.3: A *characteristic function* of the coalition C, $V(C)$, is a collection of utility vectors, such that if C can guarantee u_i to any member, $i \in N$, then u is in $V(C)$.

Definition 1.4: u dominates u' with respect to C if u is in $V(C)$ and for any member $i \in C$ $u_i > u_i'$. u dominates u' if there exists a coalition C, so that u dominates u' with respect to C.

Definition 1.5: The *core* of a game in characteristic function form is the set of undominated utility vectors in U.

The *core* serves as the main solution concept in the cooperative game theoretic approach to multi-person bargaining problems. The idea behind using the *core* as a solution concept is straightforward: if the *core* is not empty, it is reasonable to predict that only outcomes in the *core* of a game will persist precisely because they are 'undominated.' A *core* allocation is likely to be stable because, by definition, no winning coalition can offer an allocation entailing higher pay-offs to all its members.

In this book, we use cooperative game theory and the solution concept of the *core* in the analysis of elections, post elections and coalition formation processes. There are, however, several drawbacks to the use of cooperative game theory in general, and the core as a solution concept in particular. The first is that they presuppose that players can reach agreements through costless communication and go on to assume the existence of mechanisms that successfully enforce these agreements (Binmore and Dasgupta, 1987: 5). This may be a good assumption to make in analyzing well-regulated activities such as majority rule decisions in parliaments, or market interactions when property rights are well-defined. We know, however, that many social bargaining contexts do not have such obvious enforcement mechanisms. The challenge in the analysis of the emergence of institutions that induce law and order in society is that we cannot assume the pre-existence of such enforcement mechanisms.

Another disadvantage of cooperative game theory is that it does not help us understand the strategic interactions among agents, because the strategic behavior of agents is never explicitly analyzed. The core concept is efficient in identifying external threats to the stability of the solution. Insofar as some pay-off profiles are undominated, they will be inherently stable and the pay-off vectors that are dominated will be excluded.

In studying political bargaining, the underlying institutional structures and the strategic behavior of individual agents in society may vary considerably. At times the institutional structure allows agents to reach and maintain 'cooperative' agreements, as, for example, in the process of coalition formation. In other contexts, like international conflict, all that counts is the strategic behavior of players, whilst the institutional superstructure is virtually non-existent. In fact, in all bargaining situations characterized by a clear conflict of interests among agents, it is improper to use cooperative game theory solutions. In such games the core solutions concept cannot grasp, by definition, the complexity of the interaction among the players. In such contexts the use of non-cooperative game theory seems more appropriate. We now introduce the underlying concepts of non-cooperative game theory in the study of political bargaining.

1.4 Non-Cooperative Game Theory and Political Bargaining Theory

Unlike cooperative game theory, non-cooperative game theory pays special attention to the analysis of the strategic behavior of the individual players with no pre-commitment or any other type of agreement among the agents assumed.

As we stated earlier, a non-cooperative game is defined by three elements $\Gamma= \{N,\sigma,\Pi\}$. $N=\{1,...,n\}$ is the set of players. σ is the strategy space, or all possible combination of strategic choices of the n players involved in the interaction studied. Each agent, $i \in N$, has to choose a strategy σ_i, from his or her strategy set, σ_i, with $\sigma_i \in \sigma_i$.[2] σ is a Cartesian product $\sigma=\sigma_1 X...X \sigma_n$ that describes the set of all possible combinations of individual strategic choices by all the agents involved in the game. Π is a pay-off function: $\Pi: \sigma => U \subseteq \Re^n$ that assigns to each vector of strategic choices by the agents involved, a pay-off vector that specifies the utility that each player gets from the outcome that results if this combination of strategic choices is chosen by the agents in the game.

The idea behind the non-cooperative, game theoretic approach is that each agent chooses a strategy out of his or her strategy set, trying to guarantee that the resulting n-tuple of strategic choices determining the outcome of the game will yield the highest pay-off s/he can hope for, given the set of agents N, the strategy space σ, the pay-off function Π, and what s/he expects the strategic choices of other players may be. Unlike the cooperative approach, here players make their choices independently, without being able to conclude prior binding agreements.

As mentioned above, the commonly used solution concept in this approach is known as the Nash Equilibrium. To understand this solution concept, recall that we denote a strategy of player i by σ_i and the set of feasible strategies for i by σ_i, with $\sigma_i \in \sigma_i$. Recall that σ denotes the Cartesian product of the strategy sets of all the relevant players, known also as the strategy space, and $\sigma = (\sigma_1, \ldots \sigma_n) \in \sigma$ denotes a strategy vector that specifies a particular strategic choice for every agent $i \in N$. Finally, recall that $\sigma_{-i} = (\sigma_1, \ldots \sigma_{i-1}, \sigma_{i+1}, \ldots \sigma_n)$ denotes the strategic choice of all agents except player i. Definition 1.6 restates Definition 1.2 of the Nash Equilibrium solution concept.

Definition 1.6: The strategy vector σ^* is a Nash Equilibrium, if and only if, for every player $i \in N$, $u_i(\sigma^*) \geq u_i(\sigma^*_{-i}, \sigma_i)$, for every $\sigma_i \in \sigma_i$.

That is, to be a Nash Equilibrium, a strategy vector σ^* must have the property that, given the strategies chosen by all the other agents σ^*_{-i}, no agent can be made better off, or get more than $u_i(\sigma^*)$, by unilaterally choosing a different strategy $\sigma_i \in \sigma_i$ than the strategy σ_i^* s/he chose.

The use of the Nash Equilibrium as a predictive concept relies on a simple intuition. A combination of strategic choices constitutes a Nash Equilibrium if, and only if, no player wants to alter his or her strategic choice, given the strategic choices of all the other players. We expect such combinations of strategic choices to be stable outcomes of the bargaining process precisely because no individual player has an incentive to change his or her behavior, as long as the other players hold on to their strategies. Since this is true for all the players, we expect all players to stick to their choices.

To make sense of these abstract concepts, consider the game presented in Figure 1.1. This game, known as the 'Prisoners' Dilemma' is perhaps the most commonly used example of game theoretic models in the social sciences. Two agents have to decide whether to cooperate in order to achieve a common goal. Thus, the set of agents in this game is $N = \{1, 2\}$. Each player has two strategies to choose from: $\sigma_i = \{C, D\}$. 'C' denotes 'cooperate' and 'D' denotes 'defect,' or 'do not cooperate'. The strategy space of this game is the Cartesian product $\sigma = \sigma_1 \times \sigma_2 = \{(D,D), (D,C), (C,D), (C,C)\}$. The pay-off function assigns a utility vector to each of these four combinations of strategic choices. It assigns $(0,0)$ to (D,D), $(2,-1)$ to (D,C), $(-1,2)$ to (C,D) and $(1,1)$ to (C,C). The interpretation of this pay-off function is that if both players defect, they get nothing, if both cooperate they share a prize of cooperation and get a utility of 1 each. If one cooperates and the other does not, the defector gets the prize without paying the cost of working for it (2) while the agent who cooperates pays the price of -1 and gets nothing in return. It is easy to see that the unique Nash Equilibrium in this game is the strategic choice (D,D). The 'defect' strategy dominates the 'cooperate' strategy. Therefore, each rational player will prefer it, regardless of the choices made by the others. As a result, a unique Nash Equilibrium outcome will prevail. The Prisoners' Dilemma game is often used in the study of politics to explain international and domestic conflicts and, more generally, to explain the failure of individuals to capture the prize of cooperation.

Players	Player No. 2		
	Strategies	Cooperate (C)	Defect (D)
Player No. 1	Cooperate (C)	1,1	–1,2
	Defect (D)	2,–1	0,0

Figure 1.1 A Two-Person Prisoners' Dilemma Game

The advantage of non-cooperative game theory is that it enables us to identify expected outcomes of complex bargaining problems. It also allows us to make detailed analyses of the strategic choices of social agents in these bargaining processes. It defines the parameters and likely outcomes of the interaction. Building the analysis on the rules of logic, it enables scientists to offer the internal verification of logical consistency and an external source of falsification, via empirical tests, to theoretical generalizations.

The main objection to this approach is that, more often than not, scientists must make arbitrary decisions as to how to structure the game in terms of the strategy space and the pay-off function. Often, an ambitious attempt at providing an account of a situation turns out to be an exercise in oversimplification of a complex phenomenon. Likewise, much of the explanatory power of games depends on the interpretation given to reality by the scientists. Does a situation resemble a prisoners' dilemma game or should it be described as a game of chicken? For example, in the analysis of the bi-polar world, students of international relations often used the two above-mentioned games to analyze identical problems without providing a differentiating explanation as to the rationale guiding their modeling choices (Brams, 1985; Schelling, 1960). One way to deal with this objection is to judge each model according to how accurately it depicts the context it purports to model. Non-cooperative models in political science must, therefore, be judged not only on whether or not they provide us with a predictive set, but also by the extent to which they capture different aspects of the reality we wish to study and the extent to which the predictive set derived from the analysis of the model is consistent with the outcomes commonly observed in the context under study.

1.5 Rubinstein's Formulation of the Bargaining Problem

In the introduction to his seminal paper on the bargaining problem, Rubinstein (1982) refers to two earlier sources that are important in the current context. First, he reminds us (p. 97) that 'Edgeworth presented [the bargaining] problem one hundred years ago, considering it [to be] the most fundamental problem in Economics.' Second, he points out that 'since then it seems to have been the

source of considerable frustration for Economic theorists.' Rubinstein proceeds
with a telling quote from Cross (1965: 67):

> economists traditionally have had little to say about pure situations in which the
> outcome is clearly dependent upon interactions among only a few individuals.

As Rubinstein (1982: 97) explains, the 'very little' is 'that the agreed contract is
individual[ly]-rational and is Pareto Optimal; i.e. it is no worse than
disagreement, and there is no agreement which both [agents] would prefer.'

Why have economists had so little to say about the 'most fundamental question
in Economics.' Answering this question may help us understand why bargaining,
the most elementary form of social interaction and the essence of the 'political'
in our lives, is so difficult to grasp and subsequently to formalize. We have
already mentioned that neo-classical economists have traditionally used the
cooperative game theoretic approach that is less suited to the study of strategic
interactions among social agents. As Roth (1979: 20, fn.1) notes:

> ...a game is considered non-cooperative if players must make their choices
> independently, without being able to conclude a prior binding agreement, [it is
> considered] cooperative if the players can conclude a [prior] binding agreement as
> to what outcome should be chosen. ...Cooperative games ... [are] not described in
> strategic form, which emphasizes the individual choices of the players, but ...by
> the set of outcomes which each coalition of players may potentially agree on.

Cooperative game theory is ill-suited to the study of some bargaining problems
inasmuch as it presupposes that 'players can conclude a binding agreement as to
what outcome should be chosen,' which is part of the question under
investigation in studying the bargaining problem. In addition, the bargaining
problem is mainly a problem of strategic choices. We do not want to use a
theoretic framework that overlooks the strategic aspects of the problem.
Consider the standard, neo-classical, theoretical treatment of the problem,
suggested by Edgeworth, the so-called Edgeworth Box in Figure 1.2:

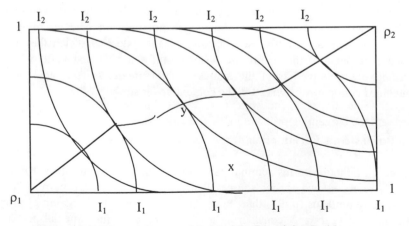

Figure 1.2 Edgeworth Box as a Model of the Bargaining Problem

Edgeworth's Box describes two players who seek to divide two goods between them. ρ_1 at the bottom left corner of the box denotes the ideal point of player 1 where she receives the most of each of the two goods, and player 2 receives the least. At point ρ_1, player 1 enjoys all the bread and butter while player 2 gets no bread or butter. At point ρ_2, player 2 gets everything while player 1 gets nothing. The arch-like lines in the box are indifference curves that describe the preferences of each player. Curves denoted by I_1 denote player 1's indifference curves. Curves denoted by I_2 denote player 2's indifference curves. These lines simply indicate that as we get closer to ρ_2, player 2's utility increases while player 1's utility decreases and as we get closer to ρ_1, player 1's utility increases and player 2's utility decreases. These lines are called indifference curves because all the points on them denote allocations that give the relevant player the same utility, as they are 'equi-distant' from the player's ideal allocation of (1,1).

The line that connects ρ_1 and ρ_2 is known as the *contract curve* and denotes all points on which the two players can agree. This line represents the line of Pareto Optimal allocations. Pareto optimal allocations are allocations that satisfy the condition that no other allocations can be found that can make all players better off. If an allocation is Pareto optimal, any other allocation that makes any of the player(s) better off must make some player(s) worse off. The contract curve of Pareto optimal allocations passes through all the points where the indifference curves of both players are tangent to each other. The idea is that points on the contract curve that connect ρ_1 and ρ_2 are preferred by both players to points off this curve. So, both players will always move to the contract curve from any point off the contract curve. The main problem with this analysis is that we get no idea how the goods will eventually be divided. We know that the allocation points on the contract curve dominate, in the sense defined in definition 1.4 above, the points off the contract curve. But both the allocation in which player 1 gets all the goods and player 2 gets nothing, and the allocation in which player 1 gets nothing and player 2 gets everything, are on the contract curves, as well as many other possible allocations. Edgeworth's Box does not tell us which of this wide range of allocations is likely to be implemented.

To be perfectly fair, if we knew the *initial endowment* – i.e. the distribution of resources among players before the bargaining process starts – then we could use the Edgeworth Box to predict the agreement point. For example, if the initial endowment is point x in Figure 1.2, the Edgeworth Box analysis predicts that the agreement point would be point y because both players prefer y to x. But where does the initial endowment point come from? Rubinstein's approach does not depend on an initial endowment point. Rubinstein (1982: 100) proposed to present the bargaining problem in the following way:

> Two players, 1 and 2, are bargaining on the partition of a pie. The pie will be partitioned only after the players reach an agreement. Each player, in turn, offers a partition and his opponent may agree to the offer 'Y' or reject it 'N'. Acceptance of the offer ends the bargaining. After rejection, the rejecting player then has to make a counter offer and so on. There are no rules [that] bind the players to any previous offer they have made.

Let F be the set of all strategies of player 1 who starts the bargaining with f∈F being one strategy in this set.[3] Similarly, let G be the set of all strategies of player 2, who starts by responding to player 1 with g∈G. Such strategies specify the offers and responses that each player intends to make throughout the sequence of possible offers and counter offers that may last to infinity.

There are two versions to the model. The first assumes a fixed bargaining cost, c_i, that each player pays for each round of bargaining. These costs might come from the time wasted in the bargaining session, the necessary arrangement for the session etc. The second version of the model assumes a fixed discount factor of $0 < \delta_i \leq 1$ that is a multiplier that diminishes the value of the 'pie' with every round of bargaining. Let T denote the set of natural numbers as a time index that goes from 0 to ∞, with t∈T. The value of the 'pie' is standardized to 1. At $t = 0$ the value of the pie for player i is 1. At time $t = 1$ the value of the pie for player i is δ_i. At time $t = 2$ the value of the pie for player i is δ_i^2 and so on. Since $0 < \delta_i \leq 1$, the value of the pie diminishes for both players as the sequence of offers and counter offers lasts longer. As t goes to infinity, $t \to \infty$, the value of the pie converges to zero. The use of discount factors in the study of individual behavior in social contexts is widespread. It is based on that lay observation and theoretical reflection indicate that individuals always seem to prefer immediate benefits to future benefits. This is why we take out bank loans – to buy something now that we will pay for later – and why we usually under-invest in our future – we are simply impatient to reap the benefits as soon as we can.

In this context, a Nash Equilibrium is defined in Definition 1.7 below.

Definition 1.7: The strategy pair (f*,g*) is a Nash Equilibrium if, and only if, for player 1 $u_1(f^*,g^*) \geq u_1(f,g^*)$, for every f ∈ F and for player 2 $u_2(f^*,g^*) \geq u_2(f^*,g)$, for every g ∈ G.

A strategy pair represents a choice by each player of a sequence of offers and counter-offers to every possible offer or counter-offer of the other player. A pair of two such sequences of offers and counter-offers is a Nash Equilibrium if no player could have chosen a different sequence of offers and counter-offers in the bargaining process and end up with a higher utility at the end of the process.

Rubinstein shows that every partition of the pie can be induced by a pair of strategies constituting a Nash Equilibrium. It is easy to understand why the Nash Equilibrium concept proves itself so weak in this context. Note that if one player insists on a certain partition forever, the other player may as well accept the offer rather than wait until the cost of each round of bargaining, c_i, or the discount factor, δ_i, erode the value of the pie to zero. Having said that, we understand, intuitively, that each agent in a bargaining situation may be more flexible and accept a compromise if the other side can credibly threaten to be as stubborn as to reject all counter offers until the value of the pie is completely eroded.

In order to overcome this difficulty, Rubinstein uses the solution concept of Subgame Perfect Nash Equilibrium, introduced by Selten (1975). Definition 1.8 defines a Subgame Perfect Nash Equilibrium (SPNE), using the notations introduced above, in non-technical terms.

Definition 1.8: A strategy vector, (f^*, g^*), is a SPNE if:
1. It is a Nash Equilibrium for the entire game, as defined in definition 1.7; and
2. Its relevant action rules are a Nash Equilibrium for every subgame.

Every SPNE is a Nash Equilibrium. The converse is not true. Subgame perfection is one of the most commonly accepted refinements of the Nash Equilibrium solution concept (Rasmusen, 1989: 87-8; Ordeshook, 1986: 141). A simple way to identify a SPNE is the method of backward induction. We check what the last player to act is likely to do at his or her last move in the game. We find out the consequent pay-off vector for all the agents, given the anticipated behavior of the last player at the end action. We then treat the anticipated behavior of the last player and its consequences as given, and repeat the exercise for the one-before-last player. One works this way up the game tree until one reaches the starting point of the original game.

In the context of the bargaining game as formalized by Rubinstein (1982), a sequence of offers and counter-offers may be infinite. At a certain point, however, the cost of another round of bargaining, c_i, threatens to diminish the pay-offs from the entire game to zero. At this stage, any rational player would prefer to compromise for any positive pay-off rather than continue the game. This may serve as the 'last round' in the analysis of the game in our context.

Using the SPNE solution concept, Rubinstein reaches two conclusions about the SPNE partition (SPNEP) of the pie at the end of the bargaining process, as he models it. The first conclusion is cited below (Rubinstein, 1982: 107).

Conclusion 1: If both players have fixed bargaining costs, c_1 and c_2:
1. If $c_1 > c_2$, [player 1 getting] c_2 is the only SPNEP.
2. If $c_1 = c_2$, [player 1 getting any share, x] $c_1 \leq x \leq 1$ is a SPNEP.
3. If $c_1 < c_2$, [player 1 getting] 1 is the only SPNEP.

This conclusion can be explained intuitively. If the cost that player 1 pays for every round, c_1, is greater than the cost, c_2, player 2 pays, then player 1 cannot credibly insist on getting anything more than c_2. This can be shown using the logic of backward induction explained above. Player 1 can continue to bargain only until he is about to pay the cost of another round, c_1, that would reduce his or her pay-offs from the game to a negative number. At this point, player 1 would agree to get a pay-off of 0 provided that they stop the bargaining process, because, if they continue, player 1 receives a negative pay-off. Since $c_1 > c_2$, player 2 can still continue and bargain at that point. But since at that critical 'last round' player 1 would settle for 0, s/he would settle for the same share at the previous round and so on to the first round. Why can player 1 extract a pay-off of c_2? Because player 1 is the first to make an offer and if player 2 would reject player 1's offer of $1-c_2$, s/he will have to pay a cost of c_2 and move to the next round. At the next round, it is player 2's turn to make an offer. As explained above, player 1 would accept at that point any offer of player 2, but player 2 already paid the cost of c_2, so s/he may as well accept to pay to player 1 a share of c_2 at the first round.

When $c_2 > c_1$ this logic turns around. Player 2 knows that player 1 can go on and bargain until player 2 can no longer bear the cost of bargaining, at which stage player 2 would accept any share of the pie including 0. For this reason player 2 would accept an offer of player 1, at the first round, that leaves the whole value, 1, of the pie to player 1 and a value of 0 to player 2.

When $c_1 = c_2$, this logic does not work because both players would lose their patience at the same time. Since at that stage player 1 can secure to himself or herself at least c_1, s/he may never get less than this, but, applying the logic of the SPNE solution, we cannot specify the outcome of the game any further.

Rubinstein's second conclusion concerns the case in which both players discount future pay-offs by factors, δ_1 and δ_2 (Rubinstein, 1982: 108):

Conclusion 2: In the case where the players have fixed discounting factors – δ_1 and δ_2 – if at least one of them is strictly less than 1 and at least one of them is strictly positive, then the only [SPNEP] is [one in which player 1 gets a share M of the pie so that] $M = (1-\delta_2)/(1-\delta_1\delta_2)$.

Rubinstein (1982) explains this conclusion as follows:

> Note that when $\delta_2 = 0$, player 2 has no threat because the pie has no worth for him after the first period. Player 1 can exploit this to get all the pie ($M = 1$). When $\delta_1 = 0$, player 1 can only get $1-\delta_2$, that is the proportion of the pie that 2 may lose if he refuses 1's offer and gets 1 in the second period [compare to the case of the fixed bargaining costs discussed earlier]. When $0 < \delta_1 = \delta_2 = \delta < 1$, one gets $1/(1+\delta) > 1/2$. As one expects, [player] 1's gain from the fact that s/he starts the bargaining process decreases as δ converges to 1.

Readers may gain a better understanding of conclusion 2, by inserting other real values to δ_1 and δ_2 and playing with the numbers and their intuitions.

1.6 Concluding Remarks: Bargaining in Political Settings

Jack Knight (1992) elaborates on the crucial political consequences of the Rubinstein model: strong and patient players, especially when they can set the agenda and make the first offer in the bargaining process, are likely to extract most of the pay-offs at stake in any bargaining process. This means that in variable social contexts, powerful initiators such as coalition framers (Doron and Sherman, 1995) or war-prone states operating in an anarchical international system (Sherman and Doron, 1997), may gain considerable bargaining advantage over potential coalition partners or liberal democratic states.

Unfortunately, the literature that emanated from Rubinstein's seminal work, as well as other economic-oriented models of bargaining process, rarely explore the political consequences of these theoretical results. A central goal of our book is to highlight how politicians, parliaments, political parties, and other relevant social agents may use, abuse or suffer from such differences in the initial endowment of their political powers.

Another feature of the bargaining problem, as modeled by economists, is the lack of complexity. It is too often modeled as a two-players' game, with a pie of only one or two dimensions to partition. As the following chapters demonstrate, political bargaining is far more complex than that. The number of players is almost always greater than 2 and the goods at stake are almost always multi-dimensional. Political players differ greatly in their economic and political endowments and they are constrained by economic and institutional factors that define the rules of the bargaining game they play. It is this complexity that we study in the remainder of this book.

Notes

1. To be precise, a binary relation **R** can be neither transitive nor cyclic. Two commonly mentioned characterizations of such binary relations are quasi-transitive and a-cyclic relations. In order not to burden the reader with technical detail, we refer the reader to Austen-Smith and Banks (1999) Definition 1.2 for precise definition and a short discussion of the distinctions among these three characterization of binary relations.

2. The discussion is restricted to 'pure' strategies that should be distinguished from 'mixed' strategies. Mixed strategies involve using, with some probability, different 'pure' strategies by the same player in a particular stage of the game. Some probabilistic procedure is presumed to be used by the agent to choose which strategy is actually played at that move. We explain the concept of mixed strategies in Chapter 3.

3. The following notations and formal presentation are a simplified version of the Rubinstein (1982) model taken from the original paper omitting much technical detail and definitions that the interested reader is encouraged to find in the original paper.

2 The Social Problem

2.1 Introduction

Employing methodological individualism as our conceptual approach means that our unit of analysis, the entity to be studied, is the individual. So long as this hypothetical individual operates on his or her own, in a world free of constraints, there need not be any theoretical problems in understanding his or her behavior. This individual, we assume, has interests, tastes, and preferences, and knows what s/he wants. Our individual also knows, by the rationality assumption, how to order all possible outcomes based on his or her preferences. Moreover, even in a constrained world s/he can make an assessment of the various options available, figure out what is best from his or her point of view and make an informed choice. The rationality assumption and the rules of logic help us identify, by a process of deduction, the expected behavior of individual agents in society. Things are not as clear, however, in the presence of a particular type of constraint – the interests and preferences of other individuals.

We already know that when individuals interact, the outcome may not be best for all. The bargaining process may or may not allow them to reach satisfactory outcomes from their point of view. The purpose of this chapter is to investigate the reasons for individuals' failure to reach their preferred outcomes. We investigate what economists often refer to as the disagreement outcome, and what political philosophers call the *state of nature*. The disagreement outcome is what we expect to see when agents involved in a bargaining process fail to reach an agreement. Crawford (1987: 122) explains this point succinctly:

> ...disagreements, whether they take the form of strikes, trade restrictions or arms races, tend to be very costly... But, before this aspect of the problem can even be approached, a theory that relates the likelihood of disagreement to the bargaining environment is needed. ...Almost all microeconomic and game-theoretic models of bargaining beg the question of what determines the probability of disagreements by *assuming* that an efficient settlement is always reached. This is probably due to the simple and elegant theoretical results often available under the efficiency assumption and to the common belief that inefficient outcomes are inconsistent with rational behavior by well-informed bargainers. But plainly, any theory of bargaining that assumes away the possibility of disagreement must fail to capture an aspect of bargaining that is of central importance...

Unlike neo-classical economists, political philosophers have been aware of the possibility of disagreement for centuries. Hobbes' reference to the pre-politics *state of nature*, as cited in the introduction, is commonly used to describe this state of affairs (Hobbes, 1968 (1651): 185-6):

> ...it is manifest, that ...without a common Power to keep them all in awe, [humans] are in that condition which is called ...Warre, where every man is enemy to every man ...And the life of man, solitaery, poore, nasty, brutish, and short.

In this chapter we present four different analytical frameworks that have been developed over the years to study the likelihood, form and consequences of disagreement among rational, social agents. These are: Arrow's Impossibility Theorem; McKelvey and Schofield's Chaos Theorem; Hobbes' Collective Action Problem; and Coase's Social Cost Problem. Each sheds a different light on the principle problem that is associated with social interactions. Together they demonstrate how and why disagreement among individual members of society is an inescapable phenomenon. The following chapters build on the methodological primitives of the previous chapter and the substantive foundations of this chapter to explore the rich theory of political bargaining that explains how social agents bargain their way out of *the state of natural disagreement* into a more civil state that we later call the *bargained social contract*.

2.2 The Arrowian Social Choice Problem

The western world has grown accustomed to the idea that democracies rely on political institutions such as elections and parliamentary structures. It is broadly believed that such institutions successfully aggregate individual preferences into coherent social choices. The ability to aggregate individual preferences into coherent social choices is the very idea of representative government.

Neo-classical economists tend to argue that markets operate efficiently and that any government intervention leads to deviations from the efficient operation of the market. Political scientists tend to portray modern, democratic, political institutions as promoting, through elections and the work of legislative bodies, the adequate (Wittman, 1995, added 'efficient') operation of representative government.

Approaching the same fundamental problem of aggregating individual preferences into social choices, economists have argued for decades that some 'social welfare function' could be devised to yield optimal states of societal affairs. The idea was that some mechanism for aggregating individual preferences (e.g. a voting scheme) should be used to find the optimal outcome that maximizes the aggregate utility of members in society under existing technological and scarcity constraints (Samuelson, 1947: 219-49; 1954, 1955).

Of course, if such a social welfare function could be found and put to use, there would be little room for bargaining in society and only a negligible role for political institutions in general. In the same way, if free markets actually worked as smoothly as they should, according to neo-classical economic orthodoxy, there would be no room for economic bargaining. Producers would produce to satisfy demand and the market would clear – i.e. the quantity produced would be sold – at the price of the lowest marginal cost of production possible under existing demographic and technological conditions.

Unfortunately, Arrow (1951) proved that if we impose plausible conditions on social choice mechanisms, the task of constructing an appropriate, social welfare function is a logical impossibility (Buchanan, 1988).

Arrow's result is important to our argument inasmuch as it demonstrates that society cannot rely on straightforward mechanisms to aggregate the preferences of its members into social choices. Dictatorial regimes do not need such mechanisms because the preferences of the single ruler are aggregated with no other preferences. Hence, the dictator's choice is the social choice. Western liberal societies, on the other hand, because they base their social choices on the aggregation of individual preferences, have been using several sorts of summation schemes for more than two centuries, but with only limited success. The difficulty inherent in democratic mechanisms that attempt to aggregate individual preferences into social choices, such as general elections and parliaments, necessarily leads special interests and other agents in society to rely on different bargaining mechanisms to complement the institutions that western society has devised to help reach social choices. To understand this point we turn to a brief discussion of *Arrow's Impossibility Theorem*.

In the previous chapter we introduced the following notations: $O=\{a,b,c...\}$ is the set of outcomes; $N=\{1,...,n\}$ is the set of agents with $i \in N$ being a generic member of this set. R denotes a weak preference relation, where aR_ib denotes that outcome a is at least as good for i as outcome b. If aR_ib and bR_ia, then aI_ib denotes that i is indifferent between a and b. If aR_ib but not bR_ia, aP_ic denotes that i strictly prefers a to c. A preference order, R_i, orders the set of outcomes $O=\{a,b,c,...\}$ according to i's preferences. R_i is complete if for any pair of outcomes, $a,b \in O$, either aR_ib, or bR_ia or both – i.e. if for every possible pair of outcomes i prefers one or the other, or is indifferent. The preference order, R_i is transitive if for every three outcomes $\{a,b,c\} \subseteq O$, if aR_ib and bR_ic then aR_ib. This means that if i weakly prefers a to b and b to c, then i weakly prefers a to c. R_i is reflexive if for every outcome $a \in O$, aR_ia, i.e. every outcome is at least as good for i as this same outcome. Completeness requires that individuals know what they want, making choices among pairs of possible outcomes. Transitivity requires that individuals have logical preferences. If a person weakly prefers fish to meat and meat to bread, transitivity requires that this person weakly prefers fish to bread. If agents' preferences were not transitive, a person who prefers fish to meat and meat to bread, but prefers bread to fish would not be able to decide which of these to pick. Reflexivity guarantees that each outcome is always valued in the same way. It rules out trivial internal contradictions of preferences. A preference order R_i is called a *weak preference order* if it is complete, transitive and reflexive (Ordeshook, 1986: 12).

Let $\Re = \{R_1,...,R_n\}$ be a set of preference orders of individuals in society. $\Re$ is often referred to as the *preference profile* of individuals in society. We assume that all the individual preference orderings are complete transitive and reflexive as defined above. Finally, **R** (without a subscript) denotes the preference order of society. We would like to be able to aggregate $\Re$, the *preference profile* of individuals in society, into **R**, a *weak social preference order*. The aggregation should take into account, at least to some minimal extent, the preference orders of the individual agents in society. We call such an aggregation scheme, a social preference function (SPF) and denote it by $S(\Re, O) = R$. $S(\Re, O) = R$ defines the social preference relation **R** between every pair of outcomes $a, b \in O$, given the preference profile, $\Re$, of agents in society, and the set of feasible outcomes **O**.

Arrow assembled five basic conditions on $S(\Re, O)$ and **R** and showed that even if these five restrictions were the only constraints on the mechanism, we end up with a logical impossibility. Since he had proven his so-called *Impossibility Theorem*, much of the scholarly interest in Social Choice Theory has been to define, redefine and substitute conditions to Arrow's original ones. But all of these efforts have proven the robustness of Arrow's result to such iterations (see for example, Sen, 1982). The minimal set of basic requirements that Arrow imposed on the SPF could be defined as follows:

1. Collective Rationality: **R**, the social preference order that is the output of the SPF is reflexive, complete and transitive, i.e. **R** is a weak order on **O**.
2. Unrestricted Domain: Every complete, transitive and reflexive individual preference order, R_i, is admissible in $\Re$, i.e. individuals may have any weak preference order over the set of feasible outcomes **O**.
3. Pareto's criterion: if every agent in society weakly prefers **a** to **b**, then society prefers **a** to **b**. Formally: $(\forall\ i \in N\ aR_i b) \Rightarrow (aRb)$.
4. Independence of Irrelevant Alternatives: any reasonable SPF, $S(\Re, O) = R$, must be consistent in the sense that adding or eliminating outcomes from the feasible set should not alter the societal preferences over remaining alternatives in **O**. Formally, let $\Re$ and $\Re'$ be two possible preference profiles of society. Let $\Re \mid \{x, y\}$ denote the preference ordering on $x, y \in O$ in the preference profile $\Re$. Independence of Irrelevant Alternatives requires that if $\Re \mid \{x, y\} = \Re' \mid \{x, y\}$ then $S(\Re, \{x, y\}) = S(\Re', \{x, y\})$ regardless of other outcomes in **O** that may be ordered in $\Re$ differently than in $\Re'$.
5. Non-Dictatorship: no individual agent may be decisive over every pair $a, b \in O$, i.e. no agent should be allowed to impose his or her preferences on society as a whole. Formally, the set of decisive coalitions D_S is defined as: $D_S = \{\ C \subseteq N:\ \forall\ a, b \in O,\ \text{if}\ \forall\ i \in C\ aP_i b,\ \text{then}\ S(\Re, \{a, b\}) = aPb\}$ Non-Dictatorship requires that $\forall\ i \in N, i \notin D_S$.

Arrow's Impossibility Theorem 2.1 (Arrow, 1951): If $n \geq 3$ and **O** consists of 3 or more alternatives, any SPF that satisfies condition 1 through 4, violates condition 5. (See the appendix to this chapter for an outline of the proof.[1])

Each of the five conditions proposed by Arrow (1951) can be justified on technical and normative grounds. Given the importance of this result we outline below the technical and normative justifications for these conditions emphasizing how minimally restrictive they are.

The first condition requires that the output of the aggregation mechanism be a weak order. On technical grounds this requirement is necessary to make the output of the aggregating mechanism useful for the purpose of making choices at the collective level. We already stated that the transitivity assumption embedded in the requirement for a weak order to ensue of the aggregating process, is crucial for the preference order to allow for decision-making at the individual level. The same holds at the collective level. On normative grounds, it is clear that an unacceptable amount of arbitrariness would be involved in any decision made on the basis of a preference order that violates the transitivity assumption.

The second condition allows individuals to have any preference order they may. On technical grounds, restricting the domain of preference orders at the individual level restricts the applicability of the aggregation mechanism to only a subset of preference profiles making it non-generic. The normative justification is the liberal principle that individuals may have whatever preferences they may in a free society. Note that allowing individuals to have any preference order they may, is very different from allowing them to obtain their most preferred outcome or any other outcome. The idea here is that it is perfectly reasonable to restrict what individuals may do, but not what they may want to do.

The third condition only requires that if all individuals in a society prefer one outcome to another then this outcome should be preferred by society. On technical grounds, an aggregation mechanism that implements a choice that is inferior by the preferences of all individuals cannot be regarded as aggregating individual preferences in any meaningful way. On normative ground note that it is very rare that all individuals in any given society agree on the preference ordering of any two outcomes. But if all individuals in society prefer one outcome to the other it is reasonable to require that the aggregation mechanism does not reverse this unanimous preference.

The fourth condition requires that the introduction or elimination of outcomes from the feasible set of possible outcomes does not change the preference relationship between other outcomes. On technical grounds this is a consistency requirement. If the arbitrary introduction or elimination of independent possible outcomes into the feasible set would reverse preference relationships among other alternatives, then the aggregating mechanism is in danger of ensuing inconsistent preference orders as its output. At the normative level, aggregation mechanisms that are sensitive to the introduction or elimination of irrelevant alternatives into the feasible set make it easy to manipulate the social preference order by introducing arbitrary outcomes to the choice set or eliminating outcomes that no one would want to implement anyway. Plurality rule is a good example to illustrate the consequences of violating this assumption. Consider Table 2.1 that specifies the preference profile of nine individuals in a society using plurality rule to make its decisions. Plurality rule picks as the winner the outcome that receives more votes than any other outcome. In Table 2.1 this would be outcome (**a**). Since both outcomes (**b**) and (**d**) are ranked either third or fourth by six of the nine individuals, suppose we eliminated them from the set of feasible outcomes. All of a sudden, outcome (**c**) is the winner.

Table 2.1 A Nine-Person Preference Profile Over Four Possible Outcomes

Individual Preference	1	2	3	4	5	6	7	8	9
1st	a	a	a	a	b	c	d	d	d
2nd	c	c	c	c	c	a	c	c	c
3rd	b	b	b	b	a	b	a	a	a
4th	d	d	d	d	d	d	b	b	b

Now suppose that we introduce alternative (e) into the choice set as in Table 2.2. It is clear that all but two individuals rank outcome (e) as their least favorable alternative. Yet the introduction of outcome (e) makes alternative (d) the winner even though it is ranked last or one before last by six out of the nine individuals. So the introduction of an alternative with very little support in society, makes this aggregation mechanism pick yet another unpopular outcome as the most preferred outcome by society. Obviously, plurality rule violates the fourth condition put forward by Arrow (1951).

Table 2.2 A Nine-Person Preference Profile Over Five Possible Outcomes

Individual Preference	1	2	3	4	5	6	7	8	9
1st	e	e	a	a	b	c	d	d	d
2nd	a	a	c	c	c	a	c	c	c
3rd	c	c	b	b	a	b	a	a	a
4th	b	b	d	d	d	d	b	b	b
5th	d	d	e	e	e	e	e	e	e

Condition five states that no single person should dictate the final preference order for society. On technical grounds an aggregation mechanism can hardly be said to be sensitive to individual preferences if it keeps implementing the preference order of a single person in society. The normative justification to rule out the possibility of a dictator is quite obvious.

Arrow's (1951) theorem proved that if we impose minimal constraints such as conditions 2–5 discussed above, on mechanisms that are supposed to aggregate individual preferences into social choices, there would always exist preference profiles that yield cyclical social preference orders. This constitutes a violation of the transitivity condition that is so basic to any pretence of logical decision making, as we explained above. This important result suggests that the common perception of the operation of representative politics is naive. Mechanisms designed to aggregate individual preferences into social choices are bound to be indecisive, inasmuch as they yield cyclical social preference orders, or arbitrary, inasmuch as they allow 'local dictators' to manipulate the agenda and political outcomes. In short, social outcomes are not reflective of individual preferences to the extent we previously believed.

Arrow's Impossibility Theorem proves that any mechanism that tries to aggregate individual preferences into collective preference must violate at least one of Arrow's conditions. Below we show how simple majority rule almost always violates the first condition and produces cyclical preference orders in violation of the transitivity assumption. In the remainder of the book we show how institutions and bargaining mechanisms help alleviate this problem by allowing complementary and substitute procedures to take over when simple social choice mechanism, like majority rule, that are supposed to aggregate individual preferences into social choices, fail.

Meanwhile, it is important to note that Arrow provided a clear theory of the possibility of disagreement. If social order relied solely on mechanisms that aggregate individual preferences into social choices, society would be stuck in an uneasy balance. A mix of arbitrary cycles of choice, arbitrary dictates of local dictators and social choice preferences twisted by the peculiarities of the mechanism that was used to generate them. The process of political bargaining, discussed in this book, originates, among other things, in the need to alleviate the damage caused by these inherent sources of arbitrariness in political decision-making. Governments and constituents realize the damage caused by cyclical social preferences and arbitrary aggregation mechanisms and, therefore, engage in different processes of bargaining that they have designed in order to enable them to attain a more desirable state of affairs.

2.3 The Chaos Theorem

Arrow's Impossibility Theorem provides a general statement concerning the arbitrariness of social decisions. In this section we discuss an important example of how political choices may be affected by this profound observation. The typical mechanism used to aggregate individual preferences into political choices is the two-stage scheme that asks adult citizens to elect representatives to a legislative body and then requires the elected members of legislative bodies to make social choices using majority rule. How then does the problem presented by Arrow and discussed in the previous section manifest itself in the context of this commonly used political institution?

Spatial theory of electoral competition (STEC) was developed to study the problem of aggregating individual preferences into social choices via general elections and the daily work of legislative bodies. In the framework of STEC, possible outcomes are represented as points in space. Each vital aspect of the choice environment is represented as a dimension in an m-dimensional space denoted by $\mathbf{R}^m$. Alternative outcomes are represented as points in this space. The utility $u_i(\mathbf{x})$ that agent i derives from an outcome $\mathbf{x} \in \mathbf{R}^m$, is assumed to be a function of the Euclidean distance between $\mathbf{x}$ and ρ_i: $u_i(\mathbf{x}) = \varphi_i(|\mathbf{x}-\rho_i|)$, where ρ_i represents the most preferred outcome, or ideal point of i in $\mathbf{R}^m$. The central solution concept in STEC is the *simple majority core*, defined as:

Definition 2.1: $\mathbf{x}^* \in \mathbf{R}^m$ is in the *simple majority core* if for any other outcome in the choice space, $\mathbf{y} \in \mathbf{R}^m$, at least half of the agents prefer x to y.

When the core is non-empty, i.e. when there is an outcome that satisfies Definition 2.1, we expect the outcome of an interaction among rational agents using majority rule to be a *core* allocation (see again our discussion in section 1.3). This is so because, by definition, there is no position that a majority of the relevant agents would prefer to the *core* position, and, therefore, no position can defeat the *core* position in a simple majority rule game.

Based on Hotteling's early work on economic marketing (1929), STEC was introduced to political science by two seminal contributions: Downs' *Economic Theory of Democracy* (1957), and Black's *Theory of Committees* (1958). What made these works exemplary (in Kuhn's, 1970, sense of the word) is that they familiarized political scientists with the *Median Voter Theorem*.

The Median Voter Theorem (MVT) (Downs, 1957; Black, 1958):[2] In uni-dimensional political settings, using plurality rule with two candidates, if voters have single peaked preferences, voters and candidates have complete information about voters' preferences and candidates' policy positions, both candidates will endorse the position of the median voter.

This result provides a rationale for using plurality rule as a political institution inasmuch as it shows that in uni-dimensional choice environments, plurality rule promotes central positions that have the advantage of being 'as close as possible to as many voters as possible.' Black's (1958) discussion of the MVT suggests that committees that use majority rule in uni-dimensional decision environments will always endorse the position of the median legislator of the committee. Note, however, that the MVT introduced a 'new' requirement to be imposed on the profile of the preference – that of 'single peakedness.' Single peakedness requires that any individual has a single most preferred outcome and that his or her utility be a decreasing function of the Euclidean distance between this point and any point in a spatial representation of the choice set of the individual.

But how can one obtain such requirements as 'single peakedness' or 'uni-dimensionality' in an empirical context? While it is very difficult to define the exact meaning of 'political culture,' it is easy to observe that certain cultures include certain preferences and exclude others. In fact, political preferences that are common in one place are not admissible in others. For example, it is difficult to imagine a party that promotes beef, competing in elections in Hindu states, or a party advocating pork, running for a post in an Islamic country. These cultural mechanisms of inclusion and exclusion of people, ideas, issues, policies and ideologies provide a sufficient logical ground for the expectation that the theoretical requirement for single peaked, single dimensional preferences may, in some cases, also be a practical one.

In Chapter 5 we analyze electoral competition as a process of bargaining over competing social choices. Candidates promote and bargain with the electorate over different possible outcomes of the electoral process. Using this interpretation, MVT is an elegant result at both the normative and positive levels of discussion. At the normative level, the theorem suggests that under some conditions social bargaining mechanisms may yield normatively acceptable outcomes. At the positive level, it is comforting to know that we can predict the outcome of complex bargaining processes with such accuracy.

The next scientific step is to see if this result holds under a somewhat more realistic assumption of multidimensional choice environments. McKelvey and Schofield show that in policy spaces with two dimensions or more, simple majority cores rarely exist, and if a core does not exist, agendas can lead to almost any outcome (McKelvey, 1976, 1979; Schofield, 1978, 1984; McKelvey & Schofield, 1986, 1987). This conclusion is often referred to as the *Chaos Theorem* (CT).

The Chaos Theorem: In multidimensional choice spaces, using pair-wise comparisons and majority rule, a *majority core* rarely exists, and if a *core* does not exist, for every pair of outcomes $a, b \in O$, there exists a series of outcomes $<o_1, ..., o_{k-1}, o_k>$ so that by majority rule $aPo_1 ... Po_{k-1}Po_kPb$.

Figure 2.1 in the following page provides a graphic illustration of this result. Postulating a legislative body of three individuals {**1,2,3**}, with respective three ideal points {ρ_1, ρ_2, ρ_3}, it is easy to see how an able manipulator could generate an agenda that would lead changing majority coalitions of two legislators at a time, to prefer o_k to x (legislators 1 and 3), o_{k-1} to o_k (legislators 2 and 3), o_{k-2} to o_{k-1} (legislators 1 and 2) and so on until alternative y is preferred to o_{k-7} (legislator 1 and 2) even though it is easy to see that all legislators prefer x to y.

We should interpret this result as a special case of Arrow's Theorem. Arrow (1951) proved that if we impose plausible requirements on mechanisms that aggregate individual preferences into social choices, we end up with mechanisms that are bound, given some preference profiles of individuals in society, to yield cyclical, intransitive social choice orders. McKelvey and Schofield (1987) show that simple majority rule is a mechanism that, for a large family of preference profiles, 'almost always' yields such cyclical, intransitive social choice orders.

These results imply that the use of majority rule and binary comparisons to order the preferences of society over a set of alternatives is likely to yield cyclical social preference orders. Put in simple terms, if we used majority rule, unchecked by other, supplementary institutional structures, as our sole social choice mechanism, it would very likely lead to inherently unstable social choice preference orders (Riker, 1982). In the following chapters, most notable in Chapters 5 and 6, we discuss at some length these 'supplementary' institutional structures and how they help prevent the arbitrariness and instability that are inherent in majority rule as a social choice mechanism.

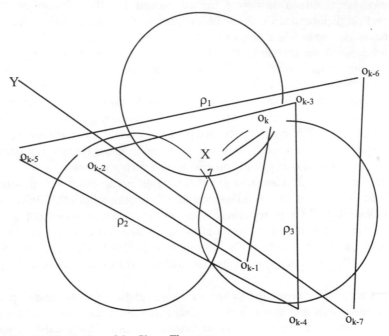

Figure 2.1 An Illustration of the Chaos Theorem

Once again we get an elegant theoretical understanding of the possibility of disagreement. The authors of the U.S. Constitution were presumably aware of the consequences of this possibility of disagreement. They therefore chose a particularly robust institutional design to guarantee the stability of constitutional provisions and amendments. There are four ways to amend the Constitution: in the first stage, a new amendment must be passed either by a two-third majority of both houses of Congress[3] or by a special constitutional convention. In the second stage, the amendment must either be approved by three-fourths of the state legislatures or ratified by special ratifying conventions in three-fourths of the states.[4] Many legal systems include similar institutional designs to protect important laws or constitutional provisions from the possibility of disagreement.

Meanwhile, we have shown how STEC provides a theoretical framework to study 'the likelihood of disagreement in the bargaining environment' of majority rule. When unchecked by complementary institutions, majority rule is likely to lead to disagreement in the form of cyclical social preference orders resulting in unstable and inefficient implementation of social policies. Niemi and Weisberg (1968) present an algorithm to calculate the actual likelihood of disagreement for different sizes of groups and sets of feasible outcomes. They find that for realistic group size and moderately diverse choice sets, the likelihood for cyclical preference orders is quite high. In the following chapters we argue that politics is often more concerned with bargaining over institutional arrangements that help reduce this high likelihood of disagreement, than with the direct aggregation of individual preferences into social preference orders.

2.4 Hobbes' Collective Action Problem[5]

Hobbes (1986 (1651)) provided us another theory of a social disagreement point. For Hobbes, humans have a natural right of self-preservation only insofar as they have a natural inclination to preserve themselves (Hobbes, 1986 (1651): 189; Bluhm, 1984: 59-60). From this natural inclination and an assumption about human rationality, Hobbes derived his justification for the necessity of governments (Hobbes, 1986 (1651): 188-91): Humans are inclined to self-preserve themselves. They know that they are basically equal in their capacity to inflict injury on one another. Therefore, they see in each other human being a potential threat.[6] So, in the *state of nature* – in the absence of governments or other 'agreement inducing' institutions – humans are expected to do anything they can to eliminate one another in a Hobbesian 'war of all against all.'

Hobbes argues that humans, as rational beings, recognize the threat of such a gloomy future. These rational expectations lead them to agree to a social contract in which they entrust the responsibility for their defense to whomever they crown as their absolute sovereign. From this point on, the sovereign – and not the individuals in society – is the guardian of all fundamental human right.

As previously described, the game theoretic model commonly used to describe and analyze what Hobbes called the state of nature is the Prisoners' Dilemma game (Taylor, 1987). For the purposes of the argument developed in subsequent chapters, it is important to understand this simple abstract model of the state of nature. Consider a two-person version of the game summarized in Figure 2.2. Each player can choose between two strategies: to respect (i.e. cooperate) or not to respect the rights of the other player. Recall that the numbers in the cells indicate the utility each player gets from any possible combination of strategies chosen, simultaneously, by the two players. The first number in every cell indicates the utility which player 1 gets. The second number indicates the utility that player 2 gets. For example, if both players chose to respect each other's rights, each would receive a utility of 1, while if both chose not to respect the other agent's rights, neither would get any utility – indeed, according to Hobbes' description of the state of nature, they would probably both be dead.

In the previous chapter we used the Prisoners' Dilemma game to explain the intuition behind the commonly used solution concept in game theory – the Nash

Players		Player No. 2	
	Strategies	Cooperate (C)	Defect (D)
Player No. 1	Cooperate (C)	1,1	-1,2
	Defect (D)	2,-1	0,0

Figure 2.2 The State of Nature as a Two-Person Prisoners' Dilemma

Equilibrium concept (Nash, 1951, 1953). To restate: a combination of strategic choices constitutes a Nash Equilibrium if no player can alter his or her strategic choice of behavior, given the strategic choice(s) of all the other player(s) and be better off. We expect Nash Equilibria to be stable outcomes in games and in the human interactions of which these games serve as abstractions, because if no player can obtain higher pay-offs by unilaterally changing his or her strategic choices, then no player has an incentive to change his or her behavior, as long as the other players stick to their strategic choices.

It is well known and we have shown in the previous chapter that the only Nash Equilibrium of a Prisoners' Dilemma game is for both players to defect. So if we think that the Prisoners' Dilemma game is an adequate representation of the *state of nature*, we would expect individuals not to respect each other's rights in this state of affairs. It is relatively easy to construct an n-person version of the game and apply this result to all members of society (Calvert, 1995; Hardin, 1982; Sened, 1997). In fact we go through this exercise in the next chapter. Note that if players could somehow commit themselves to mutual respect (all cooperate), they would be better off. Hobbes argued that rational agents should realize this advantage that each player would get if all agents respected each other's rights and opt for a social contract in which they would entrust their security to whomever they agree to regard as their absolute sovereign. This behavior, however, is not an equilibrium behavior. This simple game theoretic analysis shows the weakness of Hobbes' social contract theory. The fact that humans are rational and that they recognize the misery in which they live in the absence of a social contract, does not imply that they do anything to work their way out of their misery and into any form of a *civil society*. Protracted civil wars that rage in every corner of the globe, as well as all the gang wars in the urban centers of the U.S. serve as sad reminders of this fact. As the above game illustrates, these wars continue because it is a dominant strategy for the leader of each warring gang to perpetuate the fighting. At the international sphere we may use the Prisoners' Dilemma prediction to comprehend why so little is being done by the international community – i.e. self-interested single agents called states – to cooperate to avoid potential catastrophes that may be generated by, for example, the desecration of the rain forests or the ozone layer (Doron, 1992). We return to this subject in Chapter 7.

For the purposes of this book, it is important to realize that Hobbes was correct in arguing that only strong, stable structures of government, by enforcing law and order, can help society avoid the war of all against all. Yet, Hobbes error was to argue that such structures would emerge spontaneously from within any group of rational agents. He was also wrong to argue that the survival of these structures was dependent on the benevolence of those entrusted to govern and on the compliance of rational agents fearing the collapse of the social contract and a return to a state of nature (Sened, 1997: 18). In this way Hobbes certainly contributed an elegant theory of the likelihood and nature of the point of disagreement in the context of social interactions while teaching us very little about how human beings may bargain their way out of this disagreement point. The next two chapters address this question.

2.5 Coase's Social Cost Problem[7]

'Coase's Theorem' states that if property rights are well defined, then, in the absence of transaction costs, the efficiency of resource allocations is not affected by the initial distribution of property rights. This result has generated a body of literature known as the 'transaction cost theory of institutions' (Furubotn and Richter, 1997; Sened, 2000). Coase's (1960) theorem and the literature it generated is a good example of Crawford's (1987: 122) argument that: '...almost all ... models of bargaining beg the question of what determines the probability of disagreements by assuming that an efficient settlement is always reached.'

Coase's (1960) assumed a hypothetical world with zero transaction costs. In this world he considered two agents: a farmer growing corn, and a cattle rancher, raising cows. The question is whether it makes any difference if the rancher is liable for damages inflicted by his or her cows to the farmer's cornfields. Welfare economists often refer such damages as 'negative externalities.' That is, side-effects caused by the production of certain goods which negatively affect the utility of others, not involved in the production or purchase of the goods. Air pollution generated by factories is a prime illustration of a negative externality.

Negative externalities are often mentioned as a justification for government intervention. The argument behind such justification is that the cattle rancher does not include the damage caused to the cornfield when s/he calculates the production cost function and therefore produces more than s/he should. A government can impose a tax on the cattle rancher forcing him or her to take these costs into account and reduce the herd to a societal 'optimal' size. Coase's (1960) rejection of this argument is known as 'Coase's Theorem.'

Coase constructed his argument using the following example rephrased and augmented by a numerical illustration by Sened (1997: 92-5): let the farmer's expected revenue be p•q where p is the market price for corn and q is the quantity of corn produced. Since Caose assumes perfectly competitive markets, the price of corn and steers is unaffected by the amount produced. Suppose that the price of a ton of corn is $1.00 and that the farmer would have produced 100 tons of corn if the cornfields were undamaged by the cattle. Suppose further, that the damage, the benefits, total and marginal, to the farmer and the rancher, given different sizes of herds, are as summarized in Table 2.3. Note that marginal revenues are assumed to decrease linearly while marginal losses increase linearly. By standard analysis these implicit assumptions are not very restrictive.

By simple inspection of Table 2.3, it is clear that if the cattle-raiser were liable for damages, s/he would raise 12 steers. What previous analysts did not recognize, and Coase (1960) pointed out, is that the same is true if the rancher is not liable since the farmer is expected to pay him or her not to raise the size of the herd beyond 12 steers. Given this analysis, it does not matter if the government taxes the rancher in order to reduce production to the optimal level, if the rancher is made liable for the damages by law or if the law does not specify any liability. The legal structure of rights concerning liability for damage is not going to affect the allocation of scarce resources in the market.

Table 2.3 Total and Marginal Benefits to Farmer and Cattle-Raiser

Number of Cattle Heads	Tons/$ of Crop Lost	Marginal Loss in Crop	Net Return to Cattle-Raiser	Marginal Returns to Cattle-Raiser with no Liability (with Liability)	Total Social Return in $
7	0	0	79	9 (9)	100+79=179
8	0	0	87	8 (8)	100+87=187
9	0	0	94	7 (7)	100+94=194
10	1	1	100	6 (5)	100+100–1=199
11	3	2	105	5 (3)	100+105–3=202
12	6	3	109	4 (1)	100+109–6=203
13	10	4	112	3 (–1)	100+112–10=202
14	15	5	114	2 (–3)	100+114–15=199
15	21	6	115	1 (–5)	100+115–21=194

Table 2.4 below concludes Coase's argument and Sened's numerical example.

Table 2.4 Optimal Resource Allocation Under Different Ownership Designs

Alternative Regulations, Using Alternative Structures of Property Rights	Net Return to Cattle-Raiser	Net Return to Farmer	Net Return to Government	Total Social Return Including Government's Tax Revenue
Liability on Cattle Raiser	103	100	0	100+103=203
No Liability	109+6=115	100–12=88	0	115+88=203
One Firm Management	–	–	0	100+103=203
Government Taxes Cattle at a Rate of $ 4 per Steer	109–48=61	100–6=94	48	61+94+48=203

Crawford, however, correctly pointed out that there is one missing factor in this argument: what would happen if the cattle-raiser and the corn farmer failed to reach an agreement? Coase (1960) avoided this issue by assuming that property rights are well defined.[8] But how do we get well-defined property rights?

If governments do not interfere, we are likely to end up with the Hobbesian disagreement point. To this day we have no convincing theory as to how property rights may emerge and persist without government intervention (Sened,

1997; cf. Taylor, 1987; Sugden, 1986; Umbeck, 1981). If governments are as crucial players in this context as recent scholarship attests, we must include them in the story as self-interested, rational agents. What would be the consequences of including a government as a utility maximizing agent in the analysis? Sened (1997: 95) shows that in his numerical example a revenue maximizing government with a monopoly on law enforcement and tax collection would collect $ 8 per steer as specified in Table 2.5.

Table 2.5 Resource Allocations with Governments that Maximize Revenues

Alternative Regulations, Using Alternative Structures of Property Rights	Net Return to Cattle-Raiser	Net Return to Farmer	Net Return to Government	Total Social Return Including Government's Tax Revenue
Government Taxes Cattle at a Rate of $ 8 per Steer	87–64=23	100	64	23+100+64=187

This is a typical 'inefficiency' that economists blame governments for. But these economists refuse to recognize how crucial governments are for the definition and enforcement of property rights because they ignore, as Crawford pointed out, the high likelihood for disagreement in the absence of government intervention.

2.6 Concluding Remarks: A Bargained Social Contract

Despite extensive debate about social order, remarkably little attention has been given to the simple fact that most institutions that protect law and order in society depend on the 'good will' and 'designing skills' of central governments.

In this chapter we explored what Hobbes termed the *state of nature*. We have shown that in a world without social institutions, agents tend to settle for Pareto inferior equilibrium outcomes, or no equilibrium at all. We pointed out that governments tend to intervene and alleviate such dilemmas by enforcing different structures of order. Since governments can extract – through taxation for example – some of the benefits they help generate in this way, we expect them to seek opportunities to enforce law and order (Levi, 1988; Sened, 1997).

This claim goes back at least as far as Hobbes. What has often been overlooked by the literature, however, is that governments are rational players themselves (Buchanan, 1986: 36-7). Rational governments implement policies only when their selfish needs outweigh the expected cost of enforcement.

It is a premise of this book that social contracts are enforced and maintained by central governments. But the central theme of this book is that every element of the social contract is the outcome of a long political bargaining process that leads governments to design case-specific social contracts that they are prepared to enforce (Sened, 1997). The following chapters look at these bargaining processes.

Notes

1. A tractable rigorous version of the proof is found in Blau, 1972.

2. To be perfectly accurate this result is actually due in part to Hotelling (1929). On the role of exemplary, past achievements in the development of science see Kuhn (1970: 174-5, 187-91). The median voter theorem is a good example of such an 'exemplar.' An excellent discussion of the centrality of this result in contemporary political science is found in Shepsle, 1990.

3. The inherent instability induced by majority rule as a social choice mechanism is often cited as the underlying rationale behind the choice of 'super majority rules' as alternative institutional designs. Schofield (1984a, 1984b) shows that super majority mechanisms, that require more than a simple majority to change the status quo, are less likely to yield intransitive, cyclical, social choices.

4. For further details see Aldrich et al., 1986: 51. In fact, except for the twenty-first amendment, only the Congress-state legislatures route has ever been used.

5. This section is adopted from earlier work by Sened (1997: 15-18).

6. In most modern versions of social contract theories, scarcity is the force that motivates the use of violence (e.g. Umbeck, 1981). For Hobbes the motivation to use violence is the fear of every individual, of the pursuit of reputation by other individuals in the state of nature (Hobbes, 1968 (1651): 185; Bluhm, 1984: 62-5).

7. This section is adapted from earlier work by Sened (1997: 91-5).

8. Earlier works in neo-classical theory made the assumption that such rights are well defined and well protected explicit (e.g. Stigler, 1942: 22). Recent works tend to make this assumption implicit. But all of this literature depends crucially, in one way or another, on this basic assumption (Eggertsson, 1990: 38-9).

Appendix: An Outline of the Proof to Arrow's Theorem

A relatively simple proof of Arrow's theorem is provided in Blau (1972). We outline the logic of this proof in an attempt to explain it without making it inaccessible to a broad audience. Readers with a technical background are encouraged to read Blau's (1972) original proof. The proof follows three intuitive basic steps:

1. First, we show that if SPF, $S(\Re,O)=R$, makes individual i decisive over any two outcomes a,b$\in$O then this SPF, $S(\Re,O)=R$, makes i decisive over this pair of outcomes for any set possible outcomes. Making individual i decisive means that whenever the preference profile, $\Re$, indicates that i weakly prefers **a** to **b**, i.e. aR_ib, then the SPF, $S(\Re,O)=R$, makes society weakly prefer **a** to **b**, i.e. aRb, regardless of the preferences of other individuals in society.
2. Second, we show that if an individual i$\in$N is decisive, by SPF, $S(\Re,O)=R$, over a pair of outcomes, a,b$\in$O, s/he may be, given some preference profile $\Re$, decisive over any pair c,d$\in$O, by virtue of being made decisive, by SPF, $S(\Re,O)=R$, over a,b$\in$O and the structure of the preference profile $\Re$.
3. Third, we show that any SPF, $S(\Re,O)=R$, is bound to make some individual i$\in$N decisive over some pair of outcomes **a,b$\in$O**, given a certain preference profile, $\Re$. So, given the first two steps, every SPF is bound to violate the no-dictatorship principle if it satisfies the other conditions.

To see how the proof works, recall Arrow's five basic requirements:

1. **Collective rationality: R** is reflexive, complete and transitive, i.e. it is a weak order on **O**.
2. **Unrestricted domain:** Every *weak order*, R_i, is admissible in $\Re$, i.e. individuals may have any *weak preference order* over the set of feasible outcomes **O**.
3. **Pareto:** if every individual in society prefers **a** to **b**, then society prefers **a** to **b**: Formally: if $\forall$ i$\in$N aR_ib then **aRb**.
4. **Independence of irrelevant alternatives (IIA):** adding or eliminating alternatives to or from the feasible set will not alter the social preference order **R** over existing alternatives. Formally, let $\Re$ and $\Re$' be two preference profiles. Let $\Re \mid \{x,y\}$ refer to the preference ordering of x,y $\in$ **O** in the preference profile $\Re$. IID requires that if $\Re \mid \{x,y\} = \Re' \mid \{x,y\}$ then $S(\Re,\{x,y\}) = S(\Re',\{x,y\})$ regardless of other outcomes in **O** that may be ordered in $\Re$ differently than in $\Re$'.
5. **Non-dictatorship:** no agent i is decisive for every pair **a,b$\in$O**, i.e. no agent can have society order the alternatives according to his or her preferences. Formally, define the set of decisive coalitions, $\mathbb{D}_S$ as follows:

$$\mathbb{D}_S = \left\{ C \subseteq N: \forall \ a,b \in O \ \text{if} \ (\forall \ i \in C \ aP_ib) \ \text{then, by} \ S(\Re,O)=R, \ aPb \right\}$$

Non-Dictatorship requires that $\forall$ i$\subset$N, i$\notin \mathbb{D}_S$

Arrow's Impossibility Theorem 2.1: If $n \geq 3$ and $|O| \geq 3$, then any SPF that satisfies condition 1 through 4, violates condition 5.

Outline of the proof:
The first step is an immediate derivative of requirement # 4. If $S(\Re,O)=R$ makes some individual $i \in N$ decisive over some pair of outcomes $a,b \in O$, given a certain preference profile, $\Re$, and a set of outcomes O, IIA requires that it makes i decisive over a and b given any preference profile $\Re$, since we assume that i's preferences do not change from one profile to the other.

The second step of the proof shows how an individual who is decisive over a pair of outcomes $a,b \in O$, become decisive over other feasible outcomes, such as $c,d \in O$. To see how it works, assume some preference profile $\Re$ over $O=\{a,b,c\}$:

For individual i,	R_i is: a P_i b P_i c
$\forall\, j \in N$, $j \neq i$ (read for all individuals except i)	R_j is: b P_j c P_j a

We can assume such a preference profile based on requirement # 2 of unlimited domain. Suppose $S(\Re,O)=R$ makes i decisive over **a** and **b** (step three below, shows that every SPF makes some individual decisive over some pair of outcomes, given some preference profiles). Since aP_ib, **aPb**, by the Pareto requirement, since all agents here prefer b to c – **bPc**. By requirement # 1, **R** must be a weak order – i.e. **R** must be *transitive*. Since **aPb** (by assumption) and **bPc** (by Pareto), transitivity implies that **aPc**. Note that only i prefers **a** to **c**. So, by making individual i decisive over **a** and **b** $S(\Re,O)=R$ made him or her decisive over c. Note that we have used requirement # 4 to prove the first step and requirements 1, 2 and 3 to prove this step.

To make the general argument for larger sets of feasible outcomes one needs to go through several additional permutations of the simple argument above, but the logic remains the same: if $S(\Re,O)=R$ makes an individual decisive over one pair of outcomes, then given some preference order $\Re$, this individual could become a dictator who dictates the social preference order over all the possible outcomes. All that remains, is to prove that every SPF $S(\Re,O)=R$ allows one individual, given some preference profile $\Re$, to be decisive over two possible outcomes.

To see this recall the definition of the set of decisive coalitions, D_S:

$$D_S = \left\{ C \subseteq N: \forall\, a,b \in O \text{ if } (\forall\, i \in C\; aP_ib) \text{ then, by } S(\Re,O)=R, aPb \right\}$$

A decisive coalition is a coalition wherein if all members prefer **a** to **b**, then SPF $S(\Re,O)=R$ ranks **a** as preferred to **b** in **R**. A decisive coalition is allowed by $S(\Re,O)=R$ to impose the will of its members on the rest of society. For example, if $S(\Re,O)=R$ is a simple majority rule, then the set of decisive coalitions is the set of coalitions which includes at least half the members of society.

Every $S(\Re,O)=R$ determines a set of decisive coalition D_S and every such set has a smallest member in this set which is the smallest coalition that is decisive. By Arrow's set of requirements we know that D_S is never empty because, by the Pareto requirement, the set of all the players is always decisive.

Using the notion of a minimal decisive coalition we can now conclude the outline of the proof. Let C_{min} be the minimal size decisive coalition. The following is an admissible preference profile (by Req. # 2 of unlimited domain):

The preference order of individual i who is a member in C_{min} is: aP_ibP_ic
The preference order of all the other members of C_{min} ($j\neq i$, $j \in C_{min}$) is: cP_jaP_jb
The preference order of all the agents not members in C_{min} ($k \notin C_{min}$) is: bP_kcP_ka

Since C_{min} is decisive and all members of C_{min} prefer a to b we get aPb. Only members of C_{min} excluding i prefer c to b. C_{min} excluding i is not decisive, therefore we know that we cannot have cPb, because if we did it would mean that C_{min} excluding i is decisive and we assumed C_{min} to be the minimal size decisive coalition. But if cPb cannot be, we know that bRc. In words, simple rules of logic prescribe that if c is not preferred to b then b must be at least as good as c. By Arrow's first requirement **R** must be transitive, hence we get $aPbPc$, but note that only individual i prefers a to c.

This last step proves that every $S(\mathfrak{R},O)=R$ is bound to allow an individual to be decisive over one pair of outcomes for some preference profile $\mathfrak{R}$. From steps one and two we know that if this is the case, every $S(\mathfrak{R},O)=R$ that satisfies requirements 1 through 4 will, for some preference profiles, violate the fifth, non-dictatorship requirement.

3 A Bargained Social Contract

3.1 Introduction: Spontaneous and Intentional Origins of Social Order

How does social order evolve? Hobbes' thesis rests on the hypothesis that rational agents voluntarily agree to enter a social contract. Yet, the question as to how individuals in society overcome their tendency to behave selfishly was left unanswered. This chapter seeks to fill in the gap and looks at why people are willing to forgo immediate gain in return for an abstract social contract.

The conceptual approach of game theory in addressing this question derives from the premise that the evolution of social order must be explained in terms of equilibrium outcomes of recurrent social interactions (Schotter, 1981; Sugden, 1986; Taylor, 1987; Calvert, 1995; Sened, 1997). Sugden (1986: 5), for example, argues that legal codes 'merely formalize... conventions of behavior that have evolved out of essentially anarchic situations; ...[and] reflect codes of behavior that most individuals impose on themselves'. According to this argument, social order evolves by means of a spontaneous process from informal norms to more or less formal legal codes.

It is interesting to note how deeply the social contract hypothesis and the observed voluntary-based social order have been internalized by scholars and laymen. Historical accounts, however, reveal something different. They teach us that social order rarely emerged as conventional equilibria in repeated games (cf. Calvert, 1995), and that it is almost always imposed by central governments (Simpson, 1986 (1962); Riker and Sened, 1991; Olson, 1993). In most cases central authorities enforce law and order in an attempt to gain revenues and popular support (North, 1981; Levi, 1988; North, 1990; Sened, 1997).

Hence the argument we advance in this chapter is that governments anticipate inefficiencies that result in environments we characterized as disagreement states. They therefore enter into bargaining processes with their constituents to help avoid these points of disagreement in the hope of extracting tangible benefit from the excess productivity, either through tax revenues (Levi, 1988), or through enhanced political support (Riker and Sened, 1991). The next section introduces n-person Prisoners' Dilemma games. Section 3 presents infinitely repeated games as a milestone in the spontaneous emergence theory. We also introduce the *Folk Theorem* to demonstrate the limitations of this approach. In the remainder of the chapter we develop the 'contract by design' approach.

3.2 The Origin of Social Order: The State of Nature

It was already established that the hypothetical situation labeled as the *state of nature* could be modeled as an n-person Prisoners' Dilemma game. The concept of the *state of nature* describes a fictitious situation, very much like the notion of 'perfect markets' in economics or of the 'frictionless surface' in physics. As a concept it has much intellectual and analytical value in spite of the fact that such situations do not exist in the empirical world. This concept asks us to ignore the world in which we live where each society, large or small, is ruled by a government. It studies hypothetical rational individuals and the interest-guided dynamic taking place between them in a world without government.

Could it be that governments have always existed? The Hebrew Bible comes close to providing an answer with the story of Saul. According to this story, members of the twelve tribes of Israel, each living under 'his grape tree and fig tree' [read: *state of nature*] came to Samuel asking him to 'make us a king' [read: constitute a government] so they would be as secure as 'other nations.' The old Hebrew prophet agreed to meet his people's demand but not before he explained to them the nature of the trade-off associated with their request. With the benefit of the security they wished to obtain, so he argued, there would be a real cost to be paid in terms of their personal freedom.

An even more telling illustration of a *state of nature* situation is reflected in some aspects of contemporary electronic communication. Several countries (e.g. Norway, Italy, Israel) have permitted the legally-recognized or the de-facto development of an 'open sky' scenario, especially in the area of radio transmission. It is relatively inexpensive and often quite profitable for individuals to operate a radio station. However, the more people enter this market, the less profitable it becomes. This is because profit is determined, among other factors, by the number of listeners and the quantity of advertisement. To maximize profit, operators must expand into the zones of others. Consequently, 'a war of all against all' ensues, taking the form of jammed airwaves, and exhibiting a pattern where the rich and the powerful attempt to push the poor out of the market. One way to resolve the situation would be to let market forces take their course, whence only the fittest would survive. Another way would be to appeal to the government to regulate the matter. In this chapter we argue that governments, being rational players, tend to get involved in such situations only when they expect to derive positive gain. If the cost (of involvement) outweigh the benefit (in the form of taxes, prestige, etc.), the government would remain inactive. The following analysis explains why the 'social contract' is indeed a political outcome of a bargaining process between governments and individual members of society.

Let us return to the Prisoners' Dilemma as a conceptualization of the social problem.[1] As promised earlier we will now reconstruct it as an n-person game.[2] Suppose that each agent pays some cost $c_i=1$ to respect the law. Such an agent enhances the value of life of all agents in society by some marginal benefit. For simplicity's sake, let the marginal benefit that $i \in N$ gets if any *other* agent, $j \in N$, respects the law be $b_i = 1$. So, each agent gets a pay-off, $m \cdot b_i = m \geq 0$, if m agents ($0 \leq m < n$) respect the law. Note that m is strictly smaller than n because an agent does not get the marginal benefit of respect to the law from his or her own respect to the rights of others. In other words, if all citizens in society respect the law each gets a benefit of $(n-1) \cdot b_i = (n-1)$. Let $S_i = \{0,1\}$ (with $s_i \in S_i$) be the set of pure strategies available to any agent: s/he can pay the cost and respect the law, $s_i=1$, or ignore the law, $s_i=0$.[3] Allowing for mixed strategies, a strategy space of agent i is $[0,1]$ with $\sigma_i = pr(s_i=1) \in [0,1]$ – i.e. σ_i is the probability that i respects the law. One can think of σ_i as the willingness, or level of commitment of i to respect the law. Let $\sigma = (\sigma_1,..., \sigma_n) \in \sigma$ be a strategy vector that specifies the strategy σ_i that each agent $i \in N$ chose. The pay-off for every agent $i \in N$ from any $\sigma \in \sigma$ is:

$$(3.1) \quad u_i(\sigma) = \sum_{j \neq i} b_j \cdot \sigma_j - c_i \cdot \sigma_i = \sum_{j \neq i} \sigma_j - \sigma_i \text{ (since } b_i = c_i = 1).$$

Regardless of what other agents do, all agents maximize their utility at $\sigma_i=0$. So the unique dominant-strategy equilibrium vector is $\sigma^0 = (0,...,0)$, where all agents ignore the law, with $u_i(\sigma^0)=0 \ \forall \ i \in N$. Note that if all agents respected the law, each would get: $u_i(\sigma^1 =(1,...,1)) = (n-1) -1 = n-2$. If $n>2$,[4] we get an n-person version of the Prisoners' Dilemma: every agent prefers $u_i(\sigma^1) > 0$ over $u_i(\sigma^0) = 0$, so that σ^1 Pareto dominates the unique dominant-strategy equilibrium vector σ^0. These are the defining features of the Prisoners' Dilemma: A unique, Pareto inferior Nash Equilibrium where all players play their dominant strategy of defection while all agents would have been better off if they all cooperated.

3.3 The Origin of Order: Spontaneous Emergence and the Folk Theorem

There are two approaches to explain social order. The 'spontaneous approach' outlines equilibria in which agents find their own way into a *civil society*. The 'emergence by design' approach emphasizes the empirical fact summarized by Hume (1752: 470) who stated that almost all governments were 'founded originally either on usurpation or conquest or both, without any pretense of a fair consent or voluntary subjection of the people.' If this is the case, it may be more appropriate to look less at how free agents reach a *civil state* on their own, and study instead how social contract are promoted by 'predatory' governments.

In this section we start with the spontaneous emergence approach. In the following sections we elaborate the 'emergence by design' approach, showing how we can explain the process through which a governance structure based on 'usurpation' can evolve into a relatively civil social contract of an open society.

The most prevalent line of argument in the spontaneous emergence approach is to evoke the infinitely repeated logic of the Prisoners' Dilemma game. To argue that a social contract may emerge out of a situation of 'war of all against all,' we need to find a game that would explain how cooperation evolves out of an Hobbesian *state of nature*. It is in this context that the infinitely repeated

Prisoners' Dilemma game is evoked. Let us return to our earlier presentation of the game. Figure 3.1 reproduces the two-person Prisoners' Dilemma game.

Players		Player No. 2	
	Strategies	Cooperate (C)	Defect (D)
Player No. 1	Cooperate (C)	1,1	−1,2
	Defect (D)	2,−1	0,0

Figure 3.1 The State of Nature as a Two-Person Prisoners' Dilemma game

But suppose players kept playing the game infinitely. We must emphasize that anything less than infinity won't do. If players knew when the game ends, then they would both defect in the 'end game.' Knowing that they would both defect in the last game, each would defect in the one before last game and so on till the first game. But human interaction does not continue forever, so what is the point of building a model that assumes an infinite sequence of plays? To work around this problem, we put probabilities into the definition of the game. In this way, the game 'may' continue forever, but with all likelihood it would stop at a certain point. Consider the following utility function:

$$(3.2) \quad u_i(G) = \sum_{t=0}^{t=\infty} \delta^t \bullet \rho^t \bullet u_i(g_t)$$

G represents the infinitely repeated game and g_t represents the tth iteration of the game with $t \in \{0,1,\ldots,\infty\}$. $u_i(g_t)$ represents the pay-off individual i gets in the tth iteration of the game. We introduced δ in section 1.5 as a discount factor. We pointed out that it is commonly observed and therefore commonly assumed in these models that future pay-offs are discounted by some *discount factor* δ. The utility $u_i(g_t)$ individual i expects to get at the tth iteration is discounted by δ^t. We use ρ to denote the probability that the game will be reiterated at each point in time. We assume that once the game is interrupted players do not return to play. Therefore, the probability that players will get to the tth iteration of the game is ρ^t. Note that both $0 \leq \delta \leq 1$ and $0 \leq \rho \leq 1$. Therefore, $0 \leq \delta \bullet \rho \leq 1$ and $0 \leq \delta^t \bullet \rho^t \leq 1$. Authors often do not bother to distinguish between the two parameters. We keep the distinction because of its substantive importance for our argument.

The infinitely repeated game can be any game but here we will assume that each iteration of the game is a two-person Prisoners' Dilemma game as in Figure 3.1. An excellent n-person extension of this infinitely iterated Prisoners' Dilemma game is found in Calvert (1995). We do not present it here because it requires a higher level of technical discussion than this book sets out to deliver. The results of the n-person game are very similar to the results of the two-person game outlined here, with some interesting consequences that we discuss later.

An infinitely iterated Prisoners' Dilemma game has equilibria in which the players cooperate throughout or for some periods of the game. The most famous among them is an equilibrium in which both players choose the so-called Tit-for-Tat pair of strategies (Axelrod, 1984). A Tit-for-Tat strategy is one in which the player starts by cooperating and then in each of the following stages mimics exactly what the other player has done in the previous iteration of the game.

To show that both players choosing to play the Tit-for-Tat strategy is a Nash Equilibrium we need to show that, given the strategic choice of one player, the other player cannot choose another strategy and be better off. If both players play the Tit-for-Tat strategy, they end up cooperating to infinity. So, to show that this is a Nash Equilibrium we need to show that no player has an incentive to defect at any moment of the game. Note that given that both players chose the Tit-for-Tat strategy, the consequence of one defection is that instead of cooperating to infinity, both players will move to defecting to eternity. Given that the Tit-for-Tat strategy states that each player mimics the strategy of the other player in the last iteration, if one player defects, the other will too. Knowing that the response to a defection is defection in the next round, the person who defected in one round knows that the other player will defect in the next round. The response for this anticipated defection is to defect and so both players will defect forever. If both the discount factor, δ, and the probability of meeting again, ρ, are close enough to 1, then it is easy to show that the expected future gains of continuing to cooperate outweigh the immediate gains of defecting.

The magnitude of the product of $\delta \cdot \rho$ is often referred to as the 'shadow of the future,' because it represents how valuable future gains from the game are to the players. This value is a function of how likely future interactions are and how valuable future gains from these future interactions are to the players. If 'the shadow of the future' is long enough, people may cooperate. We use this insight to explain why, for example, the young tend to drive less carefully than the old. Young people tend not to value the future. Note that while young people have a longer future ahead of them, the fact that they don't value future pay-offs as much 'shortens' the shadow of the future for them. This is because younger people discount future gains by much more than older people, translating in our analytical framework to a smaller discount factor δ. The reverse phenomenon is the so called 'grumpy old (wo)man' phenomenon. Late in their lives people get impatient not because they don't value the future so much, but because there is not much of a future out there for them. So their discount factor is probably close enough to 1 but the probability, ρ, of future interactions is reduced considerably.

In the 1980s this *possibility of cooperation* drew a lot of attention (e.g. Axelrod, 1984; Taylor, 1987). Many saw in this model an explanation for the emergence of cooperation in many contexts. This is until the, so called *Folk Theorem* surfaced, largely due to a publication by Fudenberg and Maskin (1986). Consider the following equation:

$$(3.3) \qquad AV[u_i(G)] = \left. \sum_{t=0}^{t=\infty} \delta^t \bullet \rho^t \bullet u_i(g_t) \middle/ _{(t+1)} \right.$$

$AV[u_i(G)]$ stands for average gain per iteration. Figure 3.2 presents all the possible outcomes of an infinitely repeated, two-person Prisoners' Dilemma game, in terms of average gains per iteration for the two players, in a game where each iteration is identical to the two-person Prisoners' Dilemma game described in Figure 3.1. Thus, for example, the point (1,1) in Figure 3.2 describes an average gain of 1 by both players. This outcome is reached if both players cooperate throughout the game. We already showed that this outcome can be reached if both players choose the Tit-for-Tat strategy, which is a Nash Equilibrium in this game as we explained above. The point (0,0) in Figure 3.2 corresponds to an average gain of 0 by each of the two players. This point can be reached if both choose to defect throughout the game. It is easy to show that this is a Nash Equilibrium too. *The Folk Theorem* (so-called because it is not known who proved this theorem first) simply states that every point in Figure 3.2 can be reached in a finite sequence of the infinitely iterated game by a pair of strategies that is a Nash Equilibrium.

The Folk Theorem: If $0 \leq \delta \leq 1$ and $0 \leq \rho \leq 1$ are both large enough, in infinitely repeated games with finite action sets at each repetition, any pattern of action observed in a finite number of repetition, is the outcome of some *subgame perfect* Nash Equilibrium.

Subgame perfection is a refinement of the solution concept of Nash Equilibrium that we introduced in Chapter 1 and discuss further below. To see the logic behind the *Folk Theorem*, recall our explanation of the Tit-for-Tat equilibrium. The reason why players ended up cooperating was their desire for future gain. But the same is true if several sessions have elapsed in which both players or one of the players defected. If one player is eventually going to get back to cooperate, it is worthwhile for the other player to 'forget the past' and cooperate as well.

Recall that we explained in Chapter 1 that an equilibrium can be thought of as an equilibrium of beliefs. Suppose it is in the best interests of a player to behave in a certain way given his beliefs about the other player's behavior. If it is in the best interests of the other player to behave as the first expects him or her to behave, given what he expects the first player to do, then it is an equilibrium behavior for both players to behave in that way. The same is true here: suppose one player's best response strategy in a game is to cooperate in some iterations of the game and to defect in others, given a certain expectation of a sequence of cooperation and defection by the other player. If the sequence of cooperation and defection by the other player is the best response to the sequence of cooperation and defection of the first player, then the pair of strategies describing these two sequences constitutes a Nash Equilibrium. This logic will work as long as no player expects a negative average pay-off. Each player can avoid a negative average pay-off by defecting throughout the game. However, we only get to observe finite sequences of infinitely repeated games. Finite sequences like that could have one of the players getting negative average pay-offs, if in some point in the future s/he expected to gain some positive pay-offs to offset the losses. This is the logic behind the *Folk Theorem*. So if the game is repeated infinitely, almost anything can happen. Yet, as Sened pointed out elsewhere (1997: 68):

> This discouraging conclusion... can be interpreted in a positive way: since the correct conclusion is that repeating the game [indefinitely] yields [this large set] of equilibria, repeating the game *does makes a difference*. In the one-shot prisoners' dilemma there is a unique equilibrium in which all players defect. In the [infinitely] repeated version of the game there is a multitude of equilibria. Instead of emphasizing [any particular] set of equilibria over the [rest], we should study how players may react to this multitude of possible equilibria in the [infinitely] repeated 'supergame'.

In the next section we show that government intervention can pull a group of citizens who fail to cooperate, into a cooperative *civil state*. After discussing the

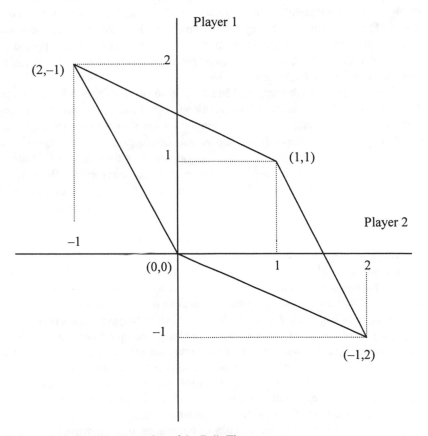

Figure 3.2 A Graphic Illustration of the Folk Theorem

Folk Theorem, our discussion there may be relevant for many equilibria that may result in the infinitely repeated game. If there is less than full and constant cooperation, government intervention can improve the state of affairs. In the next section we discuss the extreme case where no cooperation emerges at all. This is one of the many equilibria in the infinitely repeated game discussed above, and the only equilibrium in the one-shot Prisoners' Dilemma game. But our analysis below is applicable to any outcome that falls short of long-term cooperation. Our analysis should be understood as pointing to the fact that government intervention can move free agents from less to more cooperative states of affairs. As a first step we illustrate how government intervention may impose perfect cooperation on individuals who are stuck in a Hobbesian *state of nature* where no cooperation is expected at all.

At this point we should mention Calvert's (1995) version of the n-person infinitely repeated Prisoners' Dilemma game. In Sened's (1997) version of the n-person prisoners dilemma that we presented above, players were constrained to act in the same way in their interaction with other agents involved in the game. Calvert (1995) allows agents to discriminate in their reactions to different agents. He shows that in the n-person version, cooperation is likely to occur only for very high δ and ρ parameters and relatively small n. The logic behind this work is straightforward. When many agents are involved in a social interaction, the probability that each pair amongst them would get to interact at any period of time is reduced considerably. As a consequence, the expected gains from future iterations are also reduced, which takes away the incentive to cooperate.

The *Folk Theorem* (Fudenberg and Maskin, 1986) as well as work by Calvert (1995), Taylor (1987), Sugden (1986), Axelrod (1984) and others point to a very important aspect of social order. There is no longer a doubt that much of the essence of social order depends on norms and conventions that emerge in the course of the history of any society, people or a nation that constitute a fundamental dimension in the mode of interaction in these societies. We usually refer to this dimension as the *cultural* dimension or the *political culture* of a nation or a people. In the end, a comprehensive study of social order needs to incorporate the interplay of conventions and other aspects of a *political culture* with the study of the *path dependent* history of government imposed rules.

We refrain from such a study here because this book is dedicated to the understanding of political bargaining as a central aspect in the realm of politics. Norms and conventions ensue of a process of learning more than a process of bargaining. Children are being taught the prevalent norms of society at young age. Immigrants learn these rules of behavior when they embark upon a new land. Every so often, society may struggle to change accepted conventions. New trends or certain groups in society may find these norms offensive or damaging. The U.S. civil right movement in the early 1960s is a good example. Yet even here, to the extent that real bargaining took place it involved a call upon government to intervene and impose new rules in the land. No doubt the evolution of norms involves some bargaining among different interests in society. As we show below, the process of bargaining often involves a stage of learning. Yet we believe that evolution of norms is more closely related to learning and the evolution of law is more closely associated with bargaining.

We dedicate the remainder of this chapter to a close look at a model of 'emergence by design' and the role of government as proposed by Sened in his book on *The Political Institution of Private Property* (1997: 81-7).

3.4 The Origin of Order: Emergence by Design & the Role of Governments[5]

If we (re)introduce a government to the game we get a game in two stages:

Stage 1: The government chooses a strategy $g \in \{0,1\}$. $g = 1$ denotes a decision to enforce the law, $g = 0$ denotes a decision not to do so.
Stage 2: Agents choose simultaneously a probability, $\sigma_i \in [0,1]$, with which to respect the law, conditional on the government's decision in stage 1.

We represent the game as a triple $\{D,G,\Pi\}$. A strategy for a constituent, $d_i \in D_i$, is an ordered pair $((\sigma_i | g = 0),(\sigma_i | g = 1))$ specifying the probability $\sigma_i \in [0,1]$ that agent i will respect the law, conditional on whether the government enforces the law or not. As before we use $D = D_1 X...X D_n$ and $d = (d_1,...,d_n) \in D$. A strategy for the government $g \in G = \{0,1\}$ specifies whether government enforces the law – denoted by $g = 1$, or not – denoted by $g = 0$. Π is the pay-off function or a mapping $\Pi: DXG \Rightarrow U \subseteq R^{n+1}$ where U denotes the utility space of all agents involved, including the government. Any vector in this space $u = (u_1,...,u_n,u_g) \in U$ specifies a utility for each agent out of any realization of a strategic choice (d,g) of the n+1 players. The utility the government extracts of any strategic combination (d,g) is:

$$(3.4) \quad u_g(d,g) = t \cdot [\textstyle\sum_{j \in N}(b_j \cdot (\sum_{i \in N} i \neq j\, (\sigma_i | g))) - (\sigma_j | g) \cdot c_j] - g \cdot c_g$$

Equation 3.4 states that the government levies a share, $0 < t < 1$, of the added utility that agents get from law enforcement. A government can enforce law and order, $g = 1$, imposing a fine f on agents who disobey the law. An enforcement policy costs the government a fixed cost of c_g. If the government decides not to enforce the law, then $g=f=0$.[6] Accounting for government's law enforcement the utility each agent $j \in N$ gets from any strategic combination (d,g) is:

$$(3.5)\ u_j(d,g) = (1-t) \cdot [b_j \cdot (\textstyle\sum_{i \in N} i \neq j\, (\sigma_i | g))] - [(\sigma_j | g) \cdot c_j - ((f | g) \cdot (1-(\sigma_j | g)))]$$

Equation 3.5 states that the utility an agent j gets is derived from the agents in society that chose to respect the law, depending on the government's policy, less the tax collected by the government. From this expected benefit we must deduce the price an agent pays to respect the law, or the fine s/he expects to pay if s/he chose not to respect the law, given the government's strategy.

Complete Information Assumption: The set of parameters n, c_g, b_j, c_j, f and t are common knowledge with: (i) $0 < t < 1$, (ii) $t + (f | g = 1) > 1$ and (iii) $b_j = c_j = 1\ \forall\ i \in N$.[7]

In section 1.5 we introduced Subgame Perfect Nash Equilibrium [SPNE] as a solution concept. Using the notations we just introduced we define a SPNE here:

Definition 3.1: A strategy vector $(\mathbf{d},\mathbf{g})$ is a Nash Equilibrium if:
1. $u_i(\mathbf{d}^*,g^*) \geq u_i(\mathbf{d}_{-i}^*,d_i,g^*)$, $\forall$ $i \in N$ and $\forall$ $d_i \in D_i$.
2. $u_g(\mathbf{d}^*,g^*) \geq u_g(\mathbf{d}^*,g)$ $\forall$ $g \in \{0,1\}$.

Definition 3.2: A strategy vector, $(\mathbf{d}^*,g^*)$, is an SPNE if:[8]
1. It is a Nash Equilibrium for the entire game, as defined in definition 3.1; and
2. Its relevant action rules are a Nash Equilibrium for every Subgame.

Theorem 3.1 (Sened, 1997: 86 Theorem 4.1) overcomes the traditional objection to the liberal social contract theory. This objection states that governments cannot be assumed to be benevolent and selfish governments cannot be trusted to implement social order. Theorem 3.1 shows why and under what conditions, a selfish government may enforce social order to further its own selfish interest.

Theorem 3.1 (Sened, 1997: Theorem 4.1): With complete information,
1. If $t \cdot n \cdot (n-2) < c_g$,[9] the unique Subgame Perfect Nash Equilibrium outcome of the game is one in which the government does not grant the right and all agents ignore each other's property rights.
2. If $t \cdot n \cdot (n-2) > c_g$, then the unique Subgame Perfect Nash Equilibrium outcome of the game is one in which the government grants the right and all agents respect each other's rights.
3. If $t \cdot n \cdot (n-2) = c_g$, then both outcomes described in 3.1.i and 3.1.ii are SPNE.

Theorem 3.1 states the conditions under which it is an equilibrium behavior for a government to enforce a law: *a government will enforce a law if it expects the marginal benefit of enforcing this law to be higher than the cost of enforcement.*

3.5 Participation Games[10]

At least three features of the evolution of social order have not been dealt with in our discussion so far. First, individuals do not have the same preferences. A law may benefit some agents while hurting others. Second, neither government officials nor ordinary citizens possess complete information about the preferences of constituents. Third, governments are uncertain of the consequences of their policies (Austen-Smith and Riker, 1987; Krehbiel, 1992). The following three sections address these issues by introducing uncertainty about the number of constituents that may benefit from any structure of social order by including (1) different types of preferences; (2) asymmetric information: agents know their preferences but governments do not; (3) government uncertainty about the consequences of law enforcement, not knowing how many constituents would benefit from it and therefore the marginal support or tax revenues it should expect.

Enforcement agencies can solve the Prisoners' Dilemma by imposing respect of the laws. If government officials know that any particular law may benefit government officials by benefiting their constituents, they would enforce the law for their own benefit, as shown in the previous section. But when government officials believe they cannot benefit from enforcing a law, they are unlikely to do so. When this is the case and individual agents in society (be it individual citizens or economic interests – see North, 1990) expect to benefit from changing a law, they need to petition the government to do so. If a government receives enough petitions it may conclude that it could benefit from changing the law. Petitioning, however, is not only costly, it also involves *a collective action* problem: since social order is a public good, once granted, all potential beneficiaries gain from it regardless of whether they petitioned for it or not.

Palfrey and Rosenthal (1984, 1988) studied participation games that help us address this problem. Suppose each agent expects a pay-off of $b_i=1$ if a public good is provided. The public good is provided if at least ω agents contribute a cost of $0<c<1$ each. The basic structure of the game is described in Table 3.1.

Table 3.1 N-Person Participation Game

We assume that	Player i's Strategies	Number of contributions from all players except player i, α_{-i}		
b=1		$\alpha_{-i} < \omega-1$	$\alpha_{-i} = \omega-1$	$\alpha_{-i} \geq \omega$
1>c>0	Contribute	$-c$	$b-c$	$b-c$
Therefore:	Do not contribute	0	0	B
b-c>0				

If the number of all contributors except i, α_{-i}, is smaller than the threshold number by more than one, then agent i is better off not contributing, because, with or without his or her contribution, the public good will not be provided. If the number of contributors except i, α_{-i}, is greater than or equal to the threshold number, then the agent is better off not contributing, because, with or without his or her contribution, the public good is provided. Only if $\alpha_{-i}=\omega-1$, is agent i better off contributing, because without this contribution the public good is not provided, while with this contribution the public good is provided.

There are three types of Nash Equilibria in this game. In the first, no one contributes: $\alpha=0$. In the second, exactly ω agents contribute so that $\alpha=\omega$. In this type of equilibrium, identical agents facing the same game play different strategies and there is a coordination problem since agents cannot predict who will contribute. The third type of equilibrium is mixed strategy equilibria.

Symmetric mixed strategy equilibria in which all agents use the same strategy, are of particular interest. In this type of equilibria each agent believes, 'correctly,' that all the other agents are using the same strategy as s/he does. In this equilibrium all agents use a 'mixed strategy' that make other agents indifferent to either contributing or not contributing. This is the intuitive logic behind mixed strategy equilibria more generally. It is a nice example of how Nash Equilibria can be thought of as self-fulfilling mutual expectations.

A Digression on Mixed Strategy Equilibria

Given the importance of mixed strategy equilibria to our argument and in game theoretic models more generally, we make a short digression on mixed strategy equilibria. Consider the simple coordination game in Figure 3.3.

Players	Player No. 2		
	Strategies	Go First (F)	Go Second (S)
Player No. 1	Go First (F)	a=0,b=0	c=2,d=1
	Go Second (S)	e=1,f=2	g=0,h=0

Figure 3.3 A Two-Person 'Who Goes First' Game

Two players have to decide who goes first. The person who goes first gets a utility of 2 while the person who goes second gets a utility of 1. If both go first they collide and get no utility. If they both wait for the other to go first, i.e. 'both go second,' they never go anywhere and both get a utility of 0. It is easy to see that there are two pure strategy equilibria in this game, the strategy vector of (F,S) with a pay-off vector of (2,1) and the strategy vector (S,F) with the pay-off vector (1,2). However, it is clear that player 1 prefers the (2,1) equilibrium at the upper right corner of Figure 3.3 while Player 2 prefers the (1,2) equilibrium at the bottom left corner of Figure 3.3 where s/he goes first and player 1 second.

So what is likely to happen here? One possibility is that players may use 'mixed strategies.' The intuitive logic behind mixed strategy equilibria is that agents may use mixed strategies only if they are indifferent between using one or the other strategy. This is going to be the case if the other agent(s) have chosen to 'mix strategies' so as to make them indifferent.

An agent will eventually act with probability 1. So the sum of the probabilities he may use to play all pure strategies in his or her strategy set must add up to 1. In our example there are two strategies in each player's strategy set, so we can say that player 1 will choose strategy F with probability p and strategy S with probability (1-p). Similarly, player 2 would choose F with probability q and S with probability (1-q). To make player 2 indifferent between going first or going second the following must hold: p(b)+(1-p)(f) = p(d) + (1-p)(h) or: 2-2p = p which holds true when p = 2/3. However, for this mix to be an equilibrium behavior for player 1, player 2 must use a mix that leaves player 1 indifferent between going first or second. For this to be the case the following must hold: q(a)+(1-q)(c) = q(e) + (1-q)(g) or: 2-2q = q which holds true when q = 2/3.

Thus, if both players go first with probability 2/3 and second with probability 1/3 we have a mixed strategy equilibrium. The algorithm provided here allows to find the mixed strategy equilibrium in any 2×2 (two players, two strategies) for any pay-off function. Below we provide an example of a symmetric mixed strategy for the participation game discussed above, which is an n-person game.

At first sight, the notion of mixed strategy equilibria seems awkward. But if we think about it, it is probably not that hard to make sense of it. One objection is that we always take one action in the end, so what is the sense in which it makes sense to speak of a mixed strategy? The answer is that often times we take action at random. For example, people often ask us for money in the street. Sometimes we give and sometimes we don't. This is a mixed strategy. But let us return to our example in Figure 3.3. When we drive or when we have to stand in line we often give the right of way to others while at other times we insist on getting in first. If we always let others go ahead of us we would feel as being 'too nice' and waste a lot of time. If we always jumped ahead we would be rude and impolite. So the convention is to 'mix.' What mix should we use? Well, if we did not assert our right to be first often enough (use p < 2/3) we would be pushed around because others would be better off asserting themselves given the 'too low' level of assertiveness that we demonstrate. If we asserted ourselves too often (use p > 2/3) we may get our way. The best response of the other player to such a strategy is to always go second (at which case our best response is to always push and be first), but we would probably come out quite rude and there is no way to tell if the other will accept this inferior equilibrium. If we assert ourselves just often enough (p = 2/3) the other person is indifferent playing exactly the same strategy as we do and making us indifferent to play any strategy including the strategy of p = 2/3 which makes him or her indifferent as well.

Having said this, we should note that mixed strategy equilibria are often less efficient than the pure strategy ones. Note that using the mix strategy we found to be the equilibrium mix in Figure 3.3 would land the two players on a (0,0) quadrant 5/9 of the times which is more than a half. The expected pay-off for each player playing the equilibrium mixed strategy is (2/9 × 2) + (2/9 × 1) = 6/9 which is less than what each of them would get if s/he resigned to accept the second best pure strategy equilibrium. Once again one possible solution is to allow a government to coordinate action like when government regulates traffic so that we all know what to do and never end up where we do not want to end up. The point here is that government intervention is not necessarily called for only when a stark conflict of interest lead people to fight each other. Often times, government is helpful in coordinating the actions of people who wish 'to take turns' and just 'don't know how.'

In this respect it is important to make the final point in this regard: not every game has a pure strategy equilibrium and many games have way too many equilibria which makes it difficult for players to form expectation about which equilibrium is likely to ensue. Every well defined game has at least one mixed strategy equilibrium and as we discussed above, when there are many pure strategy equilibria, mixed strategy equilibria in general and symmetric mixed strategy equilibria in particular may be the way to overcome the coordination problem of choosing the 'right equilibrium' to play.

3.6 Negotiating the Social Contract Through a Bargaining Process

Palfrey and Rosenthal's participation models do not assign any role for governments. They are based on the premise that if enough agents contribute, the public good is provided. But governments do exist, and their active (and often passive) presence alters many aspects of the production of social order as a public good. Here, we are concerned with the role of governments as political entrepreneurs who specialize in protecting the law in return for political and economic support. We therefore model this interaction formally, incorporating government officials with incomplete information. We believe that the ensuing model is a good abstract presentation of how governments and social agents bargain the details of the social contract that underlies any *civil society.*

Suppose we have two types of agents. One type expect a benefit of $b_i=1$ if a law is enforced while the second type expect no benefit from this particular law so that $b_i=0$. Let $S_i=\{0,1\}$ denote the choice set of agent i with $s_i \in S_i$. $s_i=1$ denotes 'petition' and $s_i=0$ denotes 'not petition.' A normalized mixed strategy $\sigma_i:\{0,1\} \Rightarrow [0,1]^2$ is an ordered pair $\sigma_i=(pr(s_i=1|b_i=1); pr(s_i=1|b_i=0))$, specifying a probability that agent i petition, conditional on i's type. So, the strategic choice of an agent consists of choosing the probability s/he would petition if s/he is of type $b_i=1$ and the probability of petitioning if s/he is of type $b_i=0$.

The strategy space of society is denoted as $\sigma=\sigma_1 \times ... \times \sigma_n$. A particular vector of strategic choices is denoted as $\sigma=(\sigma_1,...,\sigma_n) \in \sigma$. Each agents chooses a probability σ_i of petitioning conditional on his or her type. Eventually each agent either petitions ($s_i=1$), or not ($s_i=0$). So s_i is the realization of σ_i and $s=(s_1,...,s_n)$ is the realization of $\sigma=(\sigma_1,...,\sigma_n) \in \sigma$. We define $A^1(s)=\{i \in N:s_i=1|s\}$ to be the set of agents who petition in a particular realization s of σ and α denote the number of agents in this set: $\alpha=|A^1|$. Let $0<c<1$ be the cost of petitioning. For simplicity, we assume that this cost is the same for all petitioners.

A strategy for a government is a mapping g: $\{0,1\}^n \Rightarrow \{0,1\}$. $g(A^1)=1$ denotes enforcing a law upon observing the group A^1 of petitioners that turned out. $g(A^1)=0$ denotes not enforcing it after observing the group A^1. A government's benefits, b_g, from enforcing a law, are assumed to be a linear function of β, the number of potential beneficiaries, $b_g=t \cdot \beta$, where $0<t<1$ may be interpreted as a tax rate or as a 'good will' dividend toward the next election. Again, c_g denotes a government's cost of law enforcement.

We assume that c_g, c, and t are common knowledge and that all agents, including government officials, have common prior beliefs about the probability, q, that any agent is of type $b_i=1$, i.e. $q=pr(b_i=1)$. Let $\mathbf{b}=(b_1,...,b_n)$ be a realization of n independent draws of $b_i \in \{0,1\}$ by n agents, with a probability q that each draw yield $b_i=1$. Let $B^1(\mathbf{b})=\{i \in N:b_i=1|\mathbf{b}\}$ denote the set of potential beneficiaries, and β denote the number of potential beneficiaries, of type $b_i=1$. All agents start with a common prior belief $f(\beta)$, where $f(\beta)$ is a probability density function, defined by q and n, that denotes the belief agents have about the probability that the number of potential beneficiaries, β, is any integer $k \in Z=\{0,1,...,n\}$.

We have constructed a four-stage sequential game:

Stage 1: Each agent chooses his or her strategy $\sigma_i \in \sigma_i=[0,1]^2$.
Stage 2: Agents learns thier type $b_i \in \{0,1\}$ and follow the strategy they chose.
Stage 3: The government chooses to enforce the law or not, depending on α and the prior beliefs, $(f(\beta))$, about the number of potential beneficiaries β.
Stage 4: Agents decide whether to respect the law or not given $g \in \{0,1\}$.

From the previous section we know the expected outcome of stage 4: if government officials enforce the law, all agents respect it. If the government does not enforce the law, no-one respects it. Using the logic of backward induction again, we can roll back to stage 3. Theorem 3.1 implies the following pay-off of the game: if a government enforces the law its pay-off is $u_g(g=1)=(t \cdot \beta)-c_g$. Otherwise, the pay-off is zero. The pay-off of the constituents depends on contingencies in the game, as specified in Table 3.2.

Table 3.2 Constituents' Pay-offs

i's pay-off $u_i =$	i's type $b_i =$	i's pure strategy $s_i =$	Government's strategy $g =$
$(1-t) - c$	1	1	1
$(1-t)$	1	0	1
$-c$	0	1	$g \in \{0,1\}$
$-c$	1	1	0
0	0	0	$g \in \{0,1\}$
0	1	0	0

By Theorem 3.1 if a government enforces a law all agents respect it. Each beneficiary gets a positive utility, which we standardize to be $u_i(b_i=1|g=1)=1$. Accounting for taxes, agents of type $b_i=1$ who do not petition get a pay-off of $u_i(b_i=1|g=1,s_i=0,t)=(1-t)$. Agents who petitioned, get $u_i(b_i=1|g=1,s_i=1,t)=(1-t)-c$, which we assume to be strictly positive, otherwise no-one would ever petition. Agents of type $b_i=0$, do not benefit from the law and therefore never petition.

The government gets $t \cdot \beta - c_g$, given β beneficiaries, if it enforces the law and 0 if it does not. Let $v_g(A^1, \sigma) = E(u_g | \mu(\cdot | A^1, f(\beta), \sigma))$ denote the government's expected utility after observing A^1, given its updated, posterior beliefs $\mu(\cdot | A^1, f(\beta), \sigma)$:

$$(3.6) \qquad \mu(\beta | A^1, f(\beta), \sigma) = \left(\frac{pr(A^1 | \beta, \sigma) \bullet pr(\beta | q, n)}{\sum\limits_{\beta'=0}^{n} (A^1 | \beta', \sigma) \bullet pr(\beta' | q, n)} \right)$$

Equation 3.6 states that government officials use Bayes' Rule to update their beliefs. This means that they use prior beliefs and incoming information, in this case, the fact that a group, A^1, turned out to petition, to form posterior beliefs. This mechanism may become clearer as we unfold the model and the results. If a government enforces the law its expected pay-off is:

$$(3.7) \quad v_g(g = 1 | A^1, f(\beta), \sigma) = \sum\limits_{\beta=0}^{n} \beta \bullet t \bullet \left(\frac{pr(A^1 | \beta, \sigma) \bullet pr(\beta | q, n)}{\sum\limits_{\beta'=0}^{n} (A^1 | \beta', \sigma) \bullet pr(\beta' | q, n)} \right) - c_g$$

Equation (3.7) states that the pay-off the government expects from enforcing the law is the sum, over all $\beta \in \{0, 1, ..., n\}$, of the pay-off it expects from any number, β, of beneficiaries, times the likelihood that there are β beneficiaries, by the government's posterior beliefs about β, less the cost of enforcement c_g.

If $W(g) = \{A^1 \subseteq N : (g | A^1) = 1\}$ is a set of groups that would bring a government to enforce the law if they petitioned. The expected pay-off for each agent is:

$$(3.8) \qquad v_i(\sigma, g, b_i) = E(u_i | \sigma, g, b_i) = [(1-t)(b_i) \bullet prob(A^1 \in W(g) | \sigma)] - c \bullet \sigma_i$$

In words: the expected pay-off of an agent of type $b_i = 1$ is $(1-t)$ times the probability that the government enforces the law, less the cost of petitioning, times the probability, σ_i, that the agent petitioned. The equilibrium concept used in solving this type of signaling game is as follows.[11]

Definition 3.3: A Sequential Equilibrium [SE] is a triple $(\sigma^*, g^*, \mu(\cdot))$, such that:

1. $\forall i \in N$, $\forall b_i \in \{0, 1\}$, $v_i(\sigma^*, g^*) \geq v_i(\sigma^*_{-i}, \sigma_i, g^*)$ $\forall \sigma_i \in \sigma_i$.

2. Given σ^*, $\forall A^1 \subseteq N$, $g^*(A^1) = \underset{g \in \{0,1\}}{Arg \max} \{g \bullet v_g(g = 1 | \mu(\cdot | A^1, f(\beta), \sigma^*))\}$

3. $\forall \beta \in \{0, 1, ..., n\}$, if $pr(\beta | A^1, \sigma^*) > 0$, then

$$\mu(\beta|A^1, f(\beta), \sigma^*) = \left(\frac{pr(A^1|\beta, \sigma^*) \bullet pr(\beta|q, n)}{\sum_{\beta'=0}^{n} (A^1|\beta', \sigma^*) \bullet pr(\beta'|q, n)} \right)$$

Condition 1 states that an equilibrium strategy, σ_i^*, must maximize the agent's utility, given the strategies of the government and the other agents. Condition 2 states that an equilibrium strategy by government officials, g^*, must maximize the government's expected utility given its posterior beliefs $\mu(\bullet)$, that are based on its prior beliefs and the observed group of petitioners, A^1. Condition 3 states that government's beliefs are consistent with σ^* in that government's posterior beliefs, $\mu(\bullet|A^1, \sigma^*)$, are determined by Bayes' Rule according to its prior beliefs, $f(\beta)$, the observed group of petitioners, A^1, and the strategy vector σ^*.[12]

Definition 3.4: $(\sigma^*, g^*, \mu(\bullet))$ is an agent symmetric SE (SSE) if $\forall$ i,j$\in$N $\sigma_i^* = \sigma_j^*$.

The attractive feature of symmetric equilibria is that they depend on the premise that each agent expects all other agents to behave in the same way s/he does when they face the same pay-off structure and have the same prior beliefs.

Definition 3.5: Anonymity: for any $A^1, A^{1'}$ if $|A^1| = |A^{1'}|$ if $A^1 \in W(g)$, $A^{1'} \in W(g)$.

Anonymity requires that all agents be treated the same. Restricting the analysis to SSEs implies anonymity. Since all agents use the same mixed strategy in equilibrium, it is not an equilibrium behavior for the government to interpret the behavior of different agents as resulting from different strategies. This would violate condition (3) of the definition 3.3 of sequential equilibrium. Thus, we use α instead of A^1 as the argument of the government's posterior beliefs $\mu(\alpha, f(\beta), \sigma)$. Equation (3.9) redefines expression (3.7) using α instead of A^1.

(3.9)
$$vg(g = 1|\alpha, f(\beta), \sigma) = \sum_{\beta=0}^{n} \beta \bullet t \bullet \left(\frac{pr(\alpha|\beta, \sigma) \bullet pr(\beta|q, n)}{\sum_{\beta'=0}^{n} (\alpha|\beta', \sigma) \bullet pr(\beta'|q, n)} \right) - c_g$$

3.7 The Bargained Social Contract

We are now ready to present Sened's (1997: 110-14) model of the 'bargained social contract.' Sened argument begins by proving the intuitive observation 3.1 below, that government's equilibrium strategy is always characterized by a threshold ω[13], so that if government officials observe a set of petitioners equal or greater than this threshold, they move to enact and enforces the petitioned change in the law. If they observe a number of petitioners that is smaller than this threshold, they would not bother to change the law.

Observation 3.1: (Sened, 1997: Corollary 5.1) In SSE, the government strategy is characterized by a threshold ω s.t. $g^*(\alpha)=1$ if $\alpha \geq \omega$, and $g^*(\alpha)=0$ if $\alpha < \omega$.

Since this is what agents expect government officials to do, we can roll back to the first stage of the game. Observation 3.2 characterizes the symmetric equilibrium response of the agents for each possible threshold strategy.

Observation 3.2: (Sened, 1997: Lemma 5.8) If $(\sigma^*, g^*, \mu(\bullet))$ is a mixed strategy SSE, the following must hold:[14]

$$(3.10) \quad c = (1-t) \bullet \sum_{\gamma=\omega-1}^{n-1} \left[\binom{\gamma}{\omega-1} \rho^{\omega-1}(1-\rho)^{\gamma-\omega-1} \right] \bullet \left[\binom{n-1}{\gamma} q^\gamma (1-q)^{n-\gamma-1} \right]$$

(3.10) of observation 3.2, guarantees that, given the threshold strategy of the government, every agent is using a mixed strategy, ρ. Recall from our discussion above that agents use mixed strategies in equilibrium only if they are indifferent between using different pure strategies in their choice set. The choice set for each agent here is: contributing or not contributing. We know that agents of type $b_i=0$ never contribute. Condition (3.10) is a combinatorial computation of ρ, the probability that an agent of type $b_i=1$ would contribute. Given the prior beliefs $q=pr(b_i=1)$ and n, we are looking for ρ that satisfies the requirement that if all agents of type $b_i=1$ contribute with probability ρ any agent of type $b_i=1$ would be indifferent between contributing and not contributing. Given this indifference each agent can use the mixed strategy ρ that everyone else uses which is the intuitive logic behind observations 3.2 and Theorem 3.2 as captured by equation (3.10) of observation 3.1 and condition (3.11) in Theorem 3.2 below. Condition (3.12) of Theorem 3.2 guarantees that the government uses a best response threshold strategy to this mixed strategy ρ used by all constituents of type $b_i=1$.

Theorem 3.2 (Sened, 1997: Theorem 5.1): $(\sigma^*, g^*, \mu(\bullet))$ is a mixed[15] strategy SSE if and only if:

1. $i \in N$ $\sigma_i^*(0)=0$.

2. $i \in N$ $\sigma_i^*(1)=\rho$, $g^*(\alpha)=1$ iff $\alpha \geq \omega$, and the pair (ω, ρ) satisfies simultaneously:

$$(3.11) \quad c = (1-t) \bullet \sum_{\gamma=\omega-1}^{n-1} \left[\binom{\gamma}{\omega-1} \rho^{\omega-1}(1-\rho)^{\gamma-\omega-1} \right] \bullet \left[\binom{n-1}{\gamma} q^\gamma (1-q)^{n-\gamma-1} \right]$$

$$(3.12) \quad v_g(1|\rho, \alpha) = \sum_{\beta=\alpha}^{n} (t \cdot \beta - c_g) \cdot \frac{\left[\binom{n}{\beta} q^\beta (1-q)^{n-\beta} \right] \cdot \left[\binom{\beta}{\alpha} \rho^\alpha (1-\rho)^{\beta-\alpha} \right]}{\sum_{\beta'=\alpha}^{n} \left[\binom{n}{\beta'} q^{\beta'} (1-q)^{n-\beta'} \right] \cdot \left[\binom{\beta'}{\alpha} \rho^\alpha (1-\rho)^{\beta'-\alpha} \right]} \geq 0 - \text{iff } \alpha \geq \omega$$

Theorem 3.2 captures a crucial aspect of the meaning of the social contract that we promote in this book. A social contract that evolves through a bargaining process between government officials and constituents, rely on very fragile equilibria of expectations and behavior. Governments constantly write and rewrite the contract to promote their interests. These interests often coincide with the interests of the constituents inasmuch as governments obtain popular support and tax revenues from happy and productive constituents. This interdependence allows economic and political entrepreneurs to petition for changes in the legal structure of institution that regulate the activity of society within any social order in general. As North (1990: 86) put it:

> The process of institutional change can be described as follows. A change in relative prices leads.... parties to an exchange, whether it is political or economic, to perceive that either or both could do better with an altered agreement or contract. An attempt will be made to renegotiate the contract. However, because contracts are nested in a hierarchy of rules, the renegotiation may not be possible without restructuring a higher set of rules... [a] party that stands to improve [its] bargaining position may ...devote resources to restructuring the rules at a higher level.

Sened's model of the bargained social contract that we described in the last ten pages is an attempt at a precise specification of this argument. 'The parties that stand to improve their bargaining positions' are agents of type $b_i=1$. Given the control of governments over the 'rules at the higher level,' the interested parties 'devote resources to restructuring the rules at a higher level' in petitioning government officials to change the law, as described by the model.

Theorem 3.2 generalizes Theorem 3.1 in stating that the plea of citizens to change the political institutional structure of law and order will be successful if government officials are convinced that they stand to gain from changing the law. One way to make a convincing plea for institutional change is to mobilize enough petitions from enough interested parties to convince the government that the change will bring economic growth, or increased political support.

3.8 Concluding Remarks: An Imperfect Bargained Social Contract

Theorem 3.2 has three important implications:

1. Petitions for change are expected even when common beliefs indicate that the number of those who may potentially benefit from this change is not enough to justify the change. This explains why mass demonstrations often fail to have significant consequences.

2. Government officials are likely to make two types of error in equilibrium: enforce laws that make them worse off and fail to enforce laws that could make them better off. Both type of errors are often observed in legislation.
3. Finally, the number of petitioners, α, will rarely be 'efficient.' Thus, 'political action' in the pursuit of law reform is bound to be 'wasteful.'

Possible mistakes and inefficiencies of this type have often frustrated economic and political theorists. This frustration stems from erroneously comparing ideal competitive markets with perfectly defined property rights, and complete information with the imperfect world we live in. Real political and economic games are never played in environments of complete information, perfectly well defined property rights, or zero transaction costs.

This chapter provided a model of a bargaining process through which agents reveal crucial information about their preference, and government officials create and change legal institutions to further appease their constituents.
Governments do not erect such structures out of benevolence or moral concern. They protect the law in order to promote their own interests. But in doing so, they fulfill two crucial social functions. The function of maintaining social order and the function of arbitrage among conflicting interests. Social order is promoted not by a process of aggregating individual preferences into social choices but through a bargaining process in which the government does not serve as a benevolent actor but as a self interested broker, sensitive to the interests of its client-constituents only to the extent that this sensitivity promotes the government's interests. This bargaining process allows certain preferences that may have been overlooked (or 'cycled out of sight') to enter and be counted at the political scene.

Of course, this bargaining process is more complicated than the model discussed in this chapter suggests. It involves conflicting interests that petition on opposite side of almost every issue. In the following chapter we discuss some of the issues associated with the competitive nature of a pluralistic society by introducing political entrepreneurs as intermediaries between governments and special interests. While competing interests complicate the interaction considerably, current theoretical knowledge allows us to incorporate them into the analysis. In particular, in the next chapter we introduce an extension to the model discussed above that is due to Ainsworth and Sened (1993). They show that political entrepreneurs both alleviate the collective action problem and provide constituents and government officials with crucial information that reduces the coordination problem and improves the efficiency of social interaction and of the institutions that guard and promote social order.

This is a sharp departure from the view of the 'rent-seeking' literature, which promotes the argument that the 'rent-seeking' activity of powerful economic organizations and interest groups is detrimental to the smooth functioning of the economy and the welfare of the state. We believe that this misperception is due to the fact that: 'interest-group theory of government ...does not make clear what the state is... Yet in much of the rent-seeking writings there seems to be a presumption that the state will somehow supply output maximizing property rights, if only interest groups can be contained.' (Eggertsson, 1990: 279).

In this chapter we introduced and demonstrated the usefulness of somewhat more advanced non-cooperative game theory. We also explored a relatively simple model of the state. In the following chapter we complicate the game somewhat by building into the political bargaining model an additional set of players – political entrepreneurs.

Notes

1. Our characterization of the n-person Prisoners' Dilemma is a variation on an earlier characterization by Hardin (1971), Schofield (1985), Calvert (1995) and Sened (1997).

2. This specification of the game is drawn from Sened (1997: Chapter 4).

3. As stated above, here again we implicitly assume that agents do not discriminate among players: they either respect the rights of all agents or respect the rights of none. Calvert (1995) proposed a more adequate formulation of this context. In his model, agents discriminate between other agents depending on the past behavior of each agent. While the formulation is more adequate, it considerably complicates the presentation.

4. For n=2, the unique equilibrium is still for both players to defect. It is not a classic PD because if both agents cooperate, each gets a pay-off of 0. Unlike in the PD game, both defecting is not Pareto inferior to both cooperating. To fix this we could set $b_i > 1$. We set $b_i = 1$ so that we can drop it from the equations. For n>2, we get the classic PD.

5. The model and results in this section were first published by Sened (1997: 81-7).

6. A comprehensive model should treat f as a function of c_g and compliance as a function of f. Compliance in such a model is a function of the resources invested in law enforcement. Government decision is not whether to enforce the law but to what extent to enforce it. This requires treating c_g and f as endogenous rather than exogenous variables.

7. Restrictions (3.i-3.iii) are discussed in Sened, 1990, Chapter 4.

8. Every SPNE is a Nash Equilibrium. The converse is not true. Subgame perfection is one of the most commonly used refinements of the Nash solution concept. A simple way to identify an SPNE is the method of backwards induction discussed in the first chapter of this book. The proof of Theorem 3.1 is a simple example of this method.

9. The original result had $t \cdot n^2$ instead of $t \cdot n \cdot (n-2)$ in all three articles of the Theorem. We use this occasion to correct this unfortunate, even if obvious, mistake.

10. The remainder of this chapter is based on Sened (1997: 103-16).

11. The classical reference is Kreps and Wilson, 1982. More penetrable discussions are found in Cho (1987), Cho and Kreps (1987), and Banks and Sobel (1987). The definition we use is adopted from Banks' (1991: 7). It is easy to see that the game we analyze here can be interpreted as a signaling game with the government being the 'receiver' (R), each agent $i \in N$ being a sender (S) with two types $b_i \in \{0,1\}$ and two messages $m \in \{0,1\}$ where 0 is the message of not petitioning and 1 the message of petitioning. We do not use this terminology in the text to save on unnecessary notations and technicalities.

12. This definition specifies government's beliefs only along the equilibrium path. This poses a problem if a government observes an event that according to its beliefs occurs with probability zero. This can happen if $\sigma=(1,...,1)$, but $A^1=0$. We use the Intuitive

Criterion (IC) (Cho and Kreps, 1987) to deal with this problem. IC requires that off-the-equilibrium-path beliefs place zero probability on a type who can only lose from defecting, actually going on to defect. Here it implies that $\mu(b_i=0|s_i=1)=0$, i.e. a government's out-of-equilibrium beliefs put zero probability on a type $b_i=0$ petitioning.

13. We limit our discussion to cases where the minimum number of petitioners needed to convince the government to grant the law is greater than one.

14. For every value of ω there exists zero, one or two solutions to the symmetric equilibrium condition characterized by Lemma 3.2. This follows immediately from Lemma 3.2, and Proposition 2 and Corollary 2.1 in Palfrey and Rosenthal, 1984.

15. By mixed strategy SSE we mean $\rho\in(0,1)$, thus the cases of $\rho=1$ and $\rho=0$ are left out. For these cases see Ainsworth and Sened, 1993: 844 fn. 10.

4 Special Interests and Political Entrepreneurs

4.1 Introduction: The Role of Political Entrepreneurs

The previous chapter described a simplified society in which rulers bargain with citizens directly. This polity has no mediating institutions in the form of political parties, organized special interests, or mass media. An analysis of the bargaining relationship between government and citizens in the context of such a society can thus provide only a partial picture and hence an incomplete explanation of real world of politics. To flesh out the picture we now introduce a new entity, political entrepreneurs, as generic players in the positive model of the polity.

Political entrepreneurs encompass various types of institution that serve as 'middlemen' between rulers and those they rule. In Chapters 5 and 6 we discuss two particular political institutions of this sort: elections and representative parliaments. These institutions have become the nucleus of the bargaining process between governments and their constituents in the modern polity.

In an earlier work, Ainsworth and Sened (1993) argued that political entrepreneurs function in free capacity as mediators between constituents and government officials. First, they help individuals form and crystallize preferences and beliefs about different possible outcomes. Second, by providing information about the most likely action to be taken by members of the group, they alleviate the collective action problem. Finally, they provide information about the costs and benefits of government action on one side, and group membership on the other.

The ability of entrepreneurs to influence government officials affects the ability of special interests to compete and serve their members. In addition, entrepreneurs attract constituents by helping them mobilize around a common interest, often formed and articulated by the entrepreneurs themselves. The most fundamental role of political entrepreneurs is, however, to alleviate the collective action problem by providing a focal point regarding which, of all the possible equilibrium outcomes, members of the group are going to choose.

In Chapter 1 we discussed the cooperative and non-cooperative game theoretic frameworks. We emphasized that cooperative game theory suffers from the fact that the core may often be empty. Models constructed using non-cooperative game theory often suffers from the opposite problem. In many cases the set of Nash Equilibrium outcomes turns out to be quite large or even infinite, as in the case of the *Folk Theorem* we discussed in the previous chapter (Fudenberg and Maskin, 1986). For many years scholars have tried to refine the Nash Equilibrium solution concept to find smaller subsets that would serve better as more refined predictive tools (Banks and Sobel, 1987; Banks, 1991). This strategy has recently come under attack due to the arbitrary nature of some of these refinements (Kreps, 1997). Here we follow a different strategy. We accept the multitude of equilibria as given and show how organized interests and the entrepreneurs that help organize these interests may alleviate this problem.

Why do special interest groups form? What function do political entrepreneurs serve? These questions have interested social scientists for decades. We believe that the study of *political bargaining* guided by game theoretic models provides valuable insights towards answering these questions.

In the previous chapter we noted two important implications of Theorem 3.2. First, in equilibrium, governments often enforce laws with negative marginal benefits. Second, governments may fail to enforce other laws that could yield positive marginal benefits to government officials. Such inefficiencies help explain the emergence of interest groups and political entrepreneurs as an intrinsic part of the institutional build up of the polity. Political entrepreneurs who lead organized interests help governments to assess the costs and benefits of amending the existing social order. They provide valuable information about the likelihood of obtaining institutional changes and 'focal points' concerning the actions that group members should take to achieve their goals. They also provide information about the costs and benefits of enforcing different structures of social order to group members and government officials. Thus, political entrepreneurs reduce the uncertainties surrounding the bargaining process and the environment within which social order comes to be and further evolves. In this chapter, we show how special interests and political entrepreneurs affect the set of predicted final outcomes of the political bargaining game between government officials and constituent citizens.

4.2 Special Interests and Entrepreneurs

Entrepreneurs are a common empirical phenomenon. They are people and institutions that link demands people have for some valued good and/or service and their supply. While entrepreneurs are active in various human endeavors, they are most commonly identified with the business world. There we call them brokers, bankers, traders and, more generally, businessmen. They are not the producers nor are they the consumers of any tangible product, but without them few economic transactions materialize. They are the middle wo/men.

In an exchange economy, where producers sell directly to buyers, there is limited cause for entrepreneurs to emerge. However, even in this simple model of one-to-one relationship between seller and buyer, there is miscommunication and incomplete information. Take for example a farmer who sells on his own farm a bushel of tomatoes to a consumer. Such transactions require no middleman. The farmer decides what to charge for a given quantity of vegetables and the consumer knows what price s/he is willing to pay. Bargaining then takes place in order to determine the exact price within the range of maximal values cited by the farmer and minimal values offered by the customer.

But farmers do not grow single bushels of tomatoes. They grow many bushels. To determine the price, the farmer must be aware of the intensity of a potential customer's demand for his products, the expected frequency of his/her visits to the farm, the quantities grown by competing farms and the prices charged by them. Only after obtaining knowledge about these variables would he be able to pose his marginal cost schedule against the market's demand curve and offer his products to buyers. Buyers, too, need to know what is offered by competing farms in terms of quantity, quality and price in order to bargain toward their preferred outcome.

Hence, to maximize utility, they must engage in an optimization process, taking place within two different information sets. What the farmer knows may not be known to the buyer and the former may wish to retain this information. Likewise, the farmer may want to know the guiding buying tactics that a customer may or may not want, or be able, to share with him or her. A third party, knowledgeable about both sides, may be required. A broader view of interests involved could help improve either player's position in the bargaining process. Here the role of the entrepreneur, explored conceptually in this chapter, materializes. Special traders enter the market. They specialize in buying farm products on one side and selling them to or through chain stores or other types of trading companies to urban consumers on the other.

Applying the analogy of the farmer to politics, a government is the producer of goods and services while the citizens are the buyers or consumers. Information about a government's intentions and its citizens' needs is a valued asset. In order to adjust policies to fulfill the needs of the people, a government must know what type of decisions to make and the effect of their actual implementation (Pressman and Wildavsky, 1973), necessitating a feedback mechanism (Sharkansky, 1982). It would be a lot easier for governments if, instead of acting under a veil of uncertainty concerning people's needs and desires, they could know what citizens expect of them. In other words, establishing a mechanism to mediate and channel information between the citizens and the government. With information provided by such a mechanism, governments could more precisely design their policies. No government can satisfy all needs for all people and, hence, must decide 'who gets what, and how much' (Dahl, 1963).

Entrepreneurs within parliaments, like political parties, or outside parliaments, such as organized special interests, help articulate what people want, convince citizens to press demands for these things from the government, illuminate possible ways to obtain desirable outcomes and suggest possible actors with similar preferences to carry the cost of pursuing the groups' demands. They also help to ensure that government policies meet intended goals. In doing so they find themselves in ongoing competition with other entrepreneurs, who also organize people with conflicting preferences and purposes.

Social, political and economic entrepreneurs are important players in democratic systems. Parties identify and recruit cadres to serve in governments in an attempt to bring about the implementation of their most preferred policies. We discuss this and other aspects of party politics in the next chapter. Lobbies equip lawmakers with information in order to guide them to make choices that these lobbies are promoting. Intellectuals or media people constitute bridges between citizens and governments by articulating ideas and offering new ones. Like farmers and customers, governments and citizens need entrepreneurs: governments need them to maintain power and citizens need them to obtain better laws, goods and services.

In the following section we introduce entrepreneurs with well-defined utility functions and strategic options into the model of the polity we constructed in the previous chapter. This is an example of how social scientists use formal mathematical modeling to advance an understanding of complex social phenomena. We started with a very simple model of a state with a ruler and constituents. We went on to introduce a degree of realism into the model by relaxing the assumption of complete and perfect information. We now move closer to the phenomenon we really want to understand – how law and order emerges and evolves, and how the social contract that rules modern polities came to be – by introducing a crucial additional type of player into the model: special interests and political entrepreneurs. The model may change. It may become more complex. It may lose in elegance, but our understanding will improve.

4.3 A Model of a Polity with Special Interests and Entrepreneurs[1]

The main bargaining asset that entrepreneurs usually have is 'inside information.' Ainsworth and Sened (1993) [A&S] model this relative advantage by giving the entrepreneur the ability to observe the number of agents, β, who may benefit from an amendment in the structure of the social contract. By providing some information about β to governments and their constituents, entrepreneurs reduce the uncertainty that characterizes the bargaining process. A&S allow the entrepreneur to lie about the value of β, or, in kinder terms, to be strategic about the value s/he reports. Yet, they show that regardless of what entrepreneurs may claim β to be, government officials and group members can deduce from the willingness of the entrepreneur to promote a special interest, that s/he observed a β, higher than a certain minimum $\underline{\beta}$. In this way the decision of an entrepreneur to represent an interest serves as a self-fulfilling prophecy. If s/he decides to promote an amendment to the law, s/he improves the chances that the government will react favorably to the plea of the group. If s/he chooses not to promote such an amendment, this message considerably reduces the incentive for group members to petition for change and the chance of a favorable reaction to the plea by government officials.

We can structure these considerations involving governments, citizens and entrepreneurs as a sequence of interactive steps leading to sets of possible outcomes. Ainsworth and Sened (1993) followed this strategy and introduced political entrepreneurs into the model of the polity that we explored in the previous chapter to obtain a nine-stage sequential game.

The Game (Ainsworth and Sened, 1993)

Stage 1: Each agent chooses a strategy $\sigma_i \in \sigma_i$, where σ_i is a mapping: $\sigma_i : \{0,1\} X \{0,1\} \Rightarrow [0,1]$. The first set represents the agent's types $b_i \in \{0,1\}$. The second set denotes the entrepreneur's message space $M = \{0,1\}$. The third set represents the possible values of $\rho \in [0,1]$, the probability that agent i petitions for change. An entrepreneur chooses a strategy, λ, which is a mapping from $T = \{0,1,...,n\}$, the set of types, with $\beta \in T$, to the message space M, $\lambda : \{0,1,...,n\} \Rightarrow \{0,1\}$ Government chooses a strategy which is a mapping $g : \{0,...,n\} X \{0,1\} \Rightarrow \{0,1\}$. The first set denotes the possible values of $\alpha \in \{0,1,...,n\}$, the number of petitioners. The second set is the entrepreneur's message space and the third set is the government's strategy space.

Stage 2: Each agent $i \in N$ learns his or her type $b_i \in \{0,1\}$.

Stage 3: The entrepreneur observes his or her type $\beta \in T$.

Stage 4: The entrepreneur sends a message $m \in M = \{0,1\}$, based on λ and β.

Stage 5: The government and the agents update their beliefs given m.

Stage 6: Each agent acts according to the strategy s/he chose in stage 1.

Stage 7: The government updates its beliefs after seeing m and α.

Stage 8: The government chooses its action, depending on g, m and α.

Stage 9: Pay-offs are distributed as specified below.

Strategies and Pay-offs

From the previous chapter we have a set $N = \{1,...,n\}$ of constituents with $i,j \in N$, as generic members of N. Let c be the cost of petitioning, assumed to be equal across agents. Agent i's type, $b_i \in \{0,1\}$, characterizes his or her expected benefits from amending the law. Agents of type $b_i = 1$ expect to benefit from the amendment, while agents of type $b_i = 0$ expect no benefit. The government and all the agents have common prior beliefs about a probability q that any agent $i \in N$ be of type $b_i = 1$, represented by a discrete multinomial probability density function $f(\beta)$, defined by q and n that assigns to any value of $k \in \{0,1,...,n\}$ a probability that $\beta = k$. Let $b = (b_1,...,b_n)$ denote a realization of n independent draws of $b_i \in \{0,1\}$. β represents the number of agents of type $b_i = 1$.

Let $S_i = \{0,1\}$ denote i's pure strategy set with $s_i = 1$ denoting a choice to petition and $s_i = 0$ denoting a choice not to petition. Agents' strategies are conditional on their type and the message they receive from the entrepreneur. Thus, a strategy σ_i, of agent i, is a mapping $\sigma_i : \{0,1\} X \{0,1\} \rightarrow [0,1]^4$, or an ordered quadruple: $\sigma_i = (pr(s_i = 1|b_i = 1, m = 0); pr(s_i = 1|b_i = 0, m = 0); (pr(s_i = 1|b_i = 1, m = 1); pr(s_i = 1|b_i = 0, m = 1))$, that specifies the probability that agent i may petition, depending on his or her type and on whether the entrepreneur decides to represent the group or not. Intuitively, if members learn that an entrepreneur is going to represent them, they should be more willing to turn out and petition. Finally, we know from the previous chapter that agents of type $b_i = 0$ never petition. Table 4.1 specifies constituents' pay-offs.

Table 4.1 Constituents' Pay-offs

i's pay-off $u_i =$	i's type $b_i =$	i's pure strategy $s_i =$	government's strategy $g =$
$(1-t) - c$	1	1	1
$(1-t)$	1	0	1
$-c$	0	1	$g \in \{0,1\}$
$-c$	1	1	0
0	0	0	$g \in \{0,1\}$
0	1	0	0

As in the previous chapter, let $W(g)=\{A^1 \in N:(g|A^1)=1\}$ be the set of all subsets of agents so that if government officials observe any of these subsets of agent petition, they amend the social contract to accommodate the constituents' demands. The expected pay-off of agent i is:

$$(4.1) \quad v_i(\sigma,m,g,b_i)=E(u_i|\sigma,m,g,b_i)=[(1-t)(b_i) \cdot prob(A^1 \in W(g)|\sigma,m)] - c \cdot \sigma_1$$

The expected pay-offs of an agent is a function of his or her type, his or her strategic choice and the probability that the government amend the law, given the strategic choices of the entrepreneur and other constituents. Recall that $s=(s_1,...,s_n)$, $(s_i \in \{0,1\})$ denotes a particular realization of $\sigma = (\sigma_1,...,\sigma_n)$. $A^1=\{i \in N:s_i=1|s\}$ denotes the group of agents who petition for change and α denotes the cardinality of A^1. A government strategy is a mapping $g:\{0,1,...n\}X\{0,1)\Rightarrow\{0,1\}$, where $g(\alpha,m)=1$ denotes amending the law and $g(\alpha,m)=0$ denotes not changing the law after observing α and m. The government's benefits, b_g, from amending the law are assumed to be a linear function of β, $b_g =t \cdot \beta$, with $0<t<1$. c_g denotes the costs of enforcement. We assume c_g and c to be common knowledge. The utility the government expects from amending the law, given any β is:

$$(4.2) \quad u_g = t \cdot \beta - c_g$$

The expected pay-offs to the government from changing a law, after observing message m of the political entrepreneur and a number, α, of petitioners, is:

$$(4.3) \quad v_g(\alpha,m|\lambda^*,\sigma^*)\equiv E(u_g|\mu_2(\cdot|\alpha,m,\lambda^*,\sigma^*))$$

$\mu_2(\cdot|\alpha,m,\lambda^*,\sigma^*)$ denotes the government's posterior beliefs about β after observing α and m, given the equilibrium strategy, λ^*, of the entrepreneur and the vector σ^* of equilibrium strategies of all citizens. If a government amends the law, its expected pay-off is the sum, over all $\beta \in \{0,1,...,n\}$ of the pay-off, $t \cdot \beta$, it expects if β is the number of beneficiaries, times the probability that β is the actual number of beneficiaries, given the government's updated beliefs,

$\mu_2(\cdot|\alpha,m,\lambda^*,\sigma^*)$, after observing α and m, less the cost of implementation, c_g. We know from the previous chapter that the government's strategy in equilibrium is characterized by a threshold, ω, such that if the number of agents that petition, α, is greater than or equal to ω, the government amends the law, $g(\alpha\geq\omega)=1$, while if α is smaller than ω, the government does not change the law, $g(\alpha<\omega)=0$.

Let $0<\delta<1$, be a share of the petitioning cost of each constituent that the entrepreneur keeps to himself or herself and let c_E be the cost that the entrepreneur bears if s/he decides to represent the group. Table 4.2 fully specifies the entrepreneur's pay-offs.

Table 4.2 The Entrepreneur's Pay-offs

Entrepreneur's pay-off $u_E =$	Entrepreneur's message m =	Government's strategy $g =$
$\delta\cdot\alpha\cdot c - c_E$	1	$g \in \{0,1\}$
0	0	$g \in \{0,1\}$

After observing β, if the entrepreneur chooses not to represent the group, m=0, his or her expected pay-off is 0. If s/he chooses to represent the group – i.e. m=1 – the expected pay-off is:[2]

(4.4) $v_E(\beta,m=1) = [\delta\cdot c\cdot(\rho|m=1)\cdot\beta]-c_E$.

Equation (4.4) states that the entrepreneur gets a share of what is paid by all the constituents who are expected to join the petition for change, less c_E.

Definition of a Sequential Symmetric Equilibrium[3]

Definition 4.1: A sequential equilibrium (SE) a quadruple $(\lambda^*,\sigma^*,g^*,\mu^*)$ s.t.:

1) $\forall \beta\in T$, $\lambda^*(m',\beta)>0$ only if m'$\in$ $Arg \max_{m\in M} v_E (\beta,m,\sigma^*(m),g^*(m,\sigma^*))$.

2) $\forall m\in M$, $\forall i\in N$, $\forall b_i\in\{0,1\}$,$v_i\{\sigma^*,g^*,\mu_1^*(m)\}\geq v_i\{\sigma^*_{-i},\sigma_i,g^*,\mu_1^*(m)\}$ $\forall \sigma_i\in\sigma_i$.

3) $\forall m\in M$, given σ^*, $\forall \alpha$, $g^*\{\alpha,m\}=$ $Arg \max_{g\in\{0,1\}} (g\cdot v_g (g=1|\mu_2^*(\cdot|\lambda^*,m,\alpha,\sigma^*)))$.

4) $\forall m\in M$, such that for any $\beta\in T$ $\lambda^*(m,\beta)>0$, $\mu_1^*(\cdot)$ satisfies:

$$\mu_1{}^*{}_{(f(\beta),m)} = \left(\frac{\lambda^*(m,\beta)^* pr(\beta|n,q)}{\sum_{\beta'\in T}\lambda^*(m,\beta')^* pr(\beta'|n,q)} \right)$$

5) $\forall \beta\in T$, such that $pr(\beta|\mu_1^*(f(\beta),m))>0$, $\mu_2^*(\beta|\alpha,\mu_1^*(f(\beta),m),\sigma^*)$ satisfies:

$$\mu_2{}^*{}_{(\beta|\alpha,\mu_1^*(f(\beta),m),\sigma^*)} = \left(\frac{pr(\alpha|\beta,\sigma^*)^* \mu_1^*(\beta,m)}{\sum_{\beta'\in T} pr(\alpha|\beta',\sigma^*)^* \mu_1^*(\beta',m)} \right)$$

Condition 1 requires that the entrepreneur send a message with a positive probability only if it is a best response, given his or her type, β, to the expected response of the constituents, denoted by σ*. Condition 2 states that σ_i* must maximize i's utility given his or her type, his or her updated beliefs, given the entrepreneur's message, (m | λ*), and the strategies of the government g* and the strategies of all other agents σ_{-i}*. Condition 3 states that g* must maximize the government's utility given its twice updated beliefs. Condition 4 requires that the posterior beliefs, μ_1*(.), of the government and the constituents be consistent with λ* in the sense that, after observing m, these beliefs are determined by Bayes' Rule according to the prior set of beliefs f(β) and the equilibrium strategy of the entrepreneur λ*. Condition 5 requires that the government's posterior beliefs, μ_2(.), after seeing the message of the entrepreneur and the number α of petitions, be consistent with the equilibrium strategy vector of all the agents, σ*, in the sense that after observing α, μ_2*(.) is determined by Bayes' Rule according to μ_1*(.), and the equilibrium strategy vector of constituents σ*.[4]

A sequential equilibrium as defined in Definition 4.1, is symmetric (SSE) if all agents use the same strategy in equilibrium, i.e. $\forall i,j \in N$, σ_i*=σ_j*.[5]

By now we have completed the construction of a game. We have an individual agent we call 'the entrepreneur' – that can be an individual, an organization, a party an economic corporation or a political leader. Another individual player we refer to as 'the government.' Finally, we have chosen an equilibrium solution concept that allows us to derive the set of equilibria that will serve as our predictive tool regarding expected outcomes from this type of interaction in a polity. This solution concept was introduced by Kreps and Wilson (1982). An excellent review of the use of sequential games in the contemporary study of politics is Banks' (1991) brief manuscript, *Signaling Games in Political Science*.

Results and Implications

Lemma 4.1 shows that if the entrepreneur enters, potential members of the group and government officials can infer that the entrepreneur has observed a number of potential beneficiaries, β, that is greater than a certain threshold, z (proofs of Lemma 4.1 and Theorem 4.1 are found in Ainsworth and Sened, 1993).

Lemma 4.1 (Ainsworth and Sened, 1993): If (λ*,σ*,g*,μ*) is an SSE, then λ* is characterized by a threshold, z, such that:

$$\lambda^*(m=1|\beta \geq z)=1, \ \lambda^*(m=0|\beta \geq z)=0, \ \lambda^*(m=1|\beta<z)=0, \ \lambda^*(m=0|\beta<z)=1.$$

The intuition here is that if the entrepreneur enters, group members and government officials can infer that his or her expected pay-off covers the cost of his or her expenses.[6] Since constituents and governments know everything except β, they can compute the smallest number of β that satisfies this condition. Thus, when an entrepreneur sends a message $m \in \{0,1\}$, constituents and governments can update their beliefs and act along the lines of Theorem 3.2, outlined in the previous chapter. Theorem 4.1 characterizes the set of all SSEs.

Theorem 4.1 (Ainsworth and Sened, 1993): $\{\lambda^*, \sigma^*, g^*, \mu^*(\cdot)\}$ is a mixed strategy SSE if:

1. $\forall\, i \in N\ \sigma_i^*(0)=0$.

2. $\lambda^*(m=1|\beta) = 1$ only if $\delta\cdot c\cdot(\rho|m=1)\cdot\beta \geq c_E$ otherwise $\lambda^*(m=1|\beta) = 0/$

3. If $v_g(g=1|\mu_1^*(\cdot))>c_g$, then $\forall\alpha\in\{0,1...,n\}\ g^*(\alpha)=1$ and $\forall\ i\in N\ \sigma_i^*(0)-\sigma_i^*(1)=0$ and $\lambda^*(m=1|\beta) = 0$ regardless of the size of β.

4. If $v_g(g=1|\mu_1^*(\cdot))<c_g$, $\forall i\in N\ \sigma_i^*(0)=0, \sigma_i^*(1|m=1)=(\rho|m=1), g^*(\alpha_1\geq \omega|m=1)=1$, $g^*(\alpha_1<\omega|m=1)=0$ and the pair $\{\omega,(\rho|m=1)\}$ satisfies 4.5 and 4.6 below:

$$(4.5)\ c = (1-t)\cdot\sum_{\gamma=\omega-1}^{n-1}\left[\binom{\gamma}{\omega-1}(\rho|m=1)^{\omega-1}(1-(\rho|m=1))^{\gamma-\omega-1}\right]\cdot pr(\beta=\gamma|\mu_i^*(\cdot), b_i=1)$$

(4.6)

$$v_g(g=1|(\rho|m=1),\alpha_1) = \sum_{\beta=\alpha_1}^{n}(t\cdot\beta-c_g)\cdot\left[\frac{pr(\beta|\mu_1^*(\cdot))\cdot\left[\binom{\beta}{\alpha_1}(\rho|m=1)^{\alpha_1}(1-(\rho|m=1))^{\beta-\alpha_1}\right]}{\sum_{\beta'=\alpha_1}^{n}pr(\beta'|\mu_1^*(\cdot))\cdot\left[\binom{\beta'}{\alpha_1}(\rho|m=1)^{\alpha_1}(1-(\rho|m=1))^{\beta'-\alpha_1}\right]}\right]\geq 0\ iff\ \alpha_1\geq\omega$$

5. If $v_g(g=1|\mu_1^*(\cdot))<c_g$, $\forall i\in N\ \sigma_i^*(0)=0,\ \sigma_i^*(1|m=0)=(\rho|m=0), g^*(\alpha_0\geq \omega|m=0)=1$, $g^*(\alpha_0<\omega|m=1)=0$ and the pair $\{\omega,(\rho|m=1)\}$ satisfies 4.7 and 4.8 below:

$$(4.7)\ c = (1-t)\cdot\sum_{\gamma=\omega-1}^{n-1}\left[\binom{\gamma}{\omega-1}(\rho|m=0)^{\omega-1}(1-(\rho|m=0))^{\gamma-\omega-1}\right]\cdot pr(\beta=\gamma|\mu_i^*(\cdot), b_i=1)$$

(4.8)

$$v_g(g=1|(\rho|m=1),\alpha_0) = \sum_{\beta=\alpha_0}^{n}(t\cdot\beta-c_g)\cdot\left[\frac{pr(\beta|\mu_1^*(\cdot))\cdot\left[\binom{\beta}{\alpha_0}(\rho|m=0)^{\alpha_0}(1-(\rho|m=0))^{\beta-\alpha_0}\right]}{\sum_{\beta'=\alpha_0}^{n}pr(\beta'|\mu_1^*(\cdot))\cdot\left[\binom{\beta'}{\alpha_0}(\rho|m=0)^{\alpha_0}(1-(\rho|m=0))^{\beta'-\alpha_0}\right]}\right]\geq 0\ iff\ \alpha_0\geq\omega$$

Theorem 4.1 replicates Theorem 3.2 from the previous chapter, with the important difference that now we have an entrepreneur as an additional player in the game. We learn that the introduction of this player actually helps reduce the uncertainty in the game by providing additional information that is revealed by the strategic behavior of entrepreneurs. By Lemma 4.1, the decision of the entrepreneur to represent, or not represent, the plea of the group can considerably narrow the range of possible values of β, allowing both government officials and constituents to make more educated decisions regarding their strategic actions. Given this additional information, they would act in one way if the entrepreneur decides to represent the group's interests (condition iv of Theorem 4.1), and in another if the entrepreneur decides not to represent the group (condition v of

Theorem 4.1). The ability to distinguish between these two possible cases, based on the message sent by the entrepreneur, reduces the uncertainty in this environment and the loss in social welfare associated with it.

Condition ii of Theorem 4.1 does not imply that entrepreneurs necessarily secure a positive pay-off. It only implies that their expected pay-offs are positive. This is important inasmuch as models of this sort must be able to account for political defeat. Entrepreneurs may fail to get a law amended that would grant their constituents the right they pursue, and a political party may fail to secure a law it promised its voters.

Therefore, *ex ante,* we should expect equilibria in environments with active entrepreneurs who represent organized special interests, to be more efficient than equilibria in games without entrepreneurs.

One should not overlook the discrepancy between our conclusions and the commonly accepted prejudice against special interests in the traditional 'rent seeking' literature. Most notably, in his *Rise and Decline of Nations* (1982), Olson promoted the prevalent view in the literature that well-organized special interests are likely to strangle economic activity by seeking to obtain outrageous demands. Ainsworth and Sened (1993) promote our view that special interests and the entrepreneurs that represent them serve as oxygen to the bargaining process between governments and their constituents. We believe that the discrepancy can be accounted for by the fact that we model the state as a strategic player, and the interaction between the state and the constituents as a bargaining game, whilst the 'rent seeking' literature has no model of the state at all (Eggertsson, 1990: 279).

The economic success of the U.S., Germany, and other countries where special interests are active, compared to the stagnation of economies in countries where special interests are systematically oppressed, seems to speak in favor of our argument and militates against the prevalent view of the 'rent seeking' literature. The merit of these competing arguments can indeed be tested empirically by comparing the evolution and relative success of countries with strong interest groups against those where special interests never organized or were oppressed.

This highlights one aspect of contemporary social science that for lack of space we do not adequately emphasize: formal models of social interaction must be consistent with what we know about the world in which we live.

The presence of entrepreneurs helps constituents focus on equilibria with high levels of turnout. In so doing, they reduce the probability that government officials make the mistake of amending the law when the government may be better off not doing so, or failing to amend the law when it would be better doing so. The reduced probability of error does not guarantee that only sound changes are made, but the information revealed by entrepreneurs about the likely number of potential beneficiaries helps government officials estimate when, and to what extent, the enactment of any law is likely to gain support.

Even in the reduced set of equilibria, an equilibrium almost[7] always exists wherein no potential beneficiary contributes, the entrepreneur stays out of the game and the law is not amended, regardless whether the number of potential beneficiaries warrants the amendment. Yet, the presence of self-interested entrepreneurs creates focal points away from such equilibria. After observing an entry of an entrepreneur, potential beneficiaries will rationally conclude that the group is viable. If entrepreneurs are reluctant to enter, beneficiaries should conclude that either the cost of lobbying is too high, or the number of beneficiaries observed by the entrepreneur is too small. In this way, a message from the entrepreneur helps members of the group to focus on a small subset of all the possible equilibria that exist in the absence of the institution of political, economic and social entrepreneurs.

4.4 The State as a Nexus of Information and Coordination of Special Interests[8]

The limitation of the Ainsworth and Sened (1993) model presented in the previous section is that entrepreneurs rarely work in environments devoid of competition from other entrepreneurs. In her recent work, Olson (1995) studied how competition among entrepreneurs may affect the distribution of regulatory favors. In competitive environments entrepreneurs provide information to regulators on competing groups. Special interests usually have conflicting goals regarding structures of social order, because institutional designs promote the interests of some groups at the expense of others.

Olson (1995) constructed a model of multiple interests competing to obtain regulatory favors from a regulatory agency. The regulator maximizes positive feedback from all agents involved, including politicians, industry groups and consumer groups. Olson's work can be used here to complete the model of the polity. Suppose that a government is contemplating an action $a_g(p,b) \in A_g$ as a function of some general policy, p, and a budget constraint b. Assume k interests are potentially affected by the planned amendment in the structure of the social contract that such new regulation may present. Let $\{w_1,...,w_k\}$ be a set of weights that government officials place on the vector $m=(m_1,...,m_k) \in M$ of signals received from the respective entrepreneurs representing the different interests in society with respect to the contemplated change in the legal make-up of the polity. Let the government's utility, u_g, be a function of the vector m of signals received from the entrepreneurs and the weight w_k the government officials attach to each signal m_k. These weights may represent updated beliefs of government officials concerning the number of individuals behind each entrepreneur, their economic or political wealth, the likelihood that the group will be active in pursuing its goals etc. In this way we obtain the following objective function of a government:

$$(4.9) \qquad u_g = \phi_g \left(\textstyle\sum_{i=1}^{i=k} w_i \cdot m_i (a_g(p,b)) \right) - c(a_g(p,b))$$

$c(a_g(p,b))$ is the cost of choosing an action $a_g \in A_g$, of a particular change in the law or regulatory structure of the polity. $\sum_{i=1}^{i=k} w_i \cdot m_i (a_g(p,b)) - c(a_g(p,b))$ is the sum of benefits that the government officials expect from implementing $a_g \in A_g$. $m_i(a_g(p,b))$ is the signal, $m_i \in M_i$ of the entrepreneur representing interest $i \in K$, which is a function of the action $\mathbf{a_g(p,b)}$, taken by the government. w_i is the weight that government officials attach to signals coming from any particular entrepreneur, depending on the number of individuals represented by the entrepreneur, their economic wealth or political power, the likelihood that they be active in pursuing their goals and other characteristics of special interests.

Finally, ϕ_g is a government specific utility function. Scholars often assume that all governments have the same utility functions, maximizing revenues, political support or other objectives. But different government officials are likely to have different objective functions, depending on the personality of the leaders in charge (Doron and Sherman, 1995), the wealth and political prospects of the government in power and a variety of other parameters. Government officials relatively sure of maintaining power may increase tax revenues through policies that may be unpopular. Government officials who struggle to remain in power may compromise their immediate tax revenues in an effort to maintain power. If we ignore the fact that governments differ in attitude towards policy-making, we risk trivializing the analysis of the bargaining processes by which social order emerges and evolves. This explains why we often fall into the trap of expecting government officials to grant and enforce efficient property rights. As North himself admits (1990: 52), he revised his theory recently 'to account for the obvious persistence of inefficient property rights. These inefficiencies exist because rulers would not antagonize powerful constituents by enacting efficient rules that were opposed to their interests.'

North acknowledges the non-trivial nature of the political bargaining game that determines the structure of property rights, but returns, all too often, to his earlier argument according to which 'institutions exist to reduce the uncertainties involved in human interactions' (*ibid*: 25). As Knight (1992: 33) points out, institutional structures are often erected to meet the distributional concerns of leaders and the interests that support them, and have little – if anything – to do with reducing transaction costs, uncertainties, or inefficiencies.

Unlike most literature in this area, Olson's model allows us to see what governments are really concerned with, and not how we would like them to be. We expect government officials to choose an action $\mathbf{a_g} \in \mathbf{A_g}$, to maximize $\phi_g\left(\sum_{i=1}^{i=k} w_i \cdot m_i(a_g(p,b)) - c(a_g(p,b))\right) \forall \mathbf{a_g} \in \mathbf{A_g}$. Thus, we should expect government officials to take the action $\mathbf{a_g}^* \in \mathbf{A_g}$ that maximizes ϕ_g, given the anticipated reaction of the affected interests, as presented by the vector of signals $\mathbf{m(a_g)}$ and the set of weights, w, that government officials attach to these anticipated signals. The vector of signals $\mathbf{m(a_g)}$ is the reaction that government expects from special interests, given action $\mathbf{a_g}$ they chose. Weights attached to signals translate into regulators' utility through regulators' expectations regarding the effect that the relevant special interests may have on their chances of winning elections, on maximizing future gains from tax revenues, or meeting various other economic and political goals (Riker and Sened, 1991). Utility functions differ considerably across governments. But it should be clear that all the other elements in $\phi_g\left(\sum_{i=1}^{i=k} w_i \cdot m_i(a_g(p,b)) - c(a_g(p,b))\right)$ also vary across governments. Individual government officials will put different weight on pleas coming from the business community, from groups that advocate social justice and from groups that struggle to provide minimum conditions for the poor. These differences may stem from ideological differences (North, 1990), the acquired beliefs with which every elected or non-elected official enters office, education etc.

The 'rent seeking' literature (Stigler, 1971; Peltzman, 1976) models governments as faceless, non-strategic, social welfare utility maximizers (Eggertsson, 1990: 279). If this is how governments operate, we do not need to worry about the bargaining process this book describes. However, we postulate that governments are made up of strategic agents who maximize a variety of goals with more or less 'know how' and information about the consequences of their actions. In modeling government interaction with constituents as a bargaining game, we hope to promote a more realistic study of the origin and evolution of real structures of social order.

4.5 Concluding Remarks: The Political Origin of Social Order

For centuries we have been falsely led to believe that nature, market forces, historic determinism and other obscure forces forge some optimal structure of social order. In this book we argue that institutional structures of law and social order are determined through a bargaining process between governments and individuals in society. In this process, government officials choose a legal structure that maximizes their utility given their notion of the size and strength of different interests in society and the extent to which these groups are active in the pursuit of the social order they wish the regulator to impose.

Our analysis so far has offered a general model of the emergence and evolution of social order that diverges considerably from traditional analysis. According to our model, social order evolves after a central body able to impose adequate levels of social order on society establishes its monopoly over law enforcement. Such agencies use this monopoly to structure order in society so as to maximize political and economic support, and to advance some very 'personal' goals that are 'specific' to every set of government official.

For centuries, society was organized hierarchically. With rare exceptions, the sovereign ruled the country and negotiated the condition of his or her constituents in a relatively haphazard manner. The bargaining process involved the more or less active participation of political intermediaries such as the nobility, members of the court and delegations of different interests in society, such as the church, merchants, guilds and others (North, 1986).

Between the 14th and the end of the 17th centuries, a new political institution emerged in Europe which signaled a great improvement in the institutional structure of the bargaining process between government and constituent: the parliament. In its early days, parliament was not actually intended as a body of representative delegates. The notion of representative government was introduced by English liberals in the 17th century and by French and American Republicans a century later. As an independent institution, parliament emerged to facilitate the bargaining process between monarch and nobility over the extent, mode and frequency of tax levies (North, 1986; North and Weingast, 1989).

Only much later – towards the end of the 17th century – would the notion of parliament as a representative body emerge. General suffrage became a norm in general elections to parliament only in the late 19th and early 20th centuries.

Whatever its origins and initial design may have been, parliament today forms the nucleus of the modern polity. As such it serves as the focus for the complex bargaining processes between different interests in society over the allocation of scarce resources. The following two chapters look at political bargaining as it manifests itself in elections to parliament, and political bargaining in parliament over the allocation of resources. In Chapter 5 we discuss a general model developed by Schofield and Sened (1998) that highlights the complex bargaining process that characterizes parliamentary systems. In Chapter 6 we rely on three decades of research into processes of bargaining in the U.S. system to describe some aspects of the bargaining process that characterize presidential systems.

Notes

1. This section is based on Ainsworth and Sened (1993) published again in Sened (1997: 133-44).

2. The choice of this simple message space where m can either be 0 or 1 is justified in Ainsworth and Sened (1993: 845-6).

3. The usual reference is Kreps and Wilson (1982). More penetrable discussions are found in Cho (1987), Cho and Kreps (1987) and Banks and Sobel (1987). The definition used in the text is adapted from Banks (1991: 7).

4. Definition 4.1 only specifies beliefs 'along-the-equilibrium-path.' No restrictions are imposed on the belief structure 'off-the-equilibrium path.' This poses a problem if the government observes an event that according to its beliefs should never occur. This could happen for example if $\sigma^* = \sigma^\circ$ where $\sigma^\circ = (\sigma_i^* = 0 \ \forall \ i \in N)$, but $\alpha \neq 0$. To deal with these cases, from a technical aspect, Ainsworth and Sened (1993) use the Intuitive Criterion (IC) proposed by Cho and Kreps (1987). The IC requires that beliefs 'off-the-equilibrium-path' place zero probability on the eventuality that agents that certainly stand to lose from deviating from the equilibrium behavior would ever do so. In our case it implies that if government officials observe someone petition, they assume s/he is of type $b_i = 1$. The government beliefs 'off-the-equilibrium-path' put zero probability on that an agent of type $b_i = 0$ ever petition, since such an agent can only lose by doing so.

5. Following the norm in the literature (e.g. Palfrey and Rosenthal, 1984,1988), we restricted our analysis to symmetric equilibria. Without imposing symmetry, the analysis of this type of game tends to become intractable. In addition, there is truth to the claim that we want to study agents who react in the same manner to similar circumstances, which is precisely the assumption that symmetric equilibria impose. From a more technical point of view, if we do not impose symmetry it is unrealistic to expect agents to satisfy the requirement of 'consistency of beliefs.' It is one thing to expect agents to more or less do what all agents end up doing, but if we don't impose symmetry, we have to require that agents guess which, of all possible combinations of strategic choices by large numbers of agents, is likely to materialize – an unrealistic assumption. If we assume symmetry, the expected behavior of other agents can be computed from the given parameters of the game. As Ainsworth and Sened (1993) show, in such cases, the number of possible equilibrium strategy vectors is limited. Therefore, it is realistic to expect

agents to find the equilibrium strategies and for one of all the possible equilibrium vectors to be chosen. If we do not impose symmetry, the number of equilibrium strategy vectors becomes infinite, and it makes little sense to expect agents to guess which of the infinite possible strategy combinations is likely to be chosen in any particular game.

6. Formally, it must be the case that $\delta \cdot c \cdot (\rho | m=1) \cdot \beta \geq c_E$. We assume that $\delta \cdot c \cdot n > c_E > 0$ to rule out equilibria where the entrepreneur always enters ($c_E = 0$) or never enters ($\delta \cdot c \cdot n > c_E$).

7. This is true in all cases except in the unlikely event of what Olson (1965) referred to as latent groups, where action of one activist warrants the public good to the entire group.

8. This is a revised version of a section with the same title previously published in Sened (1997: 145-8).

5 Electoral and Post Electoral Bargaining in Parliamentary Systems

5.1 Introduction

According to common wisdom, legislators represent the preferences of their constituents when making decisions as to how to allocate scarce resources. This wisdom notwithstanding, the next section argues that modern legislative bodies, as we know them today, were originally devised as bargaining mechanisms, and not as representative mechanisms. In the third section we discuss mechanisms used to block the path of different groups into parliamentary bodies. The fourth section returns to the spatial theory and shows that legislative bodies are unlikely to be effective representative arenas if, and inasmuch as they are meant to, aggregate individual preferences into social choices.

The rest of the chapter develops the argument that legislative bodies are, nevertheless, helpful in guiding and mediating the bargaining process between governments and constituents. We present a model of the bargaining process between constituents and governments that starts when legislators propose policy positions in order to get elected. The next stage of the process involves the construction of parliament with the electorate voting for their preferred candidate. Candidates then form a coalition government in order to implement policy positions and allocate resources to provide services to their constituents.

This bargaining process is very different from the process we observe in presidential systems, as, for example, that of the U.S. We discuss the logic and the process of bargaining in presidential systems in the next chapter. Building on three decades of research, we survey some seminal contributions to the understanding of the political bargaining process within and among the different branches of government in the political institutional structure of the U.S.

There are two good reasons to use the U.S. example. First, it is one of the purest presidential systems that exist. Second, decades of research have yielded a relatively good understanding of the bargaining process in the U.S. political system as we hope to demonstrate in Chapter 6.

5.2 The Historic Origins of Representative Government

Contrary to common perception, legislative bodies originated out of a bargaining process between absolute sovereigns and the most significant interests among their constituents. Furthermore, parliaments were not originally meant to be representative bodies in any sense of the word. They were constructed to institutionalize and thereby facilitate, a bargaining process between monarchs and affluent constituents concerning the taxes the constituents would pay and appropriate ways in which a monarch could use those revenues. As the Nobel laureate economic historian Douglass C. North (1986: 14-15) writes:

> ...in common with the rest of the emerging European nation states, [England and Spain] each faced a problem with far-reaching consequences. That is, that a ruler required additional revenue to survive. The tradition was that a king was supposed to live on his own, which meant that the income from his estates, together with the traditional feudal dues, were his total revenue. [However], the change in military technology associated with the effective use of the cross-bow, long-bow, pike and gun powder enormously increased the cost of warfare and led to a fiscal crisis... In order to get more revenue, the king had somehow to make a bargain with constituents.

The structural change in the relationship between rulers and constituents was caused by an external factor: technological change. New warfare technology created new opportunities and additional maintenance costs for the rulers, forcing them ultimately to construct different political institution. Failure to adapt to new inventions would mean putting at risk a ruler's ability to survive.

Until these changes affected the relationship between monarchs and constituents, they were based on well-defined rules and expectations. Monarchs were expected to take responsibility for the supply of two basic public goods: protection from external threat and maintenance of internal stability, either by imposing rules of conduct or by serving as arbitrators in disputes among constituents. In exchange, constituents were expected to follow suit: to show obedience and loyalty to the rulers. While, initially, rulers might have obtained their superior position by forcing consent of their dominion on independent chieftains or receiving their voluntary submission, holding to it over time required additional resources, such as well-equipped royal forces to deter opposition, and legitimization by the religious institutions.

The resulting equilibrium and stability led to dynasties of rulers reigning over long periods. While there could have been better institutional outcomes for both the rulers and the ruled, structural changes in the traditional relationship could also have led to worse outcomes for both. For example, rulers could have lost their power and constituents could have fallen victim to aggressive neighbors or internal instability. Thus, neither side was interested in changing the prevailing order. Significant political change resulted not from an understanding that there existed a better system of government, but rather because new options presented by technological innovation required a readjustment of the old relationship.

Basically, the king needed additional resources to function effectively as a ruler, and these could be found only among his affluent constituents. Rulers could always, and frequently did, resort to brute force to secure these resources, but such behavior over long periods generally ended up in violent opposition to the king. An alternative way to obtain the resources was to trade some of a ruler's rights for additional obligations on the part of constituents, especially in the area of taxes. Hence, a rearrangement of the old order to reflect changing needs was in the making. North (*ibid*) comments on the internal sequence of these developments and on the calculations of both sides:

> The King acts like a discriminating monopolist, offering to different groups of constituents 'protection and justice,' or at least the reduction of internal disorder and the protection of property rights in return for tax revenue. Since different constituent groups have different opportunity costs and bargaining power with the ruler, there result different bargains ...but the division of the incremental gains between ruler and constituents depends on their relative bargaining power ...The initial institutional structure that emerged in order to solve the fiscal crisis therefore looked similar in all the emerging nation states of Europe. A representative body (or bodies) [of] constituents, designed to facilitate exchange between the two parties, was created.

Note the similarity of this description to the model suggested by Olson (1995) that we discussed in the previous chapter. Meanwhile, it is clear why parliament emerged as an institution representing only those in society with whom the king had a vested interest in conducting a continual process of bargaining over revenues. In this sense, parliaments served as the loci of deals – designed establishments where kings could come to affluent members of the kingdom and trade rights for money. In his *Constitutional History of England*, Stubbs (cited by North, 1986: 15) concludes that: 'The admission of the right of parliament to legislate, to inquire into abuses and to share in the guidance of national policy, was practically purchased by the monies granted to Edward I and Edward III.'

Of course, this initial form of government was representative of only a tiny fraction of constituents drawn from the nobility and gentry. How did parliament evolve from the House of Commons of the 16th century, consisting of affluent nobility meeting sporadically to bargain over the amount of tax they were prepared to pay and their demands on the king in return, to the parliament of today which represents large segments of society? To answer this question we consult below Skottowe's *Short History of [the English] Parliament* (1886).

Parliaments around the world continue to do what they were designed to do at the outset: they bring together representatives of the tax-payer with those of the government in order to come to a bargained agreement over what constituents will pay for services or public goods. Indeed, in the power relationships that exist in modern democracies between governments and parliaments, the latter are careful not to surrender their 'power of the purse' (Fenno, 1966) to the former. Overseeing state budgets and approving the specific allocation of scarce resources is, even today, the principle business of parliamentary institutions.

To go back to the historic path that led from there to here, at the outset, the king would summon parliament only when he needed money. The following quote reveals the nature of the bargaining between the king and the House of Commons, characteristic of that era (Skottowe, 1886: 62-3):

> The House was nearly unanimous against the Crown, ...They complained ...of a long list of grievances, and showed themselves altogether so intractable, and so reluctant to grant money, until their grievances were redressed, that James at last, in a huff, dissolved them, February 9, 1611.

Of course, no exchange is possible when neither party is willing to compromise. The king could, however, sustain his uncompromising stand only as long as his financial needs were manageable. If and when these needs became unmanageable, he would have no choice but to approach his affluent constituents again and attempt a new bargain (Skottowe, *Ibid*).

> A second period of arbitrary government now ensued, and once more James had to face the difficulty of making two ends meet without the help of Parliament. His financial expedients, however, were highly unsuccessful, and at the end of three years he was glad to listen to a project ...proposed to influence the elections, to win over the leaders of the opposition by royal favors, to buy votes by flattery, force desertions by intimidation, conciliate many by small concessions, and then Parliament, thus happily converted..., would... vote unlimited supplies. The scheme... leaked out, and caused general indignation with the result that the Court candidates were rejected on all sides... when Parliament met, at last, on April 5, 1614, the Commons proved to be no more ready to be cajoled out of their money in return for nothing than their predecessors had been....James endured them for barely two months, and then dissolved them in a rage...
>
> For seven years James governed without Parliament, badly and unsuccessfully, plunging more deeply into arbitrary methods, and yet totally unable to supply himself with enough money to carry on the government with any rag of credit. The outbreak of the Thirty Years' War, however, obliged him once more to summon Parliament, and lay before them the hopeless statement of his financial difficulties. Finally after he promised to enforce the laws against Catholics and to restore privileges to Parliament, its members agreed to award him with two subsidies.

So the King and the members of Parliament were able to obtain, under duress, a temporary solution to their dispute. One way of affecting the final outcome of a bargaining process is to place people with ideas similar to your own on deciding bodies. Kings and Queens, eager to increase the generosity of the Commons and not wanting to use James' questionable tactics, opted to enlarge the set of represented communities and interests in the hope of introducing more members favorable to their constant plea for money (Skottowe, *Ibid*: 43-4):

> Parliament ... under Elizabeth... asserted itself still more boldly. It began to take upon itself the function of discussing matters of pressing import ... – in many cases even in direct defiance of a royal prohibition. These discussions, however,

Elizabeth was determined to prevent, and the modes which she adopted were ... the creation of new boroughs... to an unprecedented extent – sixty two altogether were added to the existing constituencies, solely with the view of increasing the numbers of the supporters of the government.

We leave it to others to trace the history of representative legislative bodies, from the limited representation of the powerful and affluent to the general suffrage of today. We simply argue that a major force behind increased representation is the ever-increasing need of governments for revenue, and the willingness of kings, queens, presidents, prime ministers and changing majorities in parliaments, to enlarge the set of represented constituents to support this quest. It is no coincidence that the best-represented group of constituents in most modern parliaments is also the most heavily taxed, namely, the middle class.

The essence of representative government cannot only be, as textbooks often indicate, an attempt to provide in parliament a miniature analogue of the preference profile of the individual preferences of constituents. A government can be said to be representative only to the extent that it may be a government of delegates who are mainly concerned with bargaining over the tax remittance from constituents, and over the value, quality and quantity of services that constituents expect in return. Just as in 16th century England.

5.3 Barriers to Entry into Elected Bodies

In the preceding section we argued that parliament originated not to represent the people, but to bargain over scarce resources. While the modern heirs of the old nobility, aptly referred to by C.W. Mills as 'the power elite' (1956), are still represented in disproportionate numbers, universal suffrage enables the entry of delegates representing groups with little wealth. Following the French Revolution, the right to elect and be elected was granted to everyone labeled a citizen. Once the principle of universal suffrage was adopted as a fundamental democratic value, one would expect all groups of citizens to be represented in the elected bodies of parliaments. Yet members of certain groups, say women, or minorities, are consistently under-represented. Is this a technical coincidence or is it an inherent feature of the bargaining process that characterizes all polities?

When kings transferred part of their powers to the small group of affluent members of their society, they did so because the cost of holding to their absolutism was presumably too high. The process of transfer was long and painful. According to conventional democratic wisdom, those who were selected to share power with the monarchy were expected to continue the process of transfer to the rest of the population. Only at the culmination of such a process can one speak of representation in its fullest sense. But if the affluent members of society obtained political power by buying it from kings, why would they then give it away or share it with others? One possible explanation, consistent with the logic of bargaining presented here, is that the affluent too were forced over time to share their newly acquired powers. The motivation this time for the transfer was not generated by external threat to the survival of the regime but from inside, from the masses who could, by their unruly behavior, endanger the economic and social stability and well being of the more affluent.

Once again, from a political perspective, the distribution of public goods and grants of property and other individual rights were not ignited by a normative understanding that the state belongs to its citizens or that each should have an equal share in its wealth. The process of continual transfer of political and economic rights occurred principally because it was cheaper at certain points in time to allow people into decision-making bodies than keep them outside. The first group to obtain entry into the exclusive club of rich legislators was the middle class, because they could help ease the financial burden of paying for state affairs. Other groups came later. Thus, for example, 'The War Against Poverty' or the 'Great Society' plan that commanded huge resources under President Johnson, as well as the increased representation of minorities in Congress, came about to a large extent as a result of the middle class desire to 'buy' order in urban America. This order was necessary to allow the middle class to continue its economic routine (Moyniham, 1970).

In modern democracies legislators decide what changes take place: what policies are made and what groups are included in the business of power sharing. Legislators – politicians who attempt to maximize the probability of their re-election (Mayhew, 1974) – have to find ways to keep challengers from outside from taking their positions. To do so they institute legal and structural barriers to make the entry of outsiders more difficult.

Some of these barriers are obvious, but others are more difficult to detect (Doron and Maor, 1989). One important example is the relative advantage of strong parties over weak ones that prevails in all electoral methods, but tends to be greater in plurality and simple majority systems than in proportional representation (Rae, 1967: 151). To the detriment of small groups, majority-type schemes are adopted. Even in proportional systems, the Highest Average Formula (The D'houndt system), which favors larger parties, is often preferred to the Largest Remainder method, which is more generous to small groups.

Single-member districts provide an advantage to large and established parties. The more members each district sends to parliament, the greater the chance that small groups of particular preferences will be represented. Hence, in the American and British polities where single-member districts are used, only two or three parties play a significant role in parliament. In Israel, to take an extreme case of a multi-member district (the entire country constitutes one district that sends 120 delegates to the Knesset), no less than 10 parties have ever been represented in parliament (Peretz and Doron, 1997).

There are many ways to make parliament a secure fortress against the penetration of outsiders. Consequently, many groups in society remain under-represented or unrepresented. But the most intrinsic obstacle to representation is the nature of electoral competition, to which we turn now.

5.4 The Spatial Theory of Electoral Competition

In Chapter 2 we introduced the spatial theory of electoral competition, STEC, as an analytical framework that sheds light on the problem of aggregating individual preferences into social choices. In STEC, possible outcomes are represented as points in space. Any vital issue of the choice problem is represented by one dimension of an m-dimensional space, denoted by $\Re^m$. The utility $u_i(x)$ that agent i derives from outcome $x \in \Re^m$, is assumed to be a function of the Euclidean distance between x and ρ_i, i.e. $u_i(x) = \varphi_i (|x-\rho_i|)$, where ρ_i represents the preferred outcome, or ideal point, of i in $\Re^m$. We assume that each agent seeks to realize an outcome as close as possible to his or her ideal outcome in the choice space. The central solution concept in this paradigm is the 'majority core' (Definition 2.1 in Chapter 2) defined as:

Definition 5.1: $x^* \in \Re^m$ is the *majority core* if, for any other feasible outcome in the choice space, $y \in \Re^m$, at least half of the agents prefer x to y.

In the terms introduced in Chapter 2, a majority core is just a special case of the *core* defined as the set of undominated outcomes in a simple majority rule game. In general, when the core is non-empty, i.e. if there is an outcome that satisfies definition 5.1, we expect the outcome of an interaction among rational agents using majority rule, to be the core. This is so because by definition there is no position that a majority of the relevant agents prefers to the core position, and, therefore, no position can defeat the core position in a simple majority rule game. One of the most commonly cited results in political science is the *Median Voter Theorem*, which more than any other result familiarized political scientists with STEC as a potent scientific paradigm (see discussion in Chapter 2).

If we interpret elections as a bargaining process over socials choices, the *Median Voter Theorem* suggests that, under some conditions, elections may yield normatively 'acceptable,' if not desirable, outcomes that can be predicted with accuracy and certainty.

Unfortunately, this elegant result does not hold under the more realistic assumption of multidimensional choice spaces. In Chapter 2 we introduced the so-called *Chaos Theorem* that shows that in policy spaces with two dimensions or more, the *majority core* is almost always empty, and whenever this is the case, manipulative agendas can lead to almost any outcome (McKelvey, 1979; Schofield, 1984; McKelvey and Schofield, 1987).

The 1980s were dominated by the impression that the *Chaos Theorem* left on the academic community. In the late 1980s and throughout the 1990s, major theoretical breakthroughs allowed a more systematic understanding of parliamentary systems (Huber, 1996; Laver and Schofield, 1990; Laver and Shepsle, 1990, 1996; Schofield, 1986, 1995, 1996; Sened, 1996; Schofield and Sened, 2000). In the remainder of this chapter we explain the bargaining process characteristic of multiparty proportional rule systems, using these recent analytical developments.

Let $P=\{1,...,p\}$ be a set of parties and $W=\{w_1,...,w_p\}$ be a set of weights assigned to parties in parliament. Let l be the biggest party in parliament with $w_l > w_i \ \forall \ i \in P, i \neq l$. let $x=(x_1,...,x_p) \in \Re^{m \cdot p}$ be a vector of the ideal points of parties. Finally, let $U: \Re^{m \cdot p} \rightarrow \Re^p$ be a utility function representing the preference profile of all parties over $\Re^m$. A voting rule, σ, is a social preference function that assigns to any utility function, U, a strict preference $\sigma(U)$. Recall the definition of the set of decisive coalitions from Chapter 2:

Definition 5.2: $D_\sigma = \left\{ C_r \subseteq P: \forall \ x,y \in X, (\forall \ i \in C_r \ yP_ix) \Rightarrow y\sigma_{(U)}x \right\}$.

In words: A coalition $C_r \subseteq P$ is decisive by σ if for any utility function, U, and any pair of outcomes $x,y \in \Re^m$, if all members of C_r prefer y to x – write $yP_ix \ \forall$ $i \in C_r$ – then y is preferred to x by σ. We write $y\sigma_{(U)}x$.

In this way a voting rule σ defines the set of decisive coalitions D_σ.[1] In western democracies, coalitions that are supported by more than half of the members in parliament are usually decisive. This rule is known as majority rule.

Definition 5.3: The Core, $C(\sigma,U)$, in a weighted voting game σ, given U, is defined as: $C(\sigma,U) = \{ \ y \in X \mid x\sigma_{(U)}y \text{ for no } x \in \Re^m \ \}$.

Definition 5.4: (Schofield, 1986) The core $C(\sigma,U)$ is structurally stable, denoted as $SSC(\sigma,U)$, if $C(\sigma,U)$ is not empty and for any $x \in C(\sigma,U)$ there exists a neighborhood, $u_{(x)}$ in U and a neighborhood $V_{(x)}$ in X, such that $\forall \ u' \in u_{(x)} \ \exists$ $x' \in V_{(x)}$ such that $x' \in C(\sigma,U)$.

Definition 5.3 is a generalization of Definition 5.1. Definition 5.1 states that any outcome that is preferred by at least half of the agents over any other outcome is in the 'majority core.' Definition 5.3 states that any outcome $y \in X$, that is preferred, over any other outcome $x \in X$, by a decisive coalition defined by the rule σ, given a utility profile U, is in the core. We want to alert the reader to the fact that this is equivalent to our definition 1.5 in Chapter 1 that states that the core of the game is the set of undominated utility vectors in this game. Definition 5.4 is a restriction on Definition 5.3 of the core, requiring that if agents' preferences change slightly, the core does not 'vanish' but remains in a neighborhood, $V_{(x)}$, of $C(\sigma,U)$. Schofield (1995) has since shown that typically, a point in the policy core (if non-empty) will be at the policy position of the 'strongest' party in the legislature. With few exceptions, the 'strongest' party in the legislature is the party l that has the greatest weight w_l or most seats in parliament. So, if $SSC(\sigma,U) \neq \emptyset$, we would predict that the ideal policy of the largest party in parliament, x_l will be implemented. To deal with the case in which the SSC is empty, Schofield (1993) developed the notion of the *Heart* that we denote by H and discuss in the next section.

Four stages characterize the process of aggregating individual preferences into social choices in multiparty proportional rule (MPR) systems:

1. **Pre-electoral stage:** in which parties position themselves in the relevant policy space by choosing a leader and declaring a manifesto.
2. **The election game:** in which voters choose whether and how to vote.
3. **The coalition bargaining game**.
4. **The legislative stage:** in which a policy is implemented as the social choice outcome.

A comprehensive model of an MPR electoral game must include all four stages. A good way to think about it is to use the notion of *backward induction* introduced in Chapter 1. To play the coalition game, parties must have clear expectations about what will happen at the legislative stage. To vote, voters must have clear expectations about the coalition formation game and the policy outcome of the coalition bargaining game. Finally, to position themselves so as to maximize their expected utility, parties must have clear expectations about voting behavior. In the remainder of this chapter we discuss in detail each of the four stages of this four stage bargaining game.[2] It was customary in the literature to discuss these stages separately. Here, we follow Schofield and Sened's (2000) effort to integrate all four stages in one game because we believe that the political game that characterizes parliamentary systems includes all four stages and should be analyzed as such (Austen-Smith and Banks, 1988).

5.5 The Legislative Bargaining Game – The Heart of the Polity[3]

Recall that P is the set of parties with $i \in P$ being a generic party in this set. Recall, further, that $X \subseteq \Re^m$ is the issue space with a generic $x \in X$. Each party $i \in P$ is assumed to have a smooth utility function over X so that for any $x \in X$ and any $i \in P$, we can define: $h_i(x) = \{v \in \Re^m \mid p_i(x) \cdot v > 0\}$ where $p_i(x)$ is i's gradient vector at x which measures the change in utility that accrues to a party with every move at point x in the direction of v. $h_i(x)$ is the set of all directions for which such a move entails a positive marginal change for i at point x. For any coalition $C_r \subseteq N$, the preference cone for C_r at x is defined as $h_{c_r}(x) = \cap_{i \in c_r} h_i(x)$. In words, the preference cone is the set of all directions of move from x that entail a marginal increase in utility for all members of $C_r \subseteq N$. Recall that any simple voting rule σ defines the set of decisive coalitions D_σ.

Definition 5.5: For every $x \in X$ we can define a *preference field:*

$$h_{D_\sigma}(x) = \cup_{c_r \in D_\sigma} h_{c_r}(x)$$

with the interpretation that if $v \in h_{D_\sigma}(x)$, then v is a direction in which a decisive coalition will be willing to move. By the definition of decisiveness, any such coalition can insist on moving away from x in the direction of V, so x cannot be a stable chosen point under the voting rule σ. Conversely, if no such V exists, then no decisive coalition can agree on the direction of change, and x is a stable point relative to $\mathbf{hD}_\sigma$ (Austen-Smith, 1996: 222).

Definition 5.6: (Schofield, 1993) Define the *efficient preference field:*

$$\mathbf{hpD}_\sigma(x) \equiv v \in \mathbf{hD}_\sigma(x) \cap \mathbf{p}_{c_r}(x)$$

With $\mathbf{p}_{c_r}(x) = \{v \in \Re^m \ c_r \in D_\sigma \mid \sum_{c_r} \alpha_i \, p_i(x) \ \alpha_i \geq 0 \ \forall \ i \in c_r, \sum_{c_r} \alpha_i = 1\}$.

$\mathbf{hpD}_\sigma(x)$ is the set of moves in any direction, V, reached by whatever coalition in the bargaining process, that is individually rational for each party $(v \in \mathbf{hD}_\sigma(x))$ and *locally efficient:* $v \in \mathbf{p}_{c_r}(x)$. Loosely speaking, local efficiency requires that coalitions not move in a particular direction if all members of the coalition prefer a move in another direction. We can redefine the core in terms of the correspondence $\mathbf{hpD}_\sigma$ as: $C(\sigma, U) = \{\ x \in X \mid \mathbf{hpD}_\sigma (x) = \varnothing\}$.

A *local cycle* about x exists if for any neighborhood, $V(x)$ there exists a sequence of alternatives $<y_1, y_2, \dots y_t>$, all in $V(x)$, such that $y_1 = y_t = x$ and each alternative is socially preferred, given σ and U, to the preceding alternative (Austen-Smith, 1996: 222). Given this interpretation we can define the set:

$$\Gamma(\mathbf{hpD}_\sigma) = \{x \in X \mid \exists \text{ a } \textit{local cycle} \text{ about } x \text{ under } \mathbf{hpD}_\sigma\}.$$

Definition 5.7: (Schofield, 1993) Defines the Heart $\mathcal{H}_{D_\sigma}(U)$ as:

$$\mathcal{H}_{D_\sigma}(U) = C(\sigma, U) \cup \text{clos } \Gamma(\mathbf{hpD}_\sigma)$$

In words, the Heart includes the core of the game (if one exists) and all the *local cycles* of the game. If the core is non-empty, all *local cycles* collapse to the core. Since in the absence of a core there must exist some non-empty set of *local cycles*, the Heart is never empty and it converges to the core when the core is non-empty, in which case no local cycles exist. The Heart is the 'local' equivalent (for convex preferences) and is the superset of the somewhat more commonly used *uncovered* set, inasmuch as the Heart can be interpreted as the set of points that are 'locally uncovered' (Schofield, 1999). A point $x \in X$ is *covered* if there exists some $y \in X$ that beats x and every alternative that beats y beats x as well. The *uncovered set* is the set of points not covered (Austen-Smith, 1996: 225, fn. 4). The advantage of using the Heart as a predictive set is that the heart is relatively simple to compute, while no one has so far been able to compute the uncovered set for $n > 3$ (Schofield, 1996: 192).

At the legislative stage of the game, the Heart should be interpreted as the set of *politically feasible* outcomes. Each election defines the set of relevant players, or parties, in parliament and endows them with respective weights. This defines the committee 'weighted voting game' and therefore the structure D_σ of decisive coalitions. The Heart is a subset of policy points in space that can be reached in an incremental process of pair-wise comparison of policies that is likely to take place in parliament after each election that define the set P of relevant parties that passed the entry threshold and won seats in parliament and the vector $W=(w_1,...,w_p)$ of weights assigned to these parties in parliament.

The *Chaos Theorem* discussed earlier assumes that a policy can be proposed on the floor of a parliament even if it is very distant from the policy with which it is compared. If we assume that the process allows only comparisons of relatively 'close' policy options, then Schofield's Heart may serve as a good predictive tool. It provides us with a set of 'likely' policy outcomes when the core is empty. When we say that the Heart collapses to the core when the core is non-empty, we refer to the fact that if the core is non-empty, the Heart and the core coincide.

5.6 The Coalition Bargaining Game – The General Heart of the Polity[4]

Sened (1996) uses this framework to model the coalition bargaining game:

An Outcome of the coalition bargaining game is an ordered pair $(C_r, K_r | \mathcal{H})$ where $\mathcal{H}$ is the Heart of the legislature, C_r is a coalition of parties and K_r denotes a vector $K_r = (K_{1r},...,K_{pr} | C_r, \mathcal{H})$ that specifies the share K_{ir} of K, the total *office*-related available side payments that each party gets, given the formation of coalition C_r in a legislature with a Heart of $\mathcal{H}$.

The Utility party *i* gets if it joins coalition C_r is a function of the Heart set of feasible outcomes and the distribution of office-related pay-offs: $u_{ir} = u_{ir}(K_r, \mathcal{H})$. We assume that u_{ir} is a linear function of K_{ir} and a quadratic function of $d[x_i, E(x_r)]$ the Euclidean distance between the ideal policy point, x_i, of party *i* and the expected policy, of coalition C_r, $E(x_r)$, i.e.: $u_{ir} = \alpha_i \cdot K_{ir} - \beta_i \cdot d[x_i, E(x_r)]^2$.

The extent to which parties are *office* or *policy* seeking (Budge and Laver, 1985, Laver and Schofield, 1990: Ch. 7) is captured by the parameters α_i and β_i. They are likely to differ from party to party. If $\beta_i=0$ then *i* is purely *office* seeking and if $\alpha_i = 0$, *i* is purely *policy* seeking. We assume that both parameters are strictly positive (Austen-Smith and Banks, 1988; Sened, 1996). Let $\pi(x)$ denote the probability that a legislature implements x as its policy. We get:

(5.1) $$u_{ir}(P_r, \mathcal{H}) = \alpha_i \cdot P_{ir} - \beta_i \cdot \int_{x \in H} d[x_i, x]^2 \cdot \pi(x) \, d(x)$$

With some abuse of notations we use $\beta_i(\mathcal{H})$ to denote $\beta_i \cdot \int_{x \in H} d[x_i, x)]^2 \cdot \pi(x) \, d(x)$.

$\beta_i(H)$ is a scalar, given the set of possible legislative outcomes implied by the results of the election, but it varies across parties depending on their ideal positions *vis-a-vis* the Heart and the magnitude of β_i. If the SSC(σ,U) is non-empty we know that $H = x_l$ because the Heart collapses to the *structurally stable core*, SSC(σ,U), that can only be at the ideal point of the largest party that we denote by x_l. In this case we get:

(5.2) $$u_{ir}(P_r, H) = \alpha_i \cdot P_{ir} - \beta_i \cdot d[x_i, x_l]^2$$

The utility function specified in equations (5.1) and (5.2) relies on the premise that it is costly for a party to endorse a policy, other than its own, because its constituents are likely to punish it for such deviations (Austen-Smith and Banks, 1988). Parties endorse such policies to allow the formation of coalitions, but they bargain to reduce $\beta_i(\mathcal{H})$, that captures the cost of such compromises, and to maximize the benefits of joining coalitions, captured by $\alpha_i \cdot K_{ir}$. Parties that stay in opposition do not get the benefits but avoid the cost of endorsing policies that deviate from their own. Formally: $\forall\ i \in P\ \forall\ C_r,\ u_{ir}(\cdot|\ i \notin c_r) = 0$.

The Game: Parties have to decide whether to accept a share, K_{ir}, to join C_r. If all parties in C_r accept their shares, C_r forms. C_r can distribute payments only if C_r is not *vulnerable*, by definition 5.9, or winning by definition 5.8 below. Formally: $u_{ir}(i \in C_r|\ C_r$ is *vulnerable*$) = 0\ \forall\ i \in P$.

Definition 5.8: A coalition C_r is *winning*, $C_r \in \{WC\}$, if it is not *vulnerable*.

Definition 5.9: A coalition, C_r is *vulnerable* if:

1. $\exists\ c_r$' such that $\sum_{i \in cr'} wi > 50\%$ and
2. $\exists\ (c_r',K_r'|\ H)$ such that $u_i(c_r',K_r'|\mathcal{H}) > u_i(c_r,K_r|\mathcal{H})\ \forall\ i \in c_r'$.

In many models of parliamentary bargaining, the control by a coalition C_r, of a majority of the seats in parliament (formally: $\sum_{i \in cr'} wi > 50\%$) is assumed to be a necessary and sufficient condition for C_r to be *winning*. Numerous minority governments in MPRs (Strøm, 1990) prove that this condition is neither necessary nor sufficient. Definition 5.6 states that C_r is winning only if **no** alternative, majority coalition C_r' exists so that all members of C_r' prefer C_r' to C_r. It captures the institution of no-confidence votes in MPRs (Huber, 1996) by which coalitions can be ousted of power when a majority in parliament approves a no-confidence motion. Thus, our analysis allows us to study cases in which minority government form and govern successfully (Strøm, 1990; Sened, 1996).

We now rely on the analytical tools of cooperative game theory, introduced in Chapter 1, to define a solution concept that we call the General Heart and denote by $\mathcal{GH}$. Let $u(c_r,K_r|\mathcal{H})=(u_{1r}(c_r,K_{1r}|\mathcal{H}),...,\ u_{pr}(c_r,K_{pr}|\mathcal{H}))$ be a utility vector associated with an outcome $(C_r,K_r|\mathcal{H})$. Recall that a characteristic function of a coalition C_r, $V(C_r)$, is a collection of utility vectors so that if C_r can distribute $u_{ir}(\cdot)$ to members in P then $u(\cdot)$ is in $V(c_r)$. Some members in P may get $u_{ir}(\cdot)=0$, specially if they are not members in C_r, in which case they stay in opposition. But, a coalition could and often does allocate positive pay-offs to non-members in order to gain some 'outside support.' A game in characteristic function form is a triple $\Gamma=(V,P,U)$ where P is the set of parties, U is the set of feasible utility vectors and V is a characteristic function that assigns to each coalition C_r, a collection of vectors that C_r can implement.

Definition 5.10: $u(.)$ dominates $u'(.)$ with respect to C_r if $u(.)$ is in $V(C_r)$ and $\forall$ $i \in c_r$, $u_i(.) > u_i'(.)$. $u(.)$ dominates $u'(.)$ if a *winning* C_r exists so that $u(.)$ dominates $u'(.)$ with respect to C_r.

Define the set of minimum winning coalitions $\{MWC\}$ as:

$$\{MWC\} = \{C_r \subseteq N: C_r \in \{WC\} \text{ but } \forall\ i \in C_r\ C_r \backslash i \notin \{WC\}\}.$$

We can now define the *General Heart*, $\mathcal{GH}$ as:[5]

Definition 5.11: The General Hart, $\mathcal{GH}$, is the set of *undominated* vectors in U.

Definition 5.11 is a standard definition of a core. It distinguishes itself only in the non-standard definition of $u(c_r, K_r | \mathcal{H})$ as a pay-off vector in U, as defined by the utility function of the parties engaged in the coalition bargaining game. However, Definitions 5.9, 5.10 and 5.11 build a non-standard definition of MWC. By this definition, minority governments are also viable and under certain conditions are actually likely to occur (Strøm, 1990; Sened, 1996). Let:

(5.3)

$$(SV_i | C_{r*}) = \text{Max}\left(\alpha i \bullet \left(K - \left[\sum_{j \in cr,\, j \notin cr*,\, j \neq i} \beta j(\text{H}) + \sum_{h \in cr,\, h \in cr*,\, h \neq i} \alpha h \bullet Khr^* \right] \right) \middle| \forall cr \middle| w(cr) > 50\% \right)$$

$(SV_i | C_{r*})$ denotes the maximum side payments that any coalition, C_r, to which a core coalition C_{r*} may be *vulnerable*, could pay any member of C_{r*} to lure it to defect. To avoid defection, C_{r*} must pay each member at least this 'reservation price.' Given the cooperative approach we use here, coalition partners could actually end up with higher pay-offs. We conjecture that a non-cooperative analogue game could be constructed in which the formator of a coalition would pay exactly this reservation price to each partner. To compute this *reservation price* we subtract from the total value of side payments, K, the minimum that any coalition, C_r, threatening to outset C_{r*}, must pay its members except i. The remainder of K after subtracting all that must be paid to other members is the maximum C_r can pay to party i to convince it to leave C_{r*}. If a relevant member j of C_r is not a member in C_{r*}, then to join C_r it must be paid enough to offset the cost $\beta_j(\mathcal{H})$. Summed up for all such members we get: $\sum_{j \in cr,\, j \notin cr*,\, j \neq i} \beta j$ $(\mathcal{H})$. If party h

is a member in C_{r*} it must be paid at least what it gets from C_{r*}, summed up for all members of both C_r and C_{r*} we get: $\sum_{h \in cr,\, h \in cr*,\, h \neq i} \alpha h \bullet Phr^*$. To convince party i to

join C_r and defect C_{r*}, C_r can offer at most $(SV_i | C_{r*})$. If C_{r*} pays each member $i \in C_{r*}$ the *reservation price* $(SV_i | C_{r*})$, then C_{r*} is not *vulnerable*. Theorem 5.1 states necessary and sufficient conditions of an outcome $(C_{r*}, P_{r*} | \mathcal{H})$ to be in $\mathcal{GH}$.

Theorem 5.1 (Sened, 1996): $(C_{r^*}, K_{r^*} | \mathcal{H}) \in (\mathcal{GH})$ if and only if:

1. $c_{r^*} \in \{MWC\}$
2. $\forall i \in P$, if $(SV_i | c_{r^*}) \leq \beta_i(H)$, then $K_{ir^*} = -\beta_i(\mathcal{H})$,

   otherwise: $(SV_i | C_{r^*}) \leq K_{ir^*} \leq (K - \left(\sum_{j \in cr^*, j \neq i} (SVj | cr^*) \right))$

3. $\sum_{i \in cr^*} P_{ir^*} = K$

In words: If the $\mathcal{GH}$ is non-empty it consists of **MWCs (1.i).** We emphasize again that here the set **{MWC}** may include minority governments. Each member of a coalition that may distribute an allocation that is in $\mathcal{GH}$ gets at least its *reservation price,* **$(SV_i | c_{r^*})$** and at most what is left of **K**, after all other members of **C_{r^*}** receive their *reservation prices.* If a *reservation price* of a party is smaller than the cost $\beta_i(\mathcal{H})$ this party pays to join a coalition, then the former will pay this party $\beta_i(\mathcal{H})$ because that is enough to keep it in **C_{r^*} (1.ii).** Finally, a $\mathcal{GH}$ allocation must distribute all available side payments **K (1.iii).**

$\mathcal{GH}$ does not coincide with the **SSC(σ,U).** It can be non-empty when the **SSC(σ,U)** is empty and empty when **SSC(σ,U)** is non-empty (Sened, 1996). In fact, when the sum of side payments exceeds an upper bound, $\overline{k}$, $\mathcal{GH}$ is empty because the policy concerns of parties will not be important enough to induce a core in the constant-sum side payment game. However, budget constraints and the relative importance of policy concerns should allow us to assume that the size of K is usually smaller than this upper bound of $\overline{k}$. Under this assumption GH is always non-empty regardless of whether the **SSC** is empty or not.

So, for each configuration of party positions $x^P = (x_1, \ldots, x_p)$, voters can compute $\mathcal{H}$ and $\mathcal{GH}$ and establish some expectations about the outcome of the coalition bargaining and the legislative stage of the game. Each voter can then compute the best response to any configuration $x^P = (x_1, \ldots, x_p)$ of party positions depending on his or her ideal policy point, the party positions' vector and how s/he expects others to vote. This is the subject of the next section. Before we move on, however, we provide two corollaries to Theorem 5.1 that are of some interest.

Proposition 5.1 (Sened, 1996): If SSC(σ,U)$\neq \varnothing$ and $(C_{r^*}, P_{r^*} | \mathcal{H}) \in (\mathcal{GH})$ then $l \in C_{r^*}$.

In words: when the structurally stable core is non-empty and the *General Heart* is non-empty, then the largest party is always a member of the winning coalition.

Due to the complexity of the problem, researchers have often tried to solve the coalition problem for the case of three parties (Baron, 1993; Schofield and Parks, 2000). The concept of the $\mathcal{GH}$ allows us to provide a clear solution to the three-party problem that can be generalized to cases with more than three parties – something previous models were unable to do. Assume three parties $P = \{1,2,3\}$ with Euclidean utility functions with $x_1 \neq x_3$, $x_1 \neq x_2$ and $x_2 \neq x_3$. Assume that no party receives a majority of the votes so that SSC(σ,U) $= \varnothing$ (in the three parties case we never $SSC(\sigma,U) \neq \varnothing$). Assume further that every pair of parties has a majority in parliament. With little loss of generality assume that:

$$\beta_1(\mathcal{H}) < \beta_2(\mathcal{H}) < \beta_3(\mathcal{H}), \; \beta_1(\mathcal{H}) + \beta_3(\mathcal{H}) < K, \; \beta_1(\mathcal{H}) + \beta_2(\mathcal{H}) < K.$$

Proposition 5.2: If $\mathcal{GH} \neq \varnothing$ then: If $\beta_2(\mathcal{H}) + \beta_3(\mathcal{H}) \geq K$ then $C_r^* = \{1\}$ and $K_{r1}^* = K$. If $\beta_2(\mathcal{H}) + \beta_3(\mathcal{H}) < K$ then $C_r^* = \{1,2\}$ $K_{r1}^* \geq K - \beta_3(\mathcal{H})$ and $K_{r2}^* \geq K - \beta_3(\mathcal{H})$.

Proposition 5.2 states that in the three-party case if two parties cannot form a coalition because of ideological differences between them, then one party will form a minority coalition and keep all the side payments. If the ideological differences are smaller, but big enough so that $\mathcal{GH}$ is non-empty, the core coalition will include the two parties that expect to pay the least for implementing the Heart, or whatever constitutes the set of *politically* feasible policy points in the post coalition, legislative game.

As in the case of the *Structurally Stable Core* and the *Heart*, the advantage of the concept of the *General Heart* is that it allows us to figure out the coalition that is expected to form, given the *Heart* of the polity. The logic of Proposition 5.2 should extend to any number of coalition members. A coalition will include not only the minimal number of members needed, but also the 'cheapest' set of coalition partners (Sened, 1999) in terms of the cost members assign to the expected deviations from their declared ideal points. This extends Riker's (1962) original argument of minimum winning coalitions. Coalitions want to keep the number of partners to a minimum and to spend as little as possible paying off members for their ideological concerns.

5.7 The Vote Decision

Politicians in general and parliament members in particular win their seats in parliament and get to keep them only if they can get the necessary votes. To get those votes, elected officials and parliament members must find ways to please the voters. At the individual level, each voter may not matter much, leading some political scientists to wonder why voters bother to pay the cost of voting (for a review of this literature see Aldrich, 1993). But as groups, voters make all the difference in the world (Morton, 1987). The 'paradox of no voting' (Riker and Ordeshook, 1968) notwithstanding, when we consider the process of bargaining that precedes any electoral campaign to public office, we should remember the argument of the previous chapter. Political entrepreneurs help solve the collective action problem of voting by guiding voters to equilibria with positive turnout (Potters and van Winden, 1996; Morton, 1987; Ainsworth and Sened, 1993). Viewed in this way, the act of voting is less puzzling. The ability of each voter to cast his or her vote in favor of one party or another is a bargaining chip that voters and candidates are perfectly aware of and pay much attention to in every election to public office.

The rational choice model of voting behavior starts with a set $N = \{1,...,v,...,n\}$ of individual voters. Each voter v, is characterized by a Euclidean policy preference, ρ_v on the policy space, $\Re^m$ derived from the smooth utility function $u_v(y) = - (\left| y - x_v \right|)^2$, where $x_v \in \Re^m$ is the ideal point of voter v and y is an arbitrary point in the space $\Re^m$.

The difficulty with specifying rational choice models of MPR stems from the complexity of the multi stage MPR game, which makes it hard to specify the effect that a single vote choice may have on the final outcome. The Median Voter Theorem discussed earlier states that in two-candidate, uni-dimensional, plurality rule contests, two candidates would converge to the median and the incentive to vote vanishes (Ledyard, 1984). Literature on the subject suggests reasons why candidates may diverge (Palfrey, 1984; Kollman, Miller and Page, 1992) and, thus, induce an incentive to vote. However, it is not at all clear to what extent these results extend to the case of MPR with multi parties and multi-dimensional spaces. One model that specifies voter rational behavior for a case where $P = 3$ is Austen-Smith and Banks (1988). They prove the existence of an equilibrium in which two large parties tie in vote shares and position themselves on the left and right of the median voter position. The third party positions itself at the median voter position to get just enough votes to pass the legal threshold to enter parliament. In this equilibrium all voters have an incentive to vote and the three parties position themselves in diverging positions.

Yet, given the uncertainty about how the coalition bargaining game maps vote choices into policy outcomes, it is implausible to treat voter choice as deterministic. The choice among a multitude of parties depends on the distance between the voter and some barely calculable outcome, especially since the voter may or may not be able to calculate the impact that his or her voting decision may have on this final outcome. One way to deal with this difficulty is to use stochastic models to better elucidate the vote choice process (Enelow and Hinich, 1984; Schofield, Sened and Nixon, 1998).

Let Δ_p be a $(p-1)$ unit simplex. The stochastic vote model assumes that the response by voter v to any vector $x^p \in \Re^{m \cdot p}$ of party positions is defined by a continuous probability function χ_v: $\Re^{m \cdot p} \to \Delta_p$ that assigns to any vector of party declaration x^p, a probability that any voter would vote for any party. In this way, $\chi_v(x) = (...\psi_{vi}(x^p),...)$, where $\psi_{vi}(x^p)$ is the probability that voter v vote for party i, given a manifesto profile x^p.

Let Ψ: $\Re^{m \cdot p} \to \tilde{\Delta}_p$. $\tilde{\Delta}_p$ is the set of Borel probability measures on the unit simplex Ψ represents a common belief about the electoral responses to different vectors of party positions. Neither voters nor party elite can perfectly elucidate the basis of the voter's choice. It is therefore sensible to suppose that for any set of voters whose ideal points lie in a neighborhood V of x_i the proportions who vote for each party are described by a continuous function ψ_{vi}.

To illustrate our analysis let us use the example of the 1996 electoral campaign in Israel (Doron, 1996; Sened, 1996). Ofek, Quinn and Sened (1998) estimated the voter positions via confirmatory factor analysis of mass level survey data collected by Arian and Shamir (1999). Figure 5.1 presents the estimated distributions of voter bliss points and party electoral declarations during the 1996 election in Israel. The scoring coefficients generated by the factor analyses were used to place voters in the two-dimensional policy spaces. A kernel density estimator was used to estimate the underlying density of voter ideal points on the eve of the election. These kernel density estimates are summarized by using darker shadings for higher density regions of the bliss points. Given the random sample used by Arian and Shamir, we assume that this is a representative portrait of the distribution of voter ideal points for the election. The survey questions used to construct the two factors were then circulated among experts in Israeli politics who were asked to answer the survey questions as if they were answering for the parties that won seats in the Knesset following each election. These responses were projected into the same space as the mass responses using the scoring coefficients generated by the mass-level factor analysis. The mean party position on each dimension is shown in Figure 5.1.[6]

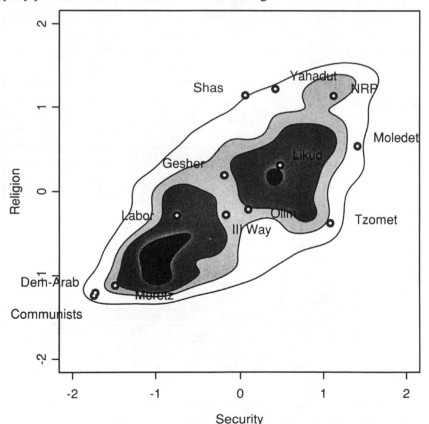

Figure 5.1 Distribution of Ideal Points and Party Positions in the 1996 Election in Israel

	Party	Posterior Mean	95% Bayezian Confidence Interval	
			Lower Bound	Upper Bound
Spatial Distance		-1.117	-1.278	-0.9742
Constant	Shas	-2.960	-7.736	1.018
	Likud	3.140	0.7091	5.800
	Labor	4.153	1.972	6.640
	NRP	-4.519	-8.132	-1.062
	Moledet	-0.8934	-4.284	2.706
	III Way	-2.340	-4.998	0.4113
Ashkenazi	Shas	0.0663	-1.831	1.678
	Likud	-0.6246	-1.510	0.2709
	Labor	-0.2191	-0.9379	0.4920
	NRP	1.055	-0.2061	2.242
	Moledet	0.8194	-0.5599	2.185
	III Way	-0.2832	-1.594	1.134
Age	Shas	0.01435	-0.05795	0.0864
	Likud	-0.0245	-0.0627	0.0082
	Labor	-0.0405	-0.0770	-0.0118
	NRP	-0.0642	-0.1108	-0.0199
	Moledet	-0.0263	-0.0878	0.0256
	III Way	0.0141	-0.0337	0.0626
Education	Shas	-0.3771	-0.6928	-0.06330
	Likud	-0.0320	-0.1804	0.1150
	Labor	0.0110	-0.0993	0.1203
	NRP	0.3861	0.1804	0.5985
	Moledet	0.0495	-0.2194	0.3045
	III Way	-0.0671	-0.2982	0.1496
Religious Observation	Shas	3.022	1.737	4.308
	Likud	0.9300	0.2702	1.629
	Labor	0.6445	0.0772	1.272
	NRP	2.161	1.299	3.103
	Moledet	0.8971	-0.05070	1.827
	III Way	0.9539	0.03055	1.869
Correctly Predicted	Shas	0.3089	0.2095	0.4139
	Likud	0.7066	0.6717	0.7403
	Labor	0.7169	0.6811	0.7518
	NRP	0.4080	0.3235	0.4925
	Moledet	0.0780	0.0461	0.1150
	III Way	0.0287	0.0168	0.0431
	Meretz	0.2850	0.2256	0.3490
	Entire Model	0.6381	0.6230	0.6540
MCMC	15,000	Source: Ofek, Quinn and Sened (1998)		
N	794			

Table 5.1 Multinomial Logit analysis of the 1996 Election in Israel
Using: Bayezian Monte Carlo Markov Chain Technique

After obtaining estimates for party positions and of the ideal points of the voters in the same policy space, Ofek, Quinn and Sened (1998) use an MNL model to obtain an estimate of Ψ. Table 5.1 lists the results for the 1996 election. Note that spatial distance, as expected, exerts a very strong negative effect on the propensity of a citizen to vote for a given party. In short, Israeli voters cast ballots, to a very large extent, on the basis of the issue positions of the parties. This is true even after checking for demographic and religious factors. That does not mean that these non-issue factors have no effect. In each election, factors such as age, education, and religious observance play a role in determining voter choice. This result suggests that some parties are more successful among some groups than they should be based solely upon the bliss points of group members and the parties' electoral declarations. One reason for this phenomenon is that voters may take informational shortcuts. To form beliefs as to current party positions they may rely on their past beliefs of party positions and on the opinions of others within their milieu (McPhee, 1963; Sprague, 1982).

Note the success of the model that correctly predicts 64% of the vote choice and 72%, 71% and 41% of survey participants who voted Labor, Likud, and NRP respectively. This success rate is particularly impressive in light of the multitude of parties that participated in this electoral campaign.

5.8 Parties' Strategic Positions at the Initial Stage of the Game

We now roll back to the first stage of the game. Any party should choose a location to maximize its utility as summarized by equation (5.1), given the location choices of all the other parties and the operator Ψ which represents a common belief about the electoral responses to different vectors of party positions. Recall that $x^p=(x_1,...,x_p)\in X^P$ is a vector of declared ideal points of parties. Note that $X\subseteq\Re^m$ s.t. $X^P\subseteq\Re^{m\cdot p}$.

Let $x^P_{-i} = (x_1,...,x_{i-1},x_{i+1},...,x_p)\in X^P_{-i}$ be a vector of all party positions except i. We can now specify the Nash Equilibrium in the electoral positioning game.

Definition 5.12: x^{p^*} is a Nash Equilibrium in the electoral positioning game iff:

$$\forall\ i\in P\ \ u_i(x^{p^*}\,|\,\Psi) \geq u_i(x_i,x^{p^*}_{-i}\,|\,\Psi)\ \ \forall\ x_i\in\Re^m$$

This condition requires that in equilibrium each party chooses a location that maximizes its utility given the positions of other parties, $x^{p^*}_{-i}$, and the common belief about voters' response operator Ψ. This condition completes our description of the bargaining process embedded in MPRs. We want to emphasize that the declared positions of parties in this model should not be expected to be vote maximizing. Schofield and Sened (2000) have clearly demonstrated the trade-off that this analysis implies between vote maximizing behavior and the prospect of the coalition bargaining game that affect the choice of the position in space, a party may want to associate itself with.

5.9 Conclusions: Representation Through Bargaining

When parliaments first appeared as innovative political institutions, they were erected to solve a simple bargaining problem: rich constituents would bargain with the king to determine how much to pay for services the king provided. The modern polity is much more complex. Government has grown considerably in size and sphere of influence and constituents pay more taxes to guarantee the continuation of these services. Consequently, the bargaining process has become more complex, involving many more constituents and services and much larger sums of money. The nucleus of the entire bargaining process in democratic systems is parliament. In the pure form of parliamentary systems, the members of parliament form coalition governments. These governments make the decisions on the distribution of resource allocations and the implementation of alternative policies.

Once a coalition government is in power, constituents have little, if any, influence on the allocation of scarce resources. Much of the bargaining process thus takes place prior to and during the electoral campaign. Candidates who run for office promise to implement different policies. Voters supposedly guard against electing candidates unless they have promised policy points to their liking. When candidates fail to deliver, voters have the next election to re-bargain the deal with the same or new candidates.

Preferences do not flow freely from the individual to parliament and then transform into social choices. There is no mechanism that can aggregate individual preferences into well-behaved social preference orders. We have demonstrated this in our discussion of Arrow's *Impossibility Theorem* in Chapter 2. Individuals' preferences are represented only inasmuch as they motivate social agents to act in the bargaining game they play with each other.

The difficulty in detecting a causal relationship between the promises made to voters and the actual distribution of national resources stems from the complexity of the process. At each level, agents enter bargaining situations that yield results that are then carried to the next stage. The complexity of each layer of the bargaining process and the multitude of layers makes it almost intractable.

Parliament members take the preferences of their constituents into account if they want to be elected or reelected. Coalition governments are made of parliament members who are bound by the commitment to their voters.

In this chapter we tried to track down the torturous road that binds government officials to take into account the preferences of their constituents in the continuous process by which they construct structures of social law and order. Democracy is representative inasmuch as it is based on institutions that make elected officials accountable to their constituents and responsible for their actions in the public domain. This accountability and responsibility are routinely tested every electoral campaign. This chapter clarified how, through the bargaining that takes place before and after each electoral campaign, individual preferences come to matter in parliamentary systems. The next chapter covers the bargaining process that characterizes presidential systems in general and the U.S. presidential system in particular.

Notes

1. Only a subset, called 'simple rules' are completely characterized by their decisive sets. To fully characterize the more general class of voting rules we need to know their 'decisive structure,' which is somewhat more complicated. For a comprehensive discussion of this issue see Austen-Smith and Banks (1999, Chapter 3).

2. The following four sections derive much of their content and analysis from Schofield and Sened (2000). For the sake of 'user friendliness' we omit much of the technical analysis and replace it with verbal explanation. The more advanced reader is encouraged to refer to the original, where Schofield and Sened (2000) prove the existence of a Nash Equilibrium for the entire four stage game outlined in the following discussion.

3. In this section we follow Austen-Smith, 1996. The more advanced reader is encouraged to refer to the original article, which is considerably more detailed.

4. This section is based on Sened (1996). For lack of space and to enhance the flow, we omit the more technical derivations and proofs. Readers more familiar with mathematical notations and derivation are encouraged to consult the original article that includes a detailed illustration based on the coalition bargaining that came before and during the tenure of Prime Minister Itzhak Rabin from the 1992 election until his assassination on November 4th 1995.

5. What we term the *General Heart* was previously named by Sened (1996) the IVCORE. The change of name can justly be called 'a change of heart.'

6. The data analysis was done by Kevin Quinn. We thank him for granting us permission to use Figure 5.1 and Table 5.1. The statistical analysis is explained in detail in Ofek, Quinn and Sened (1998).

6 Post Electoral Bargaining in Presidential Systems

6.1 Division of Power: Some Preliminary Thoughts

Parliamentary democracies and presidential democracies actually rest on fundamentally different principles. The essence of parliamentary systems is that political decisions are made in a parliament made up of representatives of the public at large. In the previous chapter we argued that the term 'representative' should not be taken literally. Representatives are elected by constituents to serve as delegates in the bargaining process that follows an election. The focal point of this bargaining process is the process of coalition formation. Parliamentary systems are usually governed by coalitions that form in parliament after the election and serve as the executive of the polity.

But the coalition is much more than just the executive. Since coalitions usually represent a parliamentary majority, and parliament is the legislative body, the coalition government also dominates the legislative process and can guarantee that its declared and hidden agendas are met.

The advantage of this centralized parliamentary system is that it makes the coalition government accountable to the voters. The disadvantage that characterizes these parliamentary systems is their lack of checks and balances. In some west European countries the judicial branch serves as a check to the coalition government since it can rule its legislation and actions unconstitutional, if a constitution is in place, or illegal if the judicial system is based on common law. However, the judicial branch has its own politics to work out. It cannot fight the government and the representatives of the people too often or it will lose its only source of power: legitimacy. It is not surprising, therefore, that studies show that courts tend to 'rule in accordance with the interests of the ruling elite, …[and] avoid constitutional confrontations with heads of states' (Barzilai and Sened, 1998).

The characteristic feature of presidential systems that distinguishes them from parliamentary systems is precisely that they are based on the principle of checks and balances. The different branches of government are genuinely independent of each other. The rule of law is less dependent on the awareness of the citizens at the day of the election and more on the constant process of bargaining between the different branches of government. Each branch pulls in its direction until a bargained compromise is achieved.

Electoral rules vary across parliamentary and presidential systems, but presidential systems tend to put less faith in the electoral process *per se,* and more in the watching eyes of elected officials. These elected officials, in addition to being delegates in the bargaining process within the branch of government to which they were elected, serve also as collective watchdogs over other branches of government. Instead of the citizens serving as watchdogs that vote their verdict on election day, the elected delegates are supposed to keep an eye on other elected officials in the various branches of government.

In this chapter we focus our attention on the bargaining process within, and among different branches of government. Since the U.S. is the most widely and carefully studied presidential system, we draw predominately on studies pertaining to the U.S. government.

6.2 A Spatial Model of Checks and Balances

Having arrived at this point in the book, we can now provide a spatial rationale for Montesquieu's (1949 (1748)) argument in favor of the checks and balances that characterize presidential systems. In light of modern scholarship, we avoid treating the judiciary as an independent branch of government (for an excellent text on *The Choices Judges Make* see Epstein and Knight, 1997). In this chapter we treat the House, the Senate and the President as the three players in the game. In the following sections we describe the internal bargaining process that is typical of the U.S. House of Representatives and the U.S. Senate. In this section we discuss a model of checks and balances as a characteristic aspect of presidential systems of government.

A commonly cited analysis of such a game is Hammond and Miller (1987). In the previous chapter we noted the danger of cyclical preferences in unicameral parliamentary systems. We pointed out that the institution of coalition governments explains how cycles may be avoided. Tangible government perquisites, conferred upon those who join a coalition, and variable costs different parties are willing to pay for these perquisites, reduce the tendency for instability in parliaments. This is because defecting parties must forego the government perquisites conferred upon them in return for their loyalty.

Presidential systems have a different incentive structure. Most presidential systems were copied from the structure of government outlined by the U.S. constitution, drafted in 1787 and ratified in 1789. In drafting the constitution, Madison (Riker, 1995) was concerned with making sure that this structure somehow induces stability (Hammond and Miller, 1987: 1956-7). Cox and McKelvey (1984) discuss at some length how multi-cameralism is a viable remedy for instability (see also Tsebelis and Money, 1997). Hammond and Miller (1987) have worked out the details of a two dimensional, spatial, game theoretic analysis that explains how the U.S. presidential system induces stability in the political process. In the remainder of this section we outline the argument using simple graphics drawn from Hammond and Miller (1987).

In Chapter 2 we used Figure 2.2 as a graphic illustration of the potential problem of cyclical preferences that may be induced by majority rule in a parliament made up of as few as three members. Figure 6.1 is taken from Hammond and Miller (1987: Figure 1). It is easy to see that it is made of two sets of agents with preference distribution very similar to the distribution of ideal points of the three agents in Figure 2.2. If we treat these two triples as representatives in the House and the Senate of a bicameral system, the core in each of the two chambers is empty (as is shown in Figure 2.2). If we treat all six players as one parliament, the core would still be empty. The general theorem from which we can conclude this is stated in Hammond and Miller (1987: 1159; see Plott, 1967, for the original argument and McKelvey and Schofield, 1987 for the general version):

Theorem 6.1 (Hammond and Miller, 1987: Theorem 1): A point x is in the core [of a two dimensional voting game assuming representatives with Euclidean preferences] if and only if no straight line [passing] through x leaves a majority of [ideal points] …to one …side of that line.

The intuition behind this theorem is straightforward. Suppose x is a contender for the core. Remember that all representatives have Euclidean preferences. If a majority of the ideal points is on one side of a line passing through x, then there is a winning coalition that would be better off by moving away from x in the direction where the majority of the ideal points are found. Therefore x is not in the core. If any such line leaves less than a majority of ideal points in any of the two 'half spaces' it produces, x is in the core precisely because there is no direction in which a winning coalition (a majority here) will be willing to move away from x.

Thus, if the configuration presented in Figure 6.1 is interpreted as representing two chambers, neither has a core; as a configuration of one parliament it would not have a core either. But in the bicameral game the core is non-empty and actually quite large. Hammond and Miller (1978: pp. 1158-60) show that the core of the bicameral game is the line segment $[p,q]$ in Figure 6.1.

Here again the intuitions are straightforward. Note that any point inside the triangle $[\rho_1, \rho_2, \rho_3]$ which is the Pareto set of the House in this example, is defeated by another point in the triangle. The same is true for the triangle $[\rho_4, \rho_5, \rho_6]$ of the Senate. However, in the bicameral game, we need to gather a majority in both the Senate and the House. Thus any point 'a' is dominated by any point 'b' if one can find a majority in the House and a majority in the Senate that prefers 'b' to 'a'. It is easy to see that the only set of points that are not dominated by other points in space are points on the line $[p,q]$. Note that the entire segment consists of points that are outside of the Pareto sets both of the Senate and of the House.

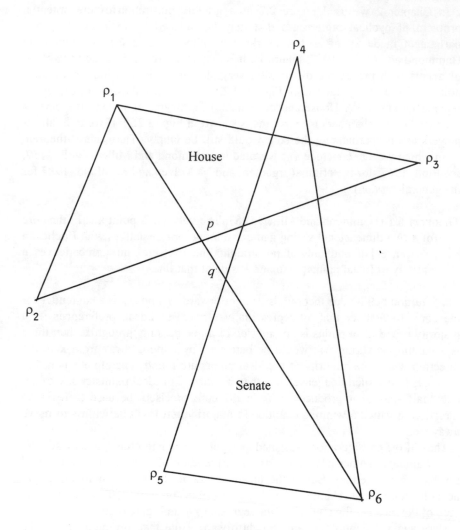

Figure 6.1 An Illustration of a Bicameral Core

While in each chamber the core is empty, the core in the bicameral game is not. At least in this example it consists of a bargained compromise between the House and Senate.

It is easy to construct examples where the core is empty in the bicameral game as well. However, what is important here is that the core may be empty in each chamber and in the two chambers acting as one parliament, and still be non-empty when the two chambers play the bicameral game of checks and balances. It would be disturbing if the contrary were true as well. That is, if we could find a case in which the core of the bicameral game was empty and the core in each chamber, or in the two chambers acting as one parliament, was not empty. Theorem 6.2 is reassuring in this regard:

Theorem 6.2 (Hammond and Miller, 1987: Theorem 4): If a unicameral game has a core, the bicameral core exists and includes the unicameral core.

Suppose we introduce an executive into this game. First, let us suppose that we have only one chamber and an executive. It is well known that the U.S. constitution gives some veto power to the president. What this means is that the president can veto any legislation that is not to his (or her) liking. This leads directly to the following two theorems:

Theorem 6.3 (Hammond and Miller, 1987: Theorem 5): The executive-veto game has a core that includes the executive's ideal point.

Theorem 6.4 (Hammond and Miller, 1987: Theorem 6): If the chamber has no core and if the executive has centrist preferences, the core of a unicameral executive game contains only the executive's ideal point.

It turns out that the core of the unicameral executive game can contain points other than the executive's ideal point. Hammond and Miller (1987: 1162) provide some examples in the game they construct. More generally and more intuitively, the extent to which a president is likely to veto anything other than a policy that coincides exactly with his (or her) ideal point depends on the expectations of what happens after the veto is enacted. Frequently the president is not really choosing between his (or her) ideal point and the policy put forward by the unicameral legislature, but between the proposal of the legislature and whatever default may be left in place after the veto. If the veto is overridden, then the president's veto is meaningless. If the veto is not overridden, the president may end up with a 'status quo' that may be closer or farther away from his (or her) ideal point than the policy put forward by the legislature. Thus, the legislature should be able to promote any policy closer to the president's ideal point than the outcome the president expects if s/he vetoes the bill.

Since the U.S. constitution imposed a bicameral legislature with an executive that is independently elected, theorem 6.5 below is probably the most relevant:

Theorem 6.5 (Hammond and Miller, 1987: 1163): The bicameral executive-veto core includes (but is not restricted to) the House executive-veto core, the Senate executive-veto core and the House-Senate bicameral core when it exists.

The bargaining process leads presidential systems to implement positions that do not represent the ideal point of anyone in particular, but are compromises reached through a process of bargaining between the branches of government.

In parliamentary systems we saw that the bargaining process took place mostly between groups of delegates we call parties. In presidential systems, a key aspect of the process is the bargaining that takes place among the different branches of government (Tsebelis and Money, 1997). But bargaining also takes place within the legislative bodies. For historic and structural reasons, this process is very different in each of the two chambers. The next three sections look at these differences.

6.3 Organization of U.S. House of Representatives: The Role of Committees

Throughout this book we refer to the contribution made by Shepsle to the study of politics, citing his most widely quoted remark (Shepsle, 1986: 51-5) that:

> The relationship between social choices and individual values is a mediated one. Standing between the individual bundle of tastes and ... available choices are institutions... – frameworks of rules, procedures, and arrangements – [that] prescribe and constrain the ...way in which business is conducted.

This observation was originally made in 1979. Shepsle was puzzled by the contrast between the mathematics of voting behavior and his observations on the floor of the U.S. House of Representatives. At the time McKelvey and Schofield were working on the second version of what later came to be known as the *Chaos Theorem*, discussed at some length in Chapter 2. The *Chaos Theorem* could be (and so often was) interpreted to suggest that the decision process in the U.S. House of Representatives would be characterized by an endless path of cycling. But Shepsle observed remarkable order and very rare occurrences of cycles. He went on to propose the notion of *Structure Induced Equilibrium* [SIE] (Shepsle, 1979). Given its remarkable effect on the evolution of political science, as we know it today, this basic concept needs elaboration.

We start again with $N = \{1,2,...,n\}$ individuals each $i \in N$ is endowed with a binary preference relation $\geq_i$ defined on all $x,y \in \Re^m$ and represented by a utility function $u_i: \Re^m \to \Re$ which is maximized at i's ideal point x_i. $\Re^m$ is assumed to be a compact, convex subset of an m-dimensional Euclidean space.[1] Shepsle (1979) defines the core using a slightly different notational framework borrowed from McKelvey and Wendell (1976). Let $C(x,y)$ be a binary choice procedure. The core includes any x such that $x \in \bigcap_{y \in R^m} C(x,y)$, where $\bigcap_{y \in R^m} C_m(x,y)$ is the intersection of all the binary choices between x and any $y \in \Re^m$. Of course, different rules will impose different restrictions on the choice procedure. For our purposes, we can continue to restrict our attention to majority rule. Majority rule is a binary choice procedure where $x = C_m(x,y)$ if and only if the number of members who weakly prefer x to y is greater than the number of those who prefer y to x. For simplicity, let us ignore members who have no preference for y over x at that point. Having (re)introduced majority rule as a binary choice procedure $\mathbf{C_m(x,y)}$, we see why if $\mathbf{x} \in \bigcap_{y \in R^m} C_m(x, y)$ then $\mathbf{x}$ would be in the majority core. If $\mathbf{x}$ is a binary majority winner against all other alternative outcomes, then $\mathbf{x}$ is obviously in the core.

Recall that a non-empty core rarely exists in multi-dimensional settings, so how can we explain so much stability in the U.S. House of Representatives? In this context Shepsle (1979) introduces the notion of *Structurally Induced Equilibrium*. Three aspects of the procedural rules of the U.S. House of Representatives help Shepsle (1979: 27) explain the excess stability:

1. The division of labor embedded in the committee system.
2. The germaneness requirement and the committees' jurisdictional arrangements.
3. The monitoring, or House rules, that provide amendment control.

The division of labor usually assigns relatively narrow 'uni-dimensional' jurisdictions to each committee. Germaneness prohibits the introduction of issues that are not within the jurisdiction of the committee into the discussion when the committee reports to the floor. Together they have the effect of reducing the multi-dimensional choice environment into uni-dimensional sub-jurisdictional choice sets governed by germaneness and amendment control. To understand how this structure induces equilibrium, consider Figure 6.2. The ideal points of the six legislators from Figure 6.1 are reproduced here, but instead of dividing them into two chambers we assigned them to two committees.

To the extent that it is up to the committees to bring new legislation to the floor for discussion, the status quo, denoted in Figure 6.2 as $\mathbf{x}^0$ is a *structure induced equilibrium*. Neither the Foreign Affairs committee, nor the Ways and Means committee, want to change the status quo. Recall from our earlier discussion that in uni-dimensional settings the ideal point of the median in each committee is the unique core point. In Figure 6.2 μ_f is the median of the Foreign Affairs committee that has jurisdiction on bringing new legislation on issues in foreign affairs to the floor. μ_w is the median of the Ways and Means committee that has jurisdiction on bringing legislation pertaining to budget issues. In this way, the structure of the U.S. House of Representatives induces equilibrium in a choice environment that, without the division of labor, jurisdiction arrangements and amendment control, would not have existed.

The committee system enforces division and specialization of labor by endowing committees with narrow 'uni-dimensional' jurisdiction. The amendment control prohibits members of the House to temper with or manipulate proposals brought to the floor by the committees. Thus, committees have amassed enormous power in modern democracies. The median of the committee can block (or 'kill') any legislation that might lead policy away from his or her ideal point. Alternatively, committees can introduce amendments or new legislation that may lead to policies closer to the ideal point of the median of

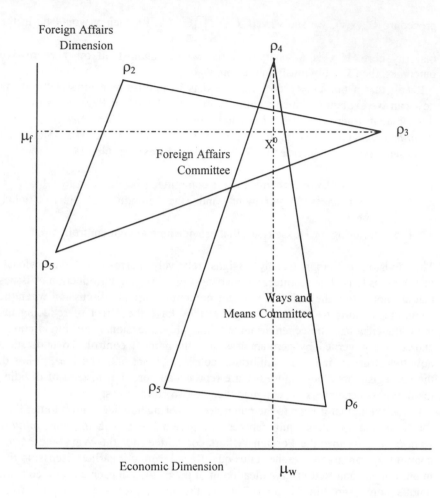

Figure 6.2 An Illustration of Structure Induced Equilibrium

the committee if they can get the support from the floor to do so (Shepsle and Weingast, 1981a). The following three theorems summarize the contribution of the original paper (Shepsle, 1979).[2] We conclude this section with a short discussion of how these results fit our general argument in this book.

Theorem 6.6 (Shepsle, 1979: Theorem 4.1): If the preferences of each $i \in N$ [can be represented] by a strict quasi-concave, continuous utility function, if the basis vectors of $\mathfrak{R}^m$ constitute committee jurisdictions, and if a germaneness rule governs the amendment process, then structure induced equilibria exist.

Theorem 6.7 (Shepsle, 1979: Theorem 3.1): [...] For one-dimensional jurisdictions, a Germaneness rule for amendments, and any committee system, x^0 is a structure induced equilibrium, if for all j, $x^0_j = \textbf{median}$ [on dimension j of the committee with jurisdiction over the jth dimension].

Theorem 6.8 (Shepsle, 1979: Theorem 2.1): If x^0 is a preference induced equilibrium then it is [also] a structure induced equilibrium, but [the] converse [is not true].

Theorem 6.6 states existence. There isn't much point in studying mathematical models if they don't yield interesting predictions about the subject of our study: political bargaining. Theorem 6.7 states that one *structure induced equilibrium* in committee systems with uni-dimensional jurisdiction is the point where the medians of all committees/jurisdiction intersect. Committee members cannot always bring the legislation to coincide with the ideal point of the committee median legislator. They will often settle for points that are as close to the ideal point of the median legislator in the committee as they possibly can.

Finally, theorem 6.8 states that all preference equilibria are also *structure induced equilibria*, but the converse is not true. This is important for two reasons. First, preference equilibria are extremely rare in multi-dimensional choice environments. Therefore, it is important to establish that the set of *structure induced equilibria* is actually bigger. Second, for the sake of consistency in this growing body of research, it is important that those equilibria that are achieved in the absence of institutional structures are maintained under the institutional structures as well. In this way Theorem 6.8 reassures us that the rare equilibria that exist under sparse institutional structures prevail under more imposing structures. The more complex structures only help individuals to achieve stable equilibria more often.

But what does all of this tell us about the bargaining process in the legislature? It tells us that bargaining does not really take place on the floor, but in the back rooms of the House after a new congress has been elected and the committee assignments have been made (cf. Krehbiel, 1992).

This notion of bargaining ahead of time is more pronounced in a recent application of this model by Laver and Shepsle (1996) to the study of coalition formation. Their remarkable effort is an alternative model to that which we introduced in the previous chapter. It applies the logic of the model outlined above to the process of coalition formation.

In the previous chapter we modeled the process of coalition formation as a bargaining process over government perquisites and policy outcomes. The trade-off between the public good of policy and the 'private' divisible good of government perquisites induces stability at the level of the final outcomes.

In the model developed by Laver and Shepsle (1996), based on the model outlined above, coalition formation remains a bargaining process over policy outcomes alone. After the elections, all parties assume that any party that gets jurisdiction over any portfolio in the ensuing coalition government will implement its ideal point in this jurisdiction. Party leaders figure out the *structure induced equilibrium* implied by any composition of any feasible coalition government and opt for the coalition that is likely to implement the policy position closest to them. A bargaining process begins where each party pushes towards the coalition that is likely to implement the position closest to its ideal point. As in the other models surveyed here and in the previous chapter, the coalition in the core will be a coalition that will satisfy the defining condition of a core allocation, namely: that no other policy-position can be implemented by a winning coalition that would prefer it over the core policy position. In other words: there is no winning coalition that prefers a distribution of portfolios that implies the implementation of a different policy position in space to the implementation of the core position.

6.4 Coalition Building in the U.S. House of Representatives

In Chapter 5 we introduced a coalition game that is based on the premise that both policy preferences and government perquisites figure as arguments in the parties' utility calculation in the bargaining game. In the previous section we discussed a model where only policy preferences mattered. In this section we complete our discussion of that matter with the seminal work of Baron and Ferejohn (1989) [B&F], who studied a coalition formation game based on the premise that only distributive implications really matter. This assumption may make sense in the U.S. House of Representatives where party loyalty is relatively weak and representatives are more interested in pork barrel politics than in abstract ideologies (Shepsle and Weingast, 1981b).

Another important feature of the B&F model distinguishes it from the model we discussed in Chapter 5 and the model promoted by Shepsle (1979, Laver and Shepsle, 1996), that we discussed in the previous section. The models we discussed earlier use cooperative game theory as the underlying analytical framework. The B&F model is derived from the non-cooperative, game theoretic, analytical framework. For an appreciation of the advantages and disadvantages of using one or the other framework, we refer the reader to the discussion of the two frameworks in Chapter 1.

Before discussing the model itself, we wish to emphasize the advantage of the B&F model in so far as it treats the strategic behavior of legislators explicitly. This is a clear advantage of the non-cooperative over the cooperative approach used in the models of coalition building surveyed earlier.

The B&F model consists of four primitives: (1) there are n legislators; (2) a neutral recognition rule that assigns equal probability to the selection of any legislator to make a proposal on the floor of the House; (3) a rule that determines whether amendments can be attached to the initial proposal before a vote is taken; (4) majority rule as the voting rule. The task of the legislators is to determine a distribution of a divisible budget for their respective constituencies.

A proposal is an n-tuple $x^i = (x_1^i, ..., x_n^i)$ with $\sum_{j=1}^{n} x_j^i \leq 1$. The set X of feasible outcomes is, thus, an n-dimensional simplex. The status quo is no allocation, represented as an n-tuple of zeros $x^0 = (0, ..., 0)$. Figure 6.3

(adopted from Baron and Ferejohn, 1989: 1184-5 Figures 1 and 2) is a graphic presentation of the legislative process as modeled by B&F. Figure 6.3a depicts the process under the *closed rule* procedure. Figure 6.3b describes the procedure under the *open rule* procedure.

Under the closed rule, each representative gets an equal probability to propose an allocation, $x^i \in X$, to the floor. Once a proposal is put to the floor, all representatives vote either in favor of or against the allocation. If a majority approves the allocation, the proposal is implemented. If a majority votes against the proposal, the status quo of no allocation ensues. The process repeats itself until a proposal is approved.

Under the *open rule*, once a proposal is made, each legislator – except the person who made the initial proposal – has an equal probability of being called to propose another allocation $x^j \in X$ as an 'amendment' to $x^i \in X$, or to call the floor to make a vote on proposal $x^i \in X$.

Figure 6.3 The Structure of the Legislative Process as Modeled by B&F

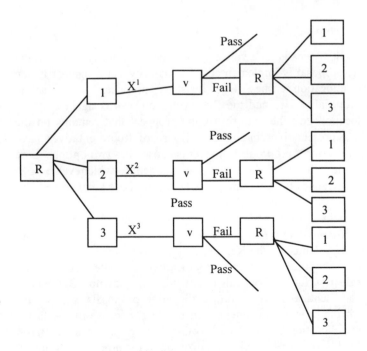

Figure 6.3a The Legislative Process Under the Closed Rule

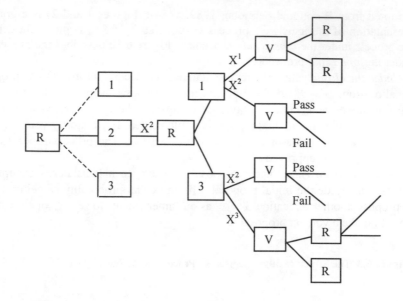

Figure 6.3b The Legislative Process Under the Open Rule

If a chosen representative calls for a vote on $x^i \in X$ and a majority approves the allocation, then the proposal is implemented. If a majority votes against it, the status quo of no allocation ensues. If a legislator proposes $x^j \in X$ as an 'amendment' to proposal $x^i \in X$, and the floor votes on $x^j \in X$ against $x^i \in X$ then whatever allocation gets the majority is the proposal that remains on the floor. Once again, representatives in the U.S. House of Representatives have equal probability of making a proposal. Whoever is chosen has two options. S/he can suggest yet another allocation $x^k \in X$ as an amendment to whichever $x^j \in X$ or $x^i \in X$ won the previous vote. Alternatively, s/he can propose a vote on $x^j \in X$ or $x^i \in X$ that won the previous vote and so on.

As in the Rubinstein (1982) model discussed in Chapter 1, members are assumed to have a discount factor $0 \leq \delta \leq 1$ over future allocations. In this way each member of the U.S. House of the Representatives has two reasons to vote in favor of an allocation proposal. If the current allocation distributes a reasonable share to his or her district, future proposals or amendments may not. But even if s/he hopes to get an identical share in future allocation proposals, s/he is still better off voting for the proposal or amendment pending, because of the factor that discounts future allocation by δ, for each voting session that goes by. Baron and Ferejohn (1989: 1186) describe their formalization of the process as follows:

> The process of proposal generation and voting yields an extensive form game
> with an infinite game tree. A *history* h_t of the game up to point **t** is a

specification of who had a move at each time, the move selected by each member …and the vote when a vote was required. A pure strategy s^i_τ at time τ is a prescription of what motion to make when [i] is recognized and of how to vote whenever a vote is required; … if H_τ denotes the set of histories, a pure strategy is $s^i_\tau : H_\tau \to X$ if τ is the beginning of a session and i is recognized. [It] is $s^i_\tau : H_\tau \to \{$yes, no$\}$ if τ is a time to vote… A strategy s^i … is a sequence of functions s^i_τ mapping H_τ into [i's] available actions at time τ. A randomized strategy σ^i_τ at time τ is a probability distribution over the strategies s^i_τ available [to i] at time τ. An important feature of this model is that whenever a member is to take an action, [s/he] knows which history has occurred; so the game is one of perfect information.

Given the similarity of this set-up to the Rubinstein (1982) model introduced in Chapter 1, it is natural to use the equilibrium concept of subgame perfection that we introduced there. Baron and Ferejohn (1989: 1186) define it as follows:

Definition 6.1: A configuration of strategies is subgame-perfect if the restriction of those strategies to any subgame constitutes a Nash Equilibrium in that subgame.

Definition 6.2: For any particular subgame-perfect equilibrium the *value* v(t,g) of subgame **g** after **t** sessions is defined as the vector of values $v_i(t,g)$ … that results from the play of that subgame-perfect equilibrium configuration. The *continuation value* $\delta v_i(t,g)$ is the value if the legislature moves to subgame **g**. The *ex ante* value at the beginning of the game is denoted by v_i.

B&F prove the following proposition:

Proposition 6.1 (B&F, 1989: 1187, Proposition 1): *A strategy configuration is a subgame-perfect equilibrium for a two-session, n-member (with n odd) legislature with a closed rule and equal probabilities of recognition if, and only if, it has the following form:*

1. *If recognized in the first session, a member makes a proposal to distribute δñ to any (n-1)/2 other members and keep 1-δ(n-1)/2n to his or her own district. If recognized in the second session, a member proposes to keep all the benefit [to his or her district].*
2. *Each member votes for any first session proposal in which the member receives at least δñ and votes for any second-session proposal.*

The first proposal is …accepted, and the legislature adjourns in the first session.

As in the Rubinstein (1982) model, B&F face the same difficulty that if the finiteness of the game is relaxed, almost any allocation can be supported by a subgame-perfect Nash Equilibrium configuration of strategies which figures as proposition 6.2 below.

Proposition 6.2 (B&F, 1989: 1189, Proposition 2): *For an n-member, majority -rule legislature with an infinite number of sessions and a closed rule, if $1>\delta(n+2)/[2(n-1)]$ and $n\geq5$ any distribution x of the benefits may be supported as a subgame-perfect equilibrium...*

We are reminded of the weakness of Nash and Subgame Nash equilibria to reduce the predictive set of expected outcomes to a manageable size. To work around this problem, B&F introduce the notion of stationary equilibria. In light both of the importance of the B&F model and the controversy that surrounds the use of the concept of stationary equilibria, we introduce the notion below.

Definition 6.3 (B&F, 1989: 1191): Two subgames are *structurally equivalent* if

1. The extant agenda at the initial nodes of the subgames are identical,
2. The set of members who may be recognized at the next recognition node are the same, [and]
3. The strategy sets of members are identical.

...[Under] the closed rule, two subgames commencing with the null agenda (i.e. no motion on the floor) are thus structurally equivalent, so all subgames commencing after the defeat of the proposal on the floor are structurally equivalent.

It should be clear that two subgames starting with two different proposals x and y where $x \neq y$ are not structurally equivalent.

Definition 6.4 (B&F, 1989: 1191): An equilibrium is said to be **stationary** if the continuation values for each structurally equivalent subgame are the same. A stationary equilibrium necessarily has strategies that are stationary; that is, they dictate that a member takes the same action in structurally equivalent subgames. Thus, if a member is recognized when there are no motions pending at each of two sessions, [s/he] makes the same proposal in both sessions.

Proposition 6.3 (B&F, 1989: 1189, Proposition 3): *For all $\delta\in[0,1]$ a configuration of pure strategies is a stationary subgame-perfect equilibrium in an infinite session, majority-rule, n-member (with n odds) legislature governed by a closed rule [and equal probabilities of recognition] if and only if it has the following form:*

1. *a member recognized proposes to receive $1-\delta(n-1)/2n$ and offer δ/n to $(n-1)/2$ other members selected at random.*
2. *each member votes for any proposal in which [s/he] receives at least δ/n.*

The first proposal receives a majority vote so the legislature completes its task in the first session. The ex ante values of the game are $v_i 1/ = n, i = 1,...,n$.

Thus, the restriction to stationary subgame-perfect equilibria reduces the set of equilibrium strategies to the one with finite numbers of sessions as in proposition 6.1 above with very much the same logic.

Accepting the assumption of stationarity[3] as B&F do, what happens if we move to the *open rule* regime? B&F (1989: 1196, Proposition 4) characterize the equilibrium for a legislature with a simple open rule in a separate proposition. We chose not to reproduce this proposition here because of space limitation and the complicated mathematical apparatus needed to make sense of the formal proposition. Instead, we discuss briefly the main features of the comparison between the two procedures.

Two basic differences emerge from the comparison. In equilibrium, under the open rule, the power of the first member to submit a proposal is considerably reduced (B&F, 1989: 1197). While the mathematics of this feature may be complicated, the logic is straightforward. Since any proposal can be amended on the floor, the first mover's proposal must satisfy members of the legislative coalition so that they motion for a vote and not for an amendment. Thus, in the final analysis, the first mover gets to keep far fewer benefits under the open rule than under the closed rule.

Second, and for very much the same reason, the first mover may choose to try and satisfy more members of the floor than just the minimum winning majority. This is a feature of the B&F model that is often overlooked. The B&F model explains the formation of larger than minimum winning coalitions in majority-rule decision environments (Groseclose and Snyder, 1996, provide an alternative model that predicts oversized coalitions). Empirically, larger than minimum winning coalitions are quite common in many presidential and parliamentary systems (Schofield, 1990). One reason why the advantage of this model is often overlooked is that B&F themselves tend to under emphasize it. They point out that as n gets bigger, the expected size of the coalition is reduced to the minimum winning – majority coalition size – commonly predicted by other models. In the U.S. House of Representatives, where party loyalty is weak, there may be good reason to undersell the prediction that larger than minimum winning coalitions may form in the B&F model. In parliamentary systems the relevant players are often parties and not individual parliament members. As we know, the number of parties in parliamentary systems is usually relatively small. Decades of studying these systems have led us to believe that the main reason for the formation of *oversize* coalitions is the logic outlined in the B&F model. The formator party often includes more than the minimum number of parties necessary to sustain a winning majority in parliament precisely because it tries to minimize the chance of future challenges to the ruling coalitions from parties that remain in opposition. Such parties may take advantage of the usual infighting that characterizes any ruling coalition to team up with outsiders – and insiders – to bring the government down. An obvious case in point is the annual process of budget approval. If the formator party allocates a little less for itself and more to additional parties in parliament, it can make it harder for opposition parties to group together as a majority against the ruling coalition government (Groseclose and Snyder, 1996).

6.5 Bargaining Over Unanimous Consent Agreements in the U.S. Senate

In the previous sections we discussed the bargaining game in the U.S. House of Representatives. The U.S. Senate is less structured. Floor rules are virtually non-existent and the committees are really advisory bodies with little 'gate keeping' power compared to the U.S. House of Representatives. How then can we explain the relatively orderly fashion in which the daily business of the U.S. Senate is conducted? Ainsworth and Flathman (1995) [A&F] use the Rubinstein (1982) bargaining model, introduced in Chapter 1, to address this puzzling question.

Modelers of political action in general and of political bargaining in particular, look at existing rules of conduct as building blocks for their models. If we want to understand how political processes work, and how they affect final outcomes, we may as well use existing rules of conduct, whether formal or informal, in constructing our formal models. The relatively sparse institutional structure of the day to day business of the U.S. Senate makes it particularly difficult to formalize in game theoretic terms. Indeed, such formalizations are rare (Ainsworth and Flathman, 1995: 179).

One aspect of the rules of conduct of the U.S. Senate that attracted some attention from formal modelers, and which is key to the A&F model, is the prevalence of 'unanimous consent agreement' [UCA]. UCAs are used to shorten the debate, whereby the freedom of senators to propose amendments to bills debated in the Senate is limited by unanimous consent. If not for UCAs, the Senate would always conduct its business under a variation of the *open rule*.

We saw earlier that the U.S. House of Representatives, even when it operates under the *open rule* procedure, is constrained by germaneness rules, other procedural rules and the gate-keeping power of House committees. The rules of conduct in the U.S. Senate put fewer constraints on U.S. senators. In this environment, UCAs play a crucial role in the smooth running of the daily business of the U.S. Senate, similar to the role played by the *closed rule* procedure on the floor of the U.S. House of Representatives.

For many years scholars argued that the role and rationale of UCAs derived from the obvious incentive of senators to reduce the time they spend on the floor. When the science of politics became more preoccupied with the problem of collective action (Olson, 1965; Hardin, 1982), UCAs became much less obvious. After all, as in the classic problem of collective action, every senator has an incentive to limit the time allocated to other senators while s/he takes as much time as s/he needs to argue his or her case or to publicize his or her image. To use Ainsworth and Flathman's (1995: 180) own language:

> There is a collective action problem at the heart of the unanimous consent [bargaining] process. Expediting floor activity benefits everyone, but individual senators have no incentive to restrict their own rights voluntarily. ...Though every senator desires an efficient solution to this collective action problem, the leader has the clearest incentive to coordinate negotiations in an attempt to reduce the chamber's inefficiencies because 'leadership gets credit or blame for how well Congress works.'[4]

The A&F model is of particular interest to us here as, consistent with our general theme in this book, A&F treat UCAs as the product of a bargaining process between the majority leaders and ordinary senators. Each senator prefers that his or her time be granted, but the majority leader must make sure that the Senate conducts its business in an orderly and efficient manner. And so a bargaining process ensues between the majority leader and the individual senators. Note that the bargaining here is not about resource allocation as it is in most of the bargaining processes discussed so far in this book. Instead, the bargaining process concerns procedure. One could argue that this bargaining concerns the allocation of the most scarce resource in politics: time in the public eye.

The model is based on two premises. First, A&F assume that the majority leader initiates the bargaining. Second, they assume that the majority leader bargains with individual senators on a one-to-one basis (Ainsworth and Flathman, 1995: 181). Based on these two premises, A&F reconstruct the Rubinstein (1982) bargaining model for this environment:

> In the model the leader and a senator bargain for debate time, which is normalized to one unit. Upon their unanimous consent, they partition the debate time, with the senator controlling 1-x and the leader preserving x for the consideration of other legislation. The bargaining process is characterized by alternating offers [for] the partition of time. Upon receiving an offer from the leader (senator), the senator (leader) must decide whether to accept the offer (thereby ending the negotiation) or reject the offer and make a counter-offer (thereby consuming time by continuing the negotiations). The negotiations are ...concluded... [once] a unanimous consent [agreement] is reached and the players allot the debate time.

A&F use the Rubinstein (1982) model with incomplete information as they assume some uncertainty on the part of the leader regarding the type of senator s/he is facing. This uncertainty manifests itself in the incomplete information about the patience parameters δ (Ainsworth and Flathman, 1995: 181):

> The leader's and senator's valuation of ...future [pay-offs] are represented by discount factors δ_L and δ_ℓ or δ_h, where $0 \leq \delta_L, \delta_\ell, \delta_h \leq 1$ with at least one being strictly less than 1 and at least one being strictly greater than 0.

The leader does not know the type of senator s/he is facing at the bargaining table. All s/he knows is that this senator is of type δ_h (or δ_ℓ) with a prior probability of p (or 1 -p). δ_h type pays a high cost for delay and δ_ℓ is the patient type who pays a low cost for delay.

If **p** is small enough, meaning that most senators are patient enough, i.e. of type δ_ℓ, the leader may just as well give up the prospects of reaching a UCA. If **p** is high enough the prospects of reaching a UCA improve. Since A&F assume that the leader initiates the bargaining process with each senator, i.e. s/he always proposes first, we can compute the expected pay-off for the leader, from each session of bargaining with any single senator, using the original results of Rubinstein's (1982) model. Let V_h (V_ℓ) denote the expected pay-offs to the leader from bargaining with high (low) cost senator of type δ_h (δ_ℓ). Rubinstein's (1982) results, introduced in the first chapter, imply equations (6.1) and (6.2) below.

$$(6.1) \quad V_h = (1-\delta_h) / (1-\delta_L\delta_h)$$
$$(6.2) \quad V_\ell = (1-\delta_\ell) / (1-\delta_L\delta_\ell)$$

Using these two equalities, A&F derive the following basic proposition:

Proposition 6.4 (A&F, 1995: 184, Proposition 1): *Bargaining Sequential Equilibrium: The leader will wait rather than concede whenever:*

$\mathbf{p} > (V_\ell - \delta_L{}^2 V_\ell)/(V_h - \delta_L{}^2 V_\ell)$ *and concede rather than wait [otherwise].*

This result is obtained by computing the expected pay-offs for the leader for a probability p (or 1–p) that the senator s/he is facing is of type δ_h (or δ_ℓ) using equalities (6.1) and (6.2).

We obtain a clear prediction that can be interpreted as follows: The leader of the Senate will tend to negotiate UCAs when s/he is strong and the senators are weak. In this model a strong leader is a patient leader and a weak senator is an impatient senator. We have already seen this general prediction of Rubinstein's (1982) model and we will meet it again in the following chapter when we discuss bargaining between nations. Political players are always stronger at the bargaining table when they are patient and weaker when they are impatient.

When will a senator be more or less patient? When s/he faces stiff competition in his or her bid for re-election, s/he may be less patient. If his or her seat is secure, s/he is likely to be more patient. After all, this is precisely the origin of the strength of the majority leader. Majority leaders are usually senior senators with little if any threat to their seat in the Senate.

With some caution we could take this argument a step further. Observers of U.S. politics often note that the U.S. Senate seems to be more responsible and less subject to effervescent moods than the U.S. House of Representatives. One example of this difference in style occurred when the Republicans took control of both the House of Representatives and the U.S. Senate in 1994. The House of Representatives, under the leadership of Newt Gingrich, immediately started a major campaign of legislation to 'undo' everything that was wrong in recent 'democratic' legislation. This campaign led to the decline of the Republican party in the 1998 election and to the resignation of Gingrich himself. Throughout this period, the U.S. Senate, under majority leader Robert Dole, proved to be much more poised and measured. Eventually, the Senate ended up blocking the Republican bid to impeach President Bill Clinton following the Lewinsky affair – no small matter given that Clinton was only the second president in the history of the U.S. to be impeached by the U.S. House of Representatives.

How can we explain this difference in style? One explanation could be Rubinstein's (1982) patience argument. All members of the U.S. House of Representatives must run for re-election every two years. Senators run for election every six years and every two years only one third of the U.S. Senate has to deal with re-election bids.

Why did the framers of the constitution create such an impatient body of representatives? Maybe they did not anticipate the consequences of their creation. But it may just as well be that the framers wished to institutionalize such a difference in style. They may have deliberately made the U.S. House of Representatives more immediately sensitive to periodic changes in the public mood and the U.S. Senate more relaxed and poised to check out any dramatic swings in the public sentiment that could cause long-term damage to the U.S. polity. To return to the impeachment of President Clinton, Republicans in the House of Representatives claimed that the Lewinsky affair demonstrated a lack of moral integrity in Clinton that made him unfit to be president. The argument of the Republicans in Senate, which helped stop the impeachment bid, did not rest on a defense of Clinton's moral integrity, but on the fact that if Clinton were impeached on these grounds, future presidents would be too much at risk of impeachment to adequately do their job as chief executives.

6.6 Bargaining Between Legislators and Special Interests

In Chapter 4 we introduced entrepreneurs as crucial players in the game of politics. We explained that entrepreneurs play a crucial role in the interchange of information between members of the groups regarding expected modes of action of the group. They also transmit information between group members and government officials about the size of the group and how seriously a group should be taken by government officials in light of its size and other parameters that determine the political power of interest groups and their willingness to take action (Ainsworth and Sened, 1993; Olson, 1995).

In the U.S. political environment, political entrepreneurs, or lobbyists as they are often called, tend to interact mostly with members of Congress. In Chapter 4 we had a government official facing one, and then a multitude of special interest groups. We now understand that each such entrepreneur faces a multitude of representatives. Each representative must, in turn, weight his or her future action in light of his or her expectations of internal politics in the U.S. House of representatives and the U.S. Senate, and of the bargaining process that eventually ensues between the U.S. House of representatives, the U.S. Senate and the President. To construct the game theoretic model of this complex interaction is beyond the scope of this book, but we hope to have given the reader insight into the complexity of modern political decision making.[5] And we hope that sooner rather than later someone in the profession will take the challenge and write the whole 'game tree' of the U.S. Presidential system as we tried to do in Chapter 5 regarding parliamentary systems in Europe.

6.7 Conclusions

The central theme of this book is that the role of bargaining between competing interests is at least as prevalent and as important to study as the well-documented and researched role of representation. Presidential government systems are usually fashioned after the U.S. governmental system outlined by the U.S. constitution. The constitution is premised on that representation *per se* is a rather weak foundation for democratic governments. Instead, it puts its faith in what we have grown accustomed to call 'checks and balances.' These checks and balances are meant to institutionalize a bargaining process at the heart of the governance structure and to safeguard against the mishaps of a 'naive' ideal, and practice, of popular representation (Riker, 1982).

In the second part of this chapter we surveyed work by Hammond and Miller to reveal how separation of power incites political players to reach compromise through bargaining. In the third section we surveyed work by Shepsle et al. 1979; Shepsle and Weingast, 1981; Laver and Shepsle, 1996. They illustrate how the division of labor in the U.S. House of Representative alleviates the tendency of representative bodies to fall into endless social choice cycles when they attempt to represent the interests of their constituents. Once again we emphasized how this division of labor translates into a bargaining process in the U.S. House of Representatives and in the context of coalition formation in parliamentary systems in Europe (Laver and Shepsle, 1996).

In section 6.4 we explained the logic behind, and the implications of the model of coalition formation in the U.S. House of Representative promoted by Baron and Ferejohn (1989). Baron and Ferejohn provide, to our mind, a picture of the legislative process that strikes a more appropriate balance between the idea of representative politics and the important practice of political bargaining.

Unlike the House of Representatives, the U.S. Senate does not have as many constraining rules, and its committees are advising bodies at best. And yet observers of American politics often concur that the U.S. Senate runs more smoothly, and frequently more responsibly, than the House of Representatives. In section 6.5 we used a simple model derived by Ainsworth and Flathman (1995) from Rubinstein's (1982) bargaining model, which goes a long way towards explaining this puzzle. Section 6.6 calls for further efforts to map into this picture the literature and theories of interest group politics (Potters and van Winden, 1996). We leave it to others to cover this angle in the detail it warrants.

As we approach our final chapter, we have traced the bargaining process from the initial abstract *state of nature* through the complex wheeling and dealing of contemporary legislative bodies to the 'checks and balances' of modern presidential systems. The final chapter looks at the bargaining that takes place at the international arena, in the absence of any rigorous formal or informal rules.

Notes

1. A set $\aleph$ is convex if for every $\lambda \in [0,1]$ and for every $x, y \in \aleph$, if $z = (1-\lambda) \cdot x + \lambda \cdot y$ then $z \in \aleph$. In simple terms, a set is convex if every point on a line that connects any two points in this set is also in the set. A set $\aleph$ is compact if it is closed and bounded (Austen-Smith and Banks, 1999: 124). A set ∂ is open relative to some set $\Im$ (with $\partial \subset \Im$) if for every point $y \in \partial$, there is some small $\varepsilon > 0$, such that any point ε away from y is also in ∂. An obvious example is an open interval $(1,2)$ that is open relative to $\Re$. This interval includes all the points between 1 and 2 except 1 and 2. If $\aleph$ is the complement of an open set, $\aleph$ is closed. Suppose for example that $\Im = [0,4]$. Let $\partial = [0,1]$, then ∂ is open relative to $\Im$ and if $\aleph$ is the complement of ∂ relative to $\Im$ then $\aleph = [1,4]$ which is closed. For a comprehensive discussion of these definitions see (Austen-Smith and Banks, 1999: 124).

2. Our intention here is to maintain clarity and transparency of exposition to the extent possible. We are omitting important technical caveats and specification for this purpose. We strongly recommend that those readers who have the time and or the technical skills and expertise return to the original work for further details.

3. The controversy over the stationarity restriction is beyond the scope of this text. Muthoo (1995) explores the existence of non-stationary equilibria in a Rubinstein's alternating-offers model. Tefler (1999) studies a similar model, introducing asymmetric information and non-stationarity. Both manuscripts are mathematically challenging and are written in a style that is beyond the level of accessibility we wish to maintain here. Rubinstein (1991) provides an excellent broader and more accessible discussion of this and other important issues on interpreting the use of game theoretic tools.

4. The quote at the end of the indented quote from A&F is from Senate stafer M. interviewed by Ainsworth in the preliminary research for the paper with Flathman.

5. An excellent short introduction to this emerging sub-field in the literature is Potters and van Winden (1996). This essay also includes a remarkable reference list that will allow the reader to delve deeper into this line of research.

7 Bargaining at the International Arena

7.1 The Nature of Bargaining in the International Arena

This chapter analyzes the nature of bargaining and negotiation at the inter-national level, which is the highest form of aggregation in which bargaining takes place. The study of international relations differs from the study of domestic politics in its particular unit of analysis. At the international level, scholars usually utilize the nation-state, or an alliance (i.e. coalition) of some nation-states, as their principle unit of analysis. These nation-states are either in an anarchic '*state of nature*,' where no order or hierarchy prevails, or in some particular world order. Pax Romana and Pax Americana are two examples of world orders. In the first case the Roman Empire dominated the ancient world, and in the second, post-1990 'new world order', the U.S. dominates. Likewise, the Cold War reflects a bi-polar world order, wherein between 1945 and 1990 the two Superpowers – the U.S. and the Soviet Union – divided among themselves zones of influence, competing for domination and the spread to other countries of their guiding ideologies.

The study of international relations is sensitive to the structural order of the particular arena in which states relate to one other. It is thus important to know if states conduct their affairs independently, or whether they submit to the dictates or wishes of a third power. For example, following World War II, countries in Eastern Europe, although politically sovereign, were largely dependent in their foreign policy on the initiatives of Moscow. Failure to submit to Soviet directives, as in the case of Hungary in 1956 or Czechoslovakia in 1968, invited an immediate aggressive military response from their eastern overseer.

What do states bargain over? History books and the daily press provide answers. They are engaged in perpetual conflict and hence they bargain over issues such as security, economics, religion and even, at times, culture and sport. More often than not these conflicts involve land. As the great educator Montessori (1932) noted:

> The primary motive of wars of antiquity, in fact, was the conquest of land...
> Although man's environment is no longer the actual physical land but rather the
> social organization in and of itself, resting on economic structure, territorial
> conquest is still regarded as the real reason for which wars are being waged.

In this sense, people have not moved far from the so-called 'territorial imperative' of the animal world. They continue to define boundaries over territories (i.e. the international borders). And inside these they try to live safely. Consequently, the prime focus of study for many students and practitioners in this area revolves around state violence and its resolution. Although the resolution of violent conflict through bargaining is but one aspect of interactive conduct at the international level, it is to a large degree our focus in this chapter.

There are two ways of looking at bargaining phenomena at the international level. Narrowly, attention is given to the particular incident and to the way the negotiating parties arrive at a solution. Widely, attention could be given to the intentional or unintentional change in conditions that ultimately lead to a solution, or to the makeup of the negotiating schemes, and to what the parties bring to the bargaining table. In this respect, actual wars or threats of war could be perceived as a point of leverage used by one side against the other. They should be considered as steps in a longer process of bargaining, a process which is conducted at different times and in different arenas between self maximizing actors. Consequently, the formal act of resolution, which often takes the form of a written contract between the sides, becomes just the tip of the iceberg.

The next section illustrates this wider sense of bargaining. Two game theory concepts that were reviewed in earlier chapters are presented in the context of the protracted conflict between Israel and Egypt, a conflict that started in 1948 and was 'resolved' only in 1979.

7.2 Inter-State Patterns of Equilibria: The Israeli–Egyptian Conflict

Interstate and inter-communal conflicts, including all-out wars, are familiar phenomena in the Middle East. After World War II, this region has often been perceived as the sick man of the international community – similar to the way the Balkans were perceived prior to World War I, and the Yugoslavian states during the 1990s. The salient pattern of settling matters by means of state and group aggression seems to have established itself in that region between both minor and major political movers.

The antagonistic relationship between Israel and its Arab neighbors comprised what may be defined as the main 'cycle of aggression.' Since its independence in 1948, Israel has been involved in full-scale war with some or all the Arab states at least once every decade. Likewise, however, Syria, Iraq and Egypt, the three most powerful Arab states, also initiated or were involved in wars against, amongst others, Lebanon, Kuwait, Yemen and, of course Iran. In addition, there are countless and often daily incidents of acts of terror by local groups against outsiders and against their own people.

Uneven distribution of power could perhaps be the principle determinant and the main explanation for this regional instability. Yet power differentials between local antagonists in the international arena is a problematic analytical tool, despite its popular use as a guiding analytical variable (Morgenthau, 1967). The power of a state involves not only the size and the quality of its armed forces and arsenal of weapons, but factors including the size of the effective population (i.e. the number and quality of people who could be used in warfare), and the strength of the economy. From these one can construct power indices similar to that composed by Bueno de Masquita (1981). Such indices help predict the occurrence of wars and their outcomes.

Outcomes of wars, however, are also a function of the spirit of fighters, their training and determination; the psychological makeup and the ability of the general population to withstand loss of life and material, as well as the quality of the decision-makers and the kind of choices, both tactical and strategic, they make. These elements are difficult to measure and are not necessarily derivatives of objective factors. The power approach is often based on unrealistic assumptions and inaccurate data.

Furthermore, unequal distribution of power amongst states is a general condition of the international arena. It thus cannot serve as an explanation for the causes of war. It cannot explain how protracted conflicts of the kind that characterizes the Middle East begin, progress and are (hopefully) settled.

The turbulence and instability of the Middle East have been explained in many different ways. One common explanation relates to the manner in which international borders, arbitrarily designed by foreign colonialists, separated one state from another and hence failed to reflect historically-grounded national aspirations. These may be claimed in the case of Syria and Lebanon and the concept of Greater Syria. Syria sought to correct the French mandate decision of the 1930s to carve an independent state for the Christian minority from traditional Islamic Syrian soil. Likewise, Iraq's claim on Kuwait is rooted in the fact that the latter was deemed the former Southern Province and an integral part of Iraq. Iraq's invasion of Kuwait in the summer of 1990 should be understood against this background (Karsh and Ruasti, 1991). Also, the entire area of Palestine (Eretz Israel) was promised to the Jews by the British Balfour Declaration, which served as the basis for the 1922 League of Nations Charter (Peretz and Doron, 1997). A little later the 'east bank' of the Jordan was cut out to form Transjordan, later becoming the Kingdom of Jordan. The Israelis and the Palestinians are yet to determine through bargaining (e.g. the 1993 Oslo Agreement) how they want to split the remainder of the land to the west of the Jordan river. Based on this explanation, it seems that the prevailing status quo among these countries is but at a temporary phase, to be altered whenever the opportunity presents itself.

Another explanation identifies the roots of regional violence in the fact that several of the region's major polities are ruled by representatives of minority groups, as is the case in Iraq, Jordan, Syria and Lebanon. Since these regimes are under permanent threat by the majority population in their countries, they are compelled to maintain themselves by force of arms. This also means that the rulers of these minority-based regimes tend to shift the blame for their domestic problems to outside sources – usually, to Israel.

Ultimately, much of the regional instability derives from the ineffectiveness of the bi-polar international system that so affected that part of the world until the late 1980s. The global rivalry between the U.S. and the Soviet Union spilled over into bitter rivalry between local states in the region. While the Superpowers were able to enforce stable relationships within their client states, they were far less effective in imposing stability between members of different groups, and between themselves and states not identified with one or the other Superpower. Stability, therefore, became for the most part a function of the efforts invested in the region by third parties that had interests in maintaining stability.

A telling example illustrates this argument. In 1970, the Soviet-oriented PLO (Palestinian Liberation Organization) threatened the stability of West-oriented Jordan, its host country. King Hussein commanded his army to solve the problem. Thousands of Palestinians were killed in what was known as the 'Black September;' others fled to Syria, Lebanon and even to Israel. Pro-Soviet Syria ordered the Jordanians to stop their attack, and began moving troops towards the border. Israel, the principle U.S. regional client, was asked to intervene on behalf of Jordan, their formal and declared enemy, and did so. Syria consequently retreated, the PLO moved to Lebanon to initiate a long period of instability there, and Israel was rewarded by the Nixon administration with weapons and loans.

When President Saddat of Egypt declared in 1977 that he was willing to end the state of war between Egypt and Israel, few, including Israeli intelligence, believed him. But conditions for peace were, by that time, ripe. Saddat's momentous arrival in Jerusalem sparked a process that culminated two years later in a peace agreement, ending the cycle of violent interaction.

Egypt's first violent engagement with Israel in 1948 is usually explained as an act motivated by a sense of solidarity with the indigenous Palestinian population. But their invasion of Palestine could not prevent the formation of the Jewish State, nor limit its expansion south. Subsequent to that war, and aside from voicing its support of the Palestinian cause on the international stage, Egypt provided very little real assistance to the Palestinians, most notably in the Gaza Strip, where many Palestinians then lived.

The 1956 Sinai campaign was the next step in the evolving antagonism between the two countries. An alliance of Israel, Great Britain and France attacked Egypt, only to pull back a little later following a joint ultimatum from the United States and the Soviet Union.

June 1967 marked the next war. Israel defeated the combined efforts of the Egyptians, Syrians, Jordanians and a symbolic Iraqi military delegation, conquering the Sinai Peninsula, the Golan Heights and West Bank. The Israeli government declared that it was waiting for Arab leaders to call for peace negotiations in return for land. Plans were made by some Israeli leaders to surrender the West Bank to Jordan (e.g. The Alon Plan), but the Arabs did not respond favorably to these initiatives. Israel thus made its hold on the occupied territories permanent by moving in civilians and constructing settlements.

In the context of the Cold War, Egypt and Syria were clients of the Soviet Union, whilst Israel was a client of the U.S. Decisions made in the region had first to be cleared in the two Superpower capitals. Neither side could conduct a war, nor withstand aggression by the other side, without the diplomatic and military support of a Superpower. The two Superpowers had an important interest in the region.

These informal rules did not and could not prevent regional instability but, until 1973, they turned the conflict into a 'game of chicken' as in Figure 7.1.

Players	USSR–Egypt		
	Strategies	A	NA
USA-Israel	A	1,1	4,2
	NA	2,4	3,3

Figure 7.1 A Game of Chicken: Israeli–Egyptian Conflict Until 1973

Note: A and NA denote an aggressive and non-aggressive strategy respectively. The numbers in the cells denote values of outcomes obtained from the strategy choices made by the players, where 4 is the best outcome and 1 is the worst.

The game of chicken has no dominant strategy. There is no strategy that yields better outcomes to a player. The game has two Nash Equilibria: (A,NA) which in Figure 7.1 is shown to be best for Israel and next to worst for Egypt, and (NA,A), which is best for Egypt but next to worst for Israel.

Since the result of the 1967 war was an (A,NA) equilibrium with a pay-off pair of (4,2) favoring Israel, Egypt, backed by the Soviet Union, tried to alter it through the 'war of attrition' between Egypt and Israel, which lasted from 1970 to 1971. The Superpowers worked to contain this aggression to avoid an escalation into an (A,A) situation, knowing that (NA,NA) is unreachable as it is not an equilibrium outcome of the game.

This structure leaves little room for bargaining, but the Egyptians had no intention to let the situation freeze at a (4,2) outcome. A war was needed to alter the equilibrium that emerged. By 1972, realizing that the Soviet Union would not assist his country in its ambition to alter the status quo, Saddat opened a secret diplomatic channel with the U.S. and expelled the Soviet 'experts' from Egypt (Aronson, 1978). He was now ready to go to war with Israel. The decision to go to war should be perceived as a stage, dramatic as it may be, in the process of bargaining between two players. This view is consistent with the popular view of war as an extension of diplomacy by other means. Both violent and non-violent means aim at improving the situation of one state in relation to another.

Recovering from a surprise attack launched by Egypt in October 1973, Israel conquered yet more land. This time, however, the Soviets were out of the game and the U.S. was the only Superpower. In 1974 it helped design the Sinai I agreement that led the two states to disengage their troops, leaving a safe neutral zone between them. In 1976, after a long period of negotiation, the Ford-Kissinger administration helped forge the Sinai II agreement – a pullback of Israeli forces in Sinai in exchange for firm security guaranties.

In this context the Camp David accord masterminded by the Carter administration in 1979, notwithstanding its symbolic, psychological and economic value, should not be perceived as a major breakthrough, but as an incremental development in a structure laid down six years earlier, when Saddat acknowledged that '99.9 percent of the cards' were in the hands of the U.S. (New York Times, February 5, 1978) and decided to move into a new structure formalized as a Prisoners' Dilemma game, as seen in Figure 7.2.

Players	Egypt	
Strategies	Cooperate (NA)	Defect (A)
Israel Cooperate (NA)	1,1	–1,2
Defect (A)	2,–1	0,0

Figure 7.2 The Game of Prisoners' Dilemma: Israel–Egypt 1973-9

Note: A and NA denote aggressive and non-aggressive strategies respectively.

As we explained earlier, this game has a dominant strategy for each player and a unique AA (0,0) equilibrium. If both players agree to hold an NA strategy, one of them is better off breaking the agreement, reverting to the aggressive mode and gaining an advantage in the form of (2;–1) or (–1;2). Since (NA,NA) is not an equilibrium in this game, to move into this more attractive (1,1) outcome, the intervention of a third party is crucial. In this case, the U.S. played the role of the third party under the Ford and Carter administrations. It was not easy. First, the Israeli government had to be convinced that a retreat from secured defensive lines in the Sinai would be conducive to future peace. To obtain flexibility from the Israeli government, the U.S. pressured it with the so-called 're-assessment policy,' which meant that these administrations were ready to reevaluate the nature of their relationships with Israel and to redefine them. That led to Sinai II and later to the Camp David accord.

In addition, monitoring stations and actual American presence in the Sinai Peninsula served as a substitute for lack of mutual trust. Finally, a long-term commitment to foreign aid and military assistance contributed to stability and cooperation between the two countries. Since 1979, both Israel and Egypt had much to lose and little to gain from violating the peace agreement.

This long-term commitment to financial and military aid as an incentive to cooperate and a credible threat to withhold it in case of defection seem to have been the tools used by the U.S. to gradually transform a finite stage 'chicken' game into an infinitely-repeated Prisoners' Dilemma game and then imposed on both sides a cooperative equilibrium of non-aggression. In a finite game, there is no equilibrium of non-aggression and even Superpowers cannot force players to use strategies that are out of equilibrium. A serious shift in the defining features of the situation was needed for peace to become even a possibility. But in the infinitely repeated game there is a multitude of equilibria. The U.S. intervention was again crucial in guiding the players into the equilibrium of non-aggression.

The example of the Israeli–Egyptian conflict shows that without trust between parties, conditions had to gradually develop until a third party, trusted by both sides, was ready and able to promote a resolution to the conflict. Bargaining in this case lasted for over 30 years, involving formal and informal signals, utilizing overt and covert diplomacy, and employing violent and non-violent acts that were played out on various regional and international stages.

Why did it take so long? Is it possible that the lack of trust so inherent in this conflict – and manifest even after the two countries had signed a peace agreement – is a function of the nature of their respective regimes? To be specific, is it possible that Israel, being a democracy, does not trust the Egyptian government because, among other things, it is not a democracy? This is the subject we turn to in the remainder of this chapter.

7.3 The Democratic Peace Hypothesis

Resting their analysis on a count of incidents of war in the last 200 years Maoz and Russett (1992) suggested that the 'democratic peace' assertion – meaning that democracies never fight each other – should be perceived as a law-like finding. By counting the number of incidents of war they concluded that democracies initiate fights only with non-democratic regimes.

In the context of the Middle East, at least one country (i.e. Israel) has often used this finding to condition its policy regarding bargaining with its neighbors. In the remainder of this chapter we examine this assertion and its relationship to bargaining in international affairs.

A reason why democracies may refrain from going to war was first mentioned in Kant's 'On Perpetual Peace' (1963). He proposed that in authoritarian regimes the subjects, who have little say in their leaders' decision, share the entire costs of war. In a democracy, everyone shares these costs. Hence, it makes sense that the larger body of citizens would block any arbitrary decision to go to war if the consequences might reduce their utility. Fearon (1994) developed this logic using a game theoretic framework that we discuss in section 7.5.

Kant's original explanation is inadequate in that he assumed that in democracies citizens are asked whether or not the country should go to war. In reality, they are never asked. At best, their representatives make choices for them. We have discussed in previous chapters how remote these choices often are from anything that might be considered meaningful representation. These choices usually reflect the preferences of the representatives, and not those of the supposedly represented (cf. Fenno, 1978). Not even a majority of citizens can block a vote for war if the leaders want one. It is, in fact, not very difficult to manipulate the agenda so that the decision to go to war becomes the preferred democratic choice (Riker, 1986). Finally, organization and communication theories teach us that decisions are usually made on the basis of information provided to the decision-makers by self-interested agents. Hence, it is not difficult to imagine that some interested groups (say, military professionals) would supply decision-makers with biased information regarding the intentions of neighboring states. This would affect the cost–benefit calculus of citizens, leading them to support a decision to go to war.

Nonetheless, while the democratic peace proposition can be supported deductively as we show below, it cannot, in light of the body of evidence accumulated over the years, be accepted as a scientific law for several reasons. First, according to Popper (1959), it is enough to confront a theory (let alone an empirical law) with one contradictory fact to render it false (1959). Thus, it is sufficient to show, even once, that democracies fight each other, for the interpretation given to this statistical finding to be changed from a law-like proposition to a probabilistic statement based on empirical evidence. The difficulty, however, associated with providing a contradictory fact, stems from the difficulty in asserting which regimes could be defined as democratic and which could not. Are India and Pakistan democracies? Is NATO (North Atlantic Treaty Organization) an alliance of democratic states? Is Yugoslavia (i.e. Serbia) democratic? According to some they are, and if that is so, their wars serve as testimony to the shortcomings of the democratic peace law-like assertion. After all, all the states (or alliances) mentioned above have free elections, vocal and overt opposition, and a relatively independent press.

Second, one cannot deduce from an outcome the reasons leading to that outcome. For example, the fact that prices for similar commodities in a given market are identical, does not mean we know whether this is an outcome of competition, or a result of a cartel arrangement. Most of the data concerning democratic behavior is based on evidence accumulated from Western Europe, North America, Australia and New Zealand. In other regions it is difficult to identify democracies that persist over time and the regimes included in them have a tendency to fight with each other incessantly. We really have no answer to why the USA and Canada have never been at war with each other.

More interesting, perhaps, is to ask why Western Europe has been at peace since World War II. It is easy to provide an explanation that is not related to the nature of west European regimes, nor for that matter to nuclear deterrence or the prohibitive cost of modern non-conventional war. After centuries of fighting and two world wars, the nations in the region have presumably learned that there are other means by which to reach their goals. They learned, in the shadow of the threat to their economic well being from both the United States and the Far East, to coordinate their activities in the EEC. Most west European countries are, post World War II, politically and economically stable. They therefore belong to the so-called First World. Muller found (1989) that the set of economically wealthy countries – which at the time of measurement (the 1980s) was larger than the set of active democracies – showed fewer war-like tendencies than their political counterparts. Perhaps rich countries refrain from war because they are afraid of losing their fortune? To maintain it, they need political stability, which is a prerequisite for long-term investment, growth and prosperity. Countries whose economic fortune is less dependent on outside investments may become more politically adventurous. An extreme case in point is Iraq, whose revenues from oil enabled it to launch several wars against its neighbors (Pelletiere, 1992).

An alternative explanation could be the fact that the German nation, the largest people in Europe, twice this century initiated war. It is hard to classify Germany as a non-democratic regime since the ascendance of Hitler took place, for the most part, within a perfectly democratic environment (Riker, 1965: 105-6). Given that this is so, World War II is an obvious example of the invalidity of the inductive basis for the 'democratic peace' hypothesis. But even if we overlook this fact, it is easy to appreciate that after World War II Germany was prevented from developing military might by the victors, with NATO acting as supervisor. So is it the mechanism of control imposed on the Germans, or is it the nature of their democratic system, that stops them from entering a third round of massive violence? When the rules of the game were broken in Europe, as in the case of Serbia in 1999, NATO assumed an aggressive mode of behavior, similar to that of non-democratic regimes.

The Romans had an interesting political arrangement. In times of peace their Senate ruled and during times of war, all authority was delegated to the emperor, only to be returned after his mission had been completed. Modern democracies follow similar arrangements. In times of war, emergency regulations substitute for normal rules and procedures, and the democratic game is tabled until the danger to the regime or to its vital interests passes. The American government's behavior towards its citizens of Japanese origin during the 1940s, England's behavior in Northern Ireland in the 1970s and 1980s, and the military rule of Israel over its Arab citizens until the mid-1960s are cases in point. They show that, right or wrong, the security of the people takes precedence over the requirement to maintain democratic procedure.

Inductively-guided arguments cannot address these problems because their method is static, requiring snap-shots of reality. Until deductively proven otherwise their statistical findings are, by definition, artifact. A more dynamic analysis would reveal that because people favor their interests over the procedures that allow them to obtain them, they change the procedures when these prevent the achievement of their interests (Riker, 1980). Hence, it should be no surprise to find that democratic regimes are often replaced by systems that are believed able to deliver basic needs to the people. King Saul was the non-democratic people's choice of the early libertarian Hebrews. Democracy could not deliver food or protection in post-Tsarist Russia; nor could the Germans counter hyperinflation, restore their honor or maintain domestic stability under the Weimar Republic. The French abandoned the unstable Forth Republic democracy, replacing it with a president whose rule included dictatorial elements. There are further examples of this sort indicating that the explanation as to why states go to war is less related to the nature of the regime itself than to other factors. Perhaps, as Sherman and Doron (1997) suggest, it is the leader's attitude towards risk that determines the decision to go to war or refrain from it.

The following two sections provide deductive explanations as to why democracies may be less prone to enter into war against each other. Unlike the inductive approach, these two alternative (or complementary) explanations do not depend on problematic definitions of democracy or on an arbitrary account of events, but on reasonable assumptions and pure logic. This section discussed the efforts made by students of international relations to understand the phenomenon of war using an inductive strategy of scientific research. The following two sections endorse the deductive approach and relate the discussion directly to political bargaining.

7.4 A Deductive Approach to the Democratic Peace Hypothesis

Deductive reasoning has one clear advantage over inductive reasoning – it need not be verified in the empirical world. In fact, it need not even reflect real world phenomena. Its falsification comes about as a result of internal inconsistency. This does not impair its explanatory utility. In fact, an explanation of the causality between the designated factors is built into the theory. For example, the perfectly competitive market is but an imaginary construct that has no analog in reality. Nonetheless, it is extremely useful in explaining economic phenomena.

In this spirit, Bueno de Masquita offered a deductive expected utility-based explanation of war called 'the war trap'(1982). In a clear departure from the prevalent 'power' explanation in the study of international systems, whereby strong states initiate wars on weaker ones, the 'war trap' principle consists of a complex set of expected cost–benefit considerations, defined along several dimensions. Thus, for example, the 'relative' power of a state is a term constructed on the basis of military capability coupled with the human and economic resources of the initiator. The inference is that wars do not occur. Someone has an interest in initiating them. The decision to go to war is taken within an observable set of constraints. It is possible to quantify the considerations made by the decision-makers as well as the set of constraints that affect them. This enables the identification and measurement of certain conditions conducive to the occurrence of war. Despite its problems, the 'war trap' principle is deductive science at its best.

Note the difference between this approach and the one presented in the former section. The composite index upon which the principle is constructed has been defined not on the basis of the author's understanding of the phenomenon of war, but on the basis of his derivations from standard expected utility theory as commonly used to explain economic and other phenomena. The statistical tests came in afterwards for validation purposes. Inductive-oriented scholars identify sets of statistical numbers representing, more or less, the issues under investigation, and when they identify high correlation among them, they propose intuitive explanations and conclusions. We have demonstrated above that for each such explanation one could easily come up with a number of others.

Sherman (1998) and Doron and Sherman (1997) followed Bueno de Masquita's approach. They integrate two paradigms commonly used to explain international problems: that of the regime-insensitive realist and that of the regime-sensitive domestic constraint. They show that when an element of uncertainty is introduced into the decision-making situation, differing domestic constraints can be translated into differing expected utility maximizing (EUM) risk preferences, and hence into differing EUM rational actor utility profiles. This means that in the anarchic international arena, independent states design foreign policies that are consistent with the nature of their polity. For that purpose Doron and Sherman (1997) constructed an imaginary political system comprising five parameters and postulates. If these are assigned maximum values they would be defined as democracies, and conversely, when they record minimal values, they would be considered dictatorships. These parameters include the legitimacy of overt and legal opposition to the government; limitations imposed on the power of the executive; public participation in elections; limits on the use of state resources; freedom of the mass media. Note that the term 'democratic regime' is generic. It is not used to refer to a regime in which periodical elections take place. Rather, the term is used to refer to hypothetical regimes characterized by a number of parameters relating to pluralism and accountability.

Because democracies and dictatorships constitute distinct structures of government, the above theory reflects these differences. But does this difference also generate a 'cleavage' of preference in their leader's choice of foreign policy? Clearly, risk averse policy-makers are less likely to initiate war against outsiders. Similarly, a group of risk averse leaders, each heading a neighboring state, would refrain from war. They would tend to support the status quo, and settle their differences in a non-aggressive manner. Of course, risk aversion is not necessarily an attribute only of democratic systems. It is quite possible that many cultures, irrespective of the nature of their polity, promote peaceful relations with outsiders.

To ascribe a peaceful attitude to democracies, one has to show that the democratic political structure adversely affects the risk preferences of the leader regarding war. This is done by imposing various limitations and restraints on the freedom of choice of the democratic decision-maker. Even if the leader is risk-taking, short of reacting to an immediate threat s/he can do little to initiate war. Also, there is growing acceptance of the notion that institutions upon which democracies depend and operate, such as constitutions, elections and separation of powers, are critical for the inducement of internal stability. This was precisely the essence of our argument in the previous chapter. More generally, this is the prime inference of the aforementioned 'neo-institutional' school of political science. Clearly then, internally stable democracies that are protected against the aggressive ambitions of other similar democratic regimes in the region are unlikely to initiate war.

It is interesting to explore whether the nature of the regime also affects the mode in which it bargains with others. This can be done by arranging the two archetypes of political regime into three forms of dyadic relationship: Democratic-Democratic; Democratic-Dictatorial; Dictatorial-Dictatorial. Let us examine each dyad and the kind of bargaining conducted between its participants. The first dyad consists of democracies. Following Sherman and Doron (1997), we assume that democratic leaders are risk averse. In addition, to prevent war from occurring, democratic regimes usually possess mechanisms – such as the American War Power Act that limits the ability of a president to declare war on some nations without the prior approval of Congress – that prevent rapid escalation towards war. It should thus be expected that in a democratic dyad, the leaders of the two nations would attempt to settle disputes in a pacific manner.

A decision-maker's utility function that reflects a risk avoiding attitude is concave. Where a conflict of interest exists, the inter-cross between two concave utility functions generates a stable equilibrium point. Small changes in the equilibrium would be negotiated and re-negotiated until either a new status quo is agreed upon, or the old one is restored. Hence, the bargaining space for risk averse decision-makers should be small and located around the existing equilibrium point.

In a dyad whose choice-makers have a convex utility function, the identification of an equilibrium point within a defined bargaining space is not easy. History teaches us that risk-taking leaders may be willing, for small pay-offs (e.g. territory or personal honor), to gamble on the lives of their subjects. They do so with no regard to the probable costs associated with potential losses, or even with gains (Sherman, 1998). Consequently, the effective equilibrium that can be obtained in this dyad is one of deterrence – 'two eyes for an eye' strategy – providing each side with clear disincentives to violate the prevailing status quo. Bargaining in this dyad usually takes place after one of the parties loses, or when both exhaust themselves in terms of lives and resources, or when a third party in the form of the international community, or a Superpower, intervenes to stop the violence. The war Paraguay launched in the nineteenth century against her neighbors is an illustration of an almost total conventional war which was stopped only after the initiator lost significant territory and many lives (Box, 1967). The war between Iran and Iraq during the 1980s exemplified a case in which, after years of fighting with no gains, the exhausted sides were willing to sit down and bargain a new framework (Karsh and Ruasti, 1991). The war that Iraq launched against Kuwait in 1990 is yet another example in point.

The last dyad is the most complicated because the nature of the regime has little effect on the relationship of the states included in it. It involves both risk-takers and risk averse decision-makers. By definition, risk-takers would tend to change the status quo whilst risk averse individuals would protect it. If the second group believes that the first is moving to alter the equilibrium, it must and will react. Hence, as the Israeli case discussed above illustrates, while democracies do not tend to initiate wars, they certainly employ preemptive strikes against dictatorships, which may amount to the same thing. Israel's preemptive strike in the war against her Arab neighbors, initiated in the first week of June 1967, is a famous example of this phenomenon.

To deter the risk-takers from moving against the status quo, the risk averse must convince them that the costs would be very high. Indeed, so high as to render a change in the status quo prohibitive. Nuclear deterrence is an effective tool employed by democracies against dictatorships. The position of Israel in relation to her Arab neighbors, or of India to Pakistan, are cases in point. In such cases, bargaining between two states with different utility functions does not, usually, lead to stable peace reinforced by domestic institutions. It could, however, lead to a state of 'no-war', a situation protected by the international community or by deterrent capabilities.[1]

In this section we built a deductive model of international relations and the advent of war to provide a theoretical grounding to the 'democratic peace' hypothesis. To provide a broad and intuitive understanding we avoided formal mathematical modeling. In the next section we survey a remarkable achievement by Fearon (1994) to provide a general game theoretic model of international bargaining that implies *deductively* the 'democratic peace' hypothesis.[2] The reader will notice that the underlying logic of the two arguments is similar and so we hope that this section has provided an intuitive introduction to the next.

7.5 A Game Theoretic Model that Implies the 'Democratic Peace' Hypothesis

The exercise of formalizing a bargaining situation in a rigorous game theoretic model necessitates a level of abstraction that forces the author to simplify the analysis considerably. Fearon's (1994) model is 'guilty' of this fault, but has the advantage and aesthetic quality of deductive reasoning at its best.

In this model two countries are involved in a crisis. They dispute a prize valued at $v > 0$. At any given time $t \in \{0,1,2,...,\infty\}$ a state can attack, quit or escalate a crisis (mobilizing troops, making harsh statements etc.). If either state initiates war, the two states get ω_1 and ω_2 respectively, where ω_1 and ω_2 denote the expected value of war including the share of the prize v but also counting the losses of fighting. For this reason ω_i is said to denote i's *resolve* to go to war. Without loss of generality, both ω_1 and ω_2 are set to be smaller than 0. If state $i \in \{1,2\}$ quits, state $j \in \{1,2\}$ gets the prize v and state i pays what Fearon (1994) calls the 'audience costs' $a_i(t)$ that is continuous and increasing function in t.

The idea behind the concept of the audience cost is straightforward. Fearon (1994) assumes that if a leader brags about war and then backs down, s/he suffers a loss of his or her reputation that may endanger his or her hold on power. These costs are increasing in t because as time goes by, the leader invests additional national resources and commitment, thereby making the so-called audience even more frustrated if s/he then backs down. Thus, if state i quits the crisis unilaterally, its opponent receives the prize while i suffers audience costs $a_i(t)$, a continuous and increasing function of t with $a_i(t = 0) = 0$.

In a game with complete information a strategy s_i specifies a finite time $t \geq 0$ at which state i decides whether to quit or to attack. $\{t, \textbf{attack}\}$ means escalate the crisis to time t and then attack. $\{t, \textbf{quit}\}$ means escalate to time t and then quit.

In a game with complete information, no crisis endures. Just like in the Rubinstein (1982) bargaining model presented in Chapter 1, both states are able to compute when the other will concede. This time of concession can be computed by taking into account both the value of the prize and the increasing audience costs. Once both states compute this point, the state which is likely to concede first is better off conceding at time $t = 0$ and avoiding audience costs.

In this model, crises escalate to full-blown war primarily because each side has incomplete information about the other side's resolve. Formally, let F_i be a cumulative distribution function with support $[\omega_i, 0]$ where $\omega_i < 0$. Assume that F_i has continuous and strictly positive density f_i. Loosely speaking, this notation means that f_1 represents the beliefs that state 2 has about the resolve of state 1 and f_2 represents the beliefs that state 1 has about the resolve of state 2. Each sate knows the exact value of its own resolve, but places some positive distribution on the level of resolve of the other state falling anywhere in the interval $[\omega_i, 0]$.

Definition 7.1: (Fearon, 1994: 583): A crisis has a *horizon* if there is a level of escalation such that neither state is expected to quit after this point is reached. Formally, let $Q_i(t)$ be the probability that state i quits on or before t in some Equilibrium. Then $t_h > 0$ is a horizon for [the game] Γ if in this equilibrium t_h is the minimum t such that neither $Q_1(t)$ nor $Q_2(t)$ increase for $t > t_h$.

The importance of the notion of the *horizon* here is that it denotes the threshold point in time after which war becomes inevitable. The logic behind this assertion is simply that if the probability of quitting is decreasing for both states, they would have quit earlier and are not going to quit now. This is the essence of the first result presented by Fearon (1994):

Lemma 7.1: (Fearon, 1994: 584): In any Equilibrium of Γ in which both states choose to escalate with positive probability, there exists a finite horizon $t_h < \infty$.

Lemma 7.1 is at the heart of all the results derived by Fearon (1994). Before describing these results, we use this occasion to introduce one last solution concept employed by Fearon (1994) to derive his results. This solution concept, commonly discussed in economics and political science literature, is only briefly introduced here. We refer interested readers to Osborn and Rubinstein (1994: 24-9; 231-43) for a comprehensive introduction of the concept.

Recall that $Q_i(t)$ is the probability that state i quits prior to or at time t if state i uses strategy s_i. Similarly let $A_i(t)$ be the probability that state i attacks prior to or at time t if state i uses strategy s_i. Define $Q_i^-(t) \equiv \lim_{t' \to t^-} Q_i(t')$. In words, $Q_i^-(t)$ is the limit of $Q_i(t')$ as t' approaches t from below, or the limit as t' approaches t with $t' < t$. State i's expected pay-off, being of type ω_i, for {t,quit} given s_j is:

$$U_i^q(t, \omega_i) \equiv Q_j^-(t)v + (Q_j(t)Q_j^-(t))((v - a_i(t))/2) + A_j(t)\omega_i + (1 - Q_j(t) - A_j(t)(-a_i(t)))$$

Similarly, i's expected pay-off, being of type ω_i, for {t, attack} given s_j is:

$$U_i^a(t, \omega_i) \equiv Q_j^-(t)v + A_j(t)\omega_i + (1 - Q_j^-(t) - A_j(t))\omega_i = Q_j^-(t)v + (1 - Q_j^-(t))\omega_i$$

It may be of interest to the reader to try and see why the above two equations follow, but here, suffice it to realize that $U_i^q(t, \omega_i)$ and $U_i^a(t, \omega_i)$ represent the expected pay-offs for state i of type ω_i for {t, quit} and {t, attack} respectively, given that state *j* has chosen to use s_j as its strategy. These notations allow Fearon (1994: 587) to define the Bayesian Nash Equilibrium for this game:

Definition 7.2: Fearon (1994: 587): {t', quit}{t', attack} is a best reply for type ω_i given s_j if: t'$\in$ $argmax_t\ U_i^q(t, \omega_i)$ and $U_i^q(t, \omega_i) \geq max_t\ U_i^a(t, \omega_i)$ or t'$\in$ $argmax_t\ U_i^a(t, \omega_i)$ and $U_i^a(t, \omega_i) \geq max_t\ U_i^q(t, \omega_i)$.

Definition 7.3: Fearon (1994: 587): (s_1, s_2) is a Bayesian Nash Equilibrium for the normal form version of [the game] Γ if (1) {F_i, s_i} $\Rightarrow$ {$Q_i(t), A_i(t)$}, and (2) under s_i, every type ω_i chooses a best reply, given s_j.

These definitions have two shortcomings. First, they fit a normal form game and this game is an extensive 'sequential' form game. Second, as we have seen time and again in previous chapters, the problem with the Nash Equilibrium concept is that too often it yields enormous equilibria sets. To deal with these two difficulties Fearon (1994: 588) provides the following definitions:

Definition 7.4: Fearon (1994: 588): In the extensive form, a complete pure strategy in [the game] Γ is a map s_i: $\Re^+ \times W_i \to \Re^+ \times \{quit, attack\}$, with the restriction that if $s_i(t', \omega_i) = \{t', quit\}$ or {t,attack} then t'$\leq$ t. For all t' $\geq$ 0 define the 'continuation game' $\Gamma(t')$ as follows: (1) pay-offs are as in [the game] Γ [described above]; and (2) 'initial beliefs' are given by a cumulative distribution function $F_i(\cdot; t')$ on W_i. A strategy s_i implies a strategy for state *i* in every continuation game $\Gamma(t')$; call this $s_i|t'$. Further, using $F_i(\cdot; t')$, $s_i|t'$ induces a pair of unique 'conditional' cumulative probability distribution $Q_i(t|t')$ and $A_i(t|t')$, analogous to $Q_i(t)$ and $A_i(t)$ already defined. From these, expected pay-off functions for $\Gamma(t')$, $U_i^q(t\,|\,t', \omega_i)$ and $U_i^a(t\,|\,t', \omega_i)$ follow as before.

This extension allows Fearon (1994: 588) to define the solution concept of a *Perfect Bayesian Nash Equilibrium* [PBNE] such that '(1) s_1 and s_2 induce Bayesian Nash Equilibria in every continuation game $\Gamma(t')$, and (2) beliefs $F_i(\cdot; t')$ are formed whenever possible using Bayes' Rule and s_i, while $F_i(\cdot; t)$ can be anything when Bayes' Rule does not apply.' The reader may want to refresh his or her memory of Bayes' rule and its use in this context by going back to section 3.6. With these notations [PBNE] is defined as follows:

Definition 7.5: (Fearon, 1994: 588): {(s_1, s_2), $F_1(\cdot; \cdot)$, $F_2(\cdot; \cdot)$}is a PBNE for Γ if:
1. (s_1, s_2) induces a Bayesian Nash Equilibrium in Γ and $\forall$ t $\geq$ 0, $(s_1|t, s_2|t)$ induces a Bayesian Nash Equilibrium in $\Gamma(t)$ using $F_1(\cdot;\cdot)$ and $F_2(\cdot;\cdot)$; and
2. for all t such that t is reached with positive probability under s_i, $F_i(\cdot; t)$ is $F_i(\cdot)$ updated using Bayes' Rule and s_i.
3. For all t > 0 such that $Q_i(t) + A_i(t) = 1$, $F_i(-a_i(t)\,; t) = 0$.

The first two conditions of Definition 7.5 are the usual restriction of the Perfect Nash Equilibrium refinement (1); the principle of Bayesian updating of beliefs in games with incomplete information (2) (Banks, 1991) and a restriction on beliefs off-the-equilibrium-path that could lead to nonsensical equilibrium behavior. To rule out such outcomes, restriction (3) is introduced.

We do not find it useful to delineate the formal results obtained by Fearon (1994) due to the technical complexity of the equilibrium conditions. Instead we cite Fearon's (1994: 585) own interpretation of these conditions in terms of the expected behavior of the players in equilibrium:

> Equilibrium behavior in the incomplete information game has the essential features of a war of nerves. At the outset, one side is expected to prefer to make concessions quietly, without public consent. This state concedes with some probability (k_1/v) at $t = 0$. If it does not ... its adversary immediately raises its estimate of the state's willingness to fight and the war of nerves begin. Neither side knows whether or exactly when the other might be locked in by increasing audience costs, but beliefs that the other prefers war ...steadily increase as audience costs accumulate. The reason is that states with low resolve are increasingly likely to have backed down, the more the crisis escalates. Ultimately, in crises that reach the horizon, the only ...states remaining have relatively high values for war... At this point, both sides prefer conflict to backing down, and both know this: attack thus becomes a rational choice.

Returning to the 'Democratic Peace' hypothesis (Fearon, 1994: 585):

> ...if Democratic leaders tend to face more powerful domestic audiences, they will be significantly more reluctant to initiate 'limited probes' in foreign policy. Showing this formally requires that we add structure to the model analyzed here, which does not represent an initial choice of one state to challenge or threaten the other. When such an option is added ... it is easily shown that the less sensitive state 1 is to audience costs, the greater the equilibrium probability that the state will try a limited probe. Finally, the equilibrium results bear on the question of how regime type influence the risk that a crisis will escalate to war. ...In the model, democratic leaders have a structural incentive to pursue more escalatory, committing strategies when they face authoritarians than when they face fellow democrats, and this can generate a greater overall chance of war.

So democracies are less likely to fight each other for three reasons. First, the signals they send are more 'revealing' because they are more costly. In this way democracies are more likely to get informed earlier and stop the escalation before it turns into full-blown war. Second, democracies bear higher audience costs and are therefore less likely to want to escalate a situation in the first place. Finally, they are more likely to escalate the situation against authoritarian regimes than against democratic ones. This last aspect of the model ties in and is consistent with empirical evidence that shows that democracies are not necessarily less prone to fight wars, but less likely to fight wars against each other as pointed out above.

We hope that the last two sections have clarified the difference between a statistical correlation followed by ad-hoc theorizing, and a deductive explanation. A statistical correlation is a fact. Just as we know how many wars have been fought in the last twenty years, we know the correlation between the regime type and the probability of war. Ad-hoc theorizing is just that. A deductive scientific explanation starts with primitive premises about the nature of the players involved and the structure of the interaction between them. If we are then able to derive from these primitives an equilibrium behavior that seems consistent with the observations collected, then we have provided a theoretical explanation for these observations. Doron and Sherman (1997) use a more verbal logical reasoning while Fearon (1994) uses applied mathematical, game theoretic derivation, but both engage in the same scientific mode of explanation.

Conclusions

We started our story with a rigorous description of individual decision-making. We moved on to describe how this individual decision-making can be assumed and shown to be logical and rational. But this rationality does not prevail at the collective decision-making level. We explained that to the extent that social decision-making processes show features of rationality and logic, it must be credited to some high level of similarity in individual preferences, or to formal and informal institutions that constrain and limit the freedom of the individuals that accept their authority. If we allowed social decision-making to mirror the diversity of preferences in the population at large, it would be unrealistic to expect it to get very far.

The constraints put on social choice processes in order to obtain reasonable decisions, limit the extent to which these decisions can be said to represent, in any meaningful way, the preference of individuals in society. But these preferences re-surface in different modes of bargaining permitted in well-ordained democracies, enabling groups and individuals to militate against and change decisions that led to outcomes far removed from their initial ideal preferences. We surveyed the logic of these bargaining processes, starting in Chapter 4 with the role of political entrepreneurs then in Chapters 5 and 6 looking at the logic of political bargaining and coalition formation in both parliamentary and bi-cameral presidential systems.

This chapter emphasized that the international arena is still, in many ways, stuck in the *state of nature*. International institutions have limited constraining effects on the behavior of individual sovereign states and thus individual states behave very much like individuals in the *state of nature*. Why then doesn't perfect chaos prevail? Because states are constrained by the 'audience costs' of their population, who prefer economic security to war, especially if war is unlikely to bring tangible advantage (Fearon, 1994), and by the natural risk aversion of their leaders (Doron and Sherman, 1997).

Notes

1. Note that there could be variations on the three types of dyadic relationships. As mentioned in the earlier section, to pursue national interests, a democracy may transform into a non-democratic regime, thus changing the shape of its decision-maker's utility function into risk taking. The conflict over Cyprus between the Turkish and the Greek armies illustrates this point.

2. In the early 1990s several such rigorous game theoretic models were advanced independently. We present here only Fearon's (1994) model for three reasons. First, it is a natural corollary to our discussion. Second, we do not have the space here to present further models. Finally, the most prominent 'competing' model (Powell, 1987, 1988, 1989, 1990) was developed and elaborated on in a book published by Cambridge University Press almost a decade ago (Powell, 1990). More recent attempts that deserve the attention of readers interested in bargaining models in international conflicts are: Morrow (1986, 1989), Powell (1993, 1996) and Schultz (1998).

Conclusion

Relationships between individuals and groups that define the essence of politics are as old as human civilization. In fact, we cannot speak of civilization in any meaningful sense without referring to its political aspects. This is so because any society is partly defined by the nature of its organizations and institutions.

Organizations and institutions induce the order and the direction of the flow of decisions made in society. They direct the choices made over collective priorities and devise means to satisfy collective needs. They determine which priorities deserve immediate attention and which can be put off to the future. These institutions may include, depending on the stage of human development, rituals, customs and manners, art, armies, police and courts, laws and regulations, symbols of identity, or schemes of distribution and redistribution of material resources.

Over time, variations among societies are merely the outcome of choices made in the context of changing circumstances. But these choices are always made through an ongoing process of bargaining between individuals.

While politics is a phenomenon that began with the first man and woman, its systematic and scientific study is relatively young – younger even than the study of economics. Perhaps the impressive advancements in the academic understanding of economics stem from the fact that this field of knowledge is better defined and delineated, in the sense that there is a clearer demarcation of what is included and what is excluded in the subject matter. It also utilizes established rules of transformation and interpretation, formal methodology and deductive logic. Political science lags way behind.

Would it make politics a more advanced science if the lessons of economics were applied to it? This was the belief and strategy in the 1950s and 1960s when efforts were being made to make the study of politics more scientific. Anthony Downs (1957) and Duncan Black (1958) were two notable economists whose methods influenced political scientists, in particular William Riker (1962) and his students. The formal language of science, the deductive logic and the rigorous methodology were adopted and applied to well-defined political phenomena such as coalitions and elections.

Ignoring the variation in starting points, the scientific study of politics still lags behind the scientific study of economics on account of difficulties in defining interpretation rules, problems in identifying stable and predictable outcomes, and a preoccupation with traditional perspectives.

Rules of Interpretation

Economists have a comprehensible medium to compare two or more items: money. Money is used to substitute for utilities, or for values of complex baskets of goods and services which otherwise, as in the case of 'apples and pairs', could not be compared. Money is a valid measuring tool, even if it often lacks accuracy and precision. Money is universally understood and widely sought after. Individuals, firms and corporations are all involved in an attempt to maximize (or optimize) revenues. We can define this attempt as aiming to gain more profit, benefit or revenue, depending on the approach used and the questions asked. Political scientists have no similar conceptual medium.

For years the study of politics has been guided by and has relied on problematic concepts. One salient example is the concept of 'power.' Politicians and nations were said to enter and play the game to maximize power. But what this concept means is not very clear (Riker, 1964b). Take another example, the concept of 'political culture'. Political culture is a subject that has attracted the attention of many students of politics. Even so, it is still not very clear what the term political culture means. While attempts have been made to mimic economists and to define a political equivalent for money, no political concept has yet been found with similar interpretation attributes.

This book does not provide a solution to this conceptualization problem. We explored the concept of political bargaining, a concept that is narrower in application, but clearer in meaning. Thus, for example, when we speak of the median voter theorem, or maximization of the probability of re-election, we are bringing the stuff of politics into the scientific sphere.

Explanations and Predications

Economists seem to have an easier task than political scientists: through their methodology and sets of assumptions they can identify general or local equilibrium points. If not in practice, then at least in theory. If not for the short term, then at least for the long term. Applying the theory, they can also predict future occurrences. Explanation and prediction is what science is all about (Hempel, 1966). It is more difficult to identify equilibrium points in political science. The reason for this is related to the nature of political phenomena.

We may approach the study of politics from the top or from the bottom. From the top, from the standpoint of politicians – those who affect the 'authoritative distribution of values'– social choices may reflect their own preferences and not those of their constituents. The economic analogue for such a situation would not last long: suppliers must meet the preferences of consumers or risk bankruptcy. From the bottom, from the standpoint of the citizens, the situation is no better. Both from a theoretical point of view and from a practical examination of reality, individual values, when aggregated into social choices, often lead to obvious inconsistencies. In fact, it has proven impossible to devise a scheme that would accurately reflect the desires of individuals in society (Arrow, 1951; Sen, 1970).

Thus there is always some measure of arbitrariness associated with the political choices arrived at by societies. The analogue in economics is the free market, where no such arbitrariness can survive. The central result that defines the very discipline of contemporary neo-classical economics states quite explicitly that in a market with enough buyers and sellers, sufficient information and well-defined property rights, the choices a society arrives at will necessarily be an optimal allocation of the scarce resources available. Not 'good', not acceptable, but deterministically *optimal*.

In politics we arrive almost at the other extreme. Because preferences over alternatives may be cyclical, it is difficult, indeed almost impossible, to evaluate whether social choices are the expression of aggregate individual preferences or if they are the result of a particular scheme employed to influence them. Thus, for any prevailing social outcome, a majority of people may prefer some other outcome. We cannot escape either from the arbitrariness associated with decisions made by politicians, nor can we be sure that those politicians selected by our democratic processes truly represent the people. Public preferences may thus be in a state of constant flux, making any political stability tenuous.

This disturbing finding and inference is not new. It was labeled by Riker (1980) as the 'disequilibrium of tastes', denoting the essence of the democratic dilemma. He writes 'outcomes are the consequences of not only institutions and tastes, but also of the political skills and artistry of those who manipulate the agendas, formulate and reformulate questions, generate 'false' issues, etc. in order to exploit the disequilibrium of tastes to their advantage' (Riker, 1980: 445). People vote, but the outcome of their choices may, at best, reflect an alternative that only tangentially represents their position.

There is today a considerable body of literature, much of which is cited in this book, suggesting that the institutional framework of the decision-making process induces equilibrium (most notably, Shepsle, 1979, 1986). Institutions in this sense are counter-cyclical mechanisms, they break cycles and produce stability. Since we can easily observe some measure of stability in the performance of the various organizations that define the fabric of a polity, we can accept the above-mentioned, so-called, neo-institutional explanation as a perfectly reasonable one. This book is built on the insights of this approach, but also develops its own explanation for the persistence of societal outcomes. The origin of social stability is maintained by social institutions, but is arrived at through an ongoing process of bargaining. To obtain stable choices (those which can be explained and thus predicted) in the framework of institutions and in the context of inconsistent preferences, people engage in a bargaining process. They bargain to stop cycles or to initiate them, they bargain over particular institutional configurations and their contents; they bargain over any aspect of what we conventionally refer to as politics.

The Political Bargaining Perspective

We believe that the particular perspective presented in this book – that of political bargaining – provides a realistic and hence a more profound explanation of politics. In spite of the impressive developments of recent years, and unlike advances made in economics, much of the study of politics remains descriptive (i.e. historical or statistical in essence) or normative. It is still dominated by answers to questions of 'what is' or 'what should be' and geared less to the positivist notion of 'why'. But without providing answers to the 'why', we cannot begin to hypothesize on the causal relationships linking the various components under investigation.

This book demonstrates how a view of politics as a bargaining process changes our understating of its nature. Utilizing several illustrations, it provides different but nonetheless verified explanations to phenomena that have been referred to as the conventional truths of the prevailing political reality. Only by emphasizing the role of bargaining in politics and in the way politicians determine the nature of the choices made in a given polity, could we begin to challenge the conventional wisdom associated with the notion of the *social contract* (Chapter 3); roles of parties and special interest groups (Chapter 4); or the nature of representation (Chapter 5).

This *social contract* is the result of an ongoing bargaining process between the rulers and the ruled, mitigated (or sometimes fueled) by the ongoing struggle between conflicting special interests. This and other political developments are outcomes of an ongoing bargaining process between various agents in any given society. The fact that on a macro level, much of the content of our political systems and their policies are similar, is perhaps proof that we are not so different from one another. We behave similarly, and arrive at more or less similar choices sooner or later because the logic of bargaining presented in this book presumably affect us all in the same way. If this is truly the case, then we have revealed potential grounds for generalization and for the advancement of the science of politics.

References

Abreu, D. and Ariel Rubinstein. 1988. 'The Structure of Nash Equilibria in Repeated Games with Finite Automata,' *Econometrica*, 56: 1259-82.

Ainsworth, Scott. 1993. 'Regulating Lobbyists and Interest Group Influence,' *The Journal of Politics*, Vol. 55: 41-56.

Ainsworth, Scott and Itai Sened. 1993. 'The Role of Lobbyists: Entrepreneurs with Two Audiences,' *American Journal of Political Science*, 37(4): 834-66.

Ainsworth, Scott and Marcus Flathman. 1995. 'Unanimous Consent Agreements as Leadership Tools,' *Legislative Studies Quarterly*, XX, 2: 177-95.

Aivazian, Varouj A. and Jeffrey L. Callen. 1981. 'The Coase Theorem and the Empty Core,' *Journal of Law and Economics*, 24: 175-81.

Aivazian, Varouj A., Jeffrey L. Callen and Irwin Lipnowski. 1986. 'The Coase Theorem and Coalition Stability,' *Economica*, 54: 517-20.

Aldrich, John H. 1993. 'Rational Choice and Turnout,' *American Journal of Political Science*, Vol. 37, 1: 246-78.

Aldrich, John H., Gary J. Miller, Charles W. Ostrom Jr. and David W. Rohde. 1986. *American Government*. Boston: Houghton Mifflin.

Anderson, Benedict. 1983. *Imagined Communities*. London: Verso.

Anderson, T.L. and J.P. Hill. 1975. 'The Evolution of Property Rights: A Study of the American West,' *Journal of Law and Economics*, 18(1): 163-79.

Arian, Asher and Michal Shamir. 1999. *The Election in Israel – 1996*, Abany: SUNY Press.

Aronson, Shlomo. 1978 *Conflict and Bargaining in the Middle East*. Baltimore: John Hopkins University Press.

Arrow, Kenneth. 1951. *Social Choice and Individual Values*. New Haven: Yale University Press.

Aumann, J. Robert and Michael Maschler. 1964. 'The Bargaining Set for Cooperative Games,' in Dreshler et al. *Advances in Game Theory*. Princeton: Princeton University Press.

Austen-Smith, David. 1983. 'The Spatial Theory of Electoral Competition: Instability, Institutions, and Information,' *Environment and Planning*, 1: 439-59.

Austen-Smith, David. 1996. 'Refinements of the Heart,' in N. Schofield (Ed) *Collective Decision-Making: Social Choice and Political Economy*. Boston: Kluwer Academic Publishers.

Austen-Smith, David and Jeffrey S. Banks. 1988. 'Elections, Coalitions and Legislative Outcomes,' *American Political Science Review*, 82: 405-22.

Austen-Smith, David and Jeffrey S. Banks. 1999. *Positive Political Theory I*. Ann Arbor: The University of Michigan Press.

Austen-Smith, David and William H. Riker. 1987. 'Asymmetric Information and the Coherence of legislation,' *American Political Science Review*, 81: 897-918.

Austen-Smith, David and John R. Wright. 1992. 'Competitive Lobbying for a Legislator's Vote,' *Social Choice and Welfare,* 19: 229-57.

Axelrod, Robert. 1980a. 'Effective Choice in the Prisoners' Dilemma,' *Journal of Conflict Resolution,* Vol. 24: 3-25.

Axelrod, Robert. 1980b. 'More Effective Choice in the Prisoners' Dilemma,' *Journal of Conflict Resolution,* Vol. 24: 379-403.

Axelrod, Robert. 1981. 'The Emergence of Cooperation Among Egoists,' *American Political Science Review,* Vol. 75: 306-18.

Axelrod, Robert. 1984. *The Evolution of Cooperation.* New York: Basic Books.

Axelrod, Robert. 1986. 'An Evolutionary Approach to Norms,' *American Political Science Review,* 80: 1095-112.

Banks, Jeffrey S. 1991. *Signaling Games in Political Science.* Chur: Harwood Academic Publisher.

Banks, Jeffrey S. and Randall L. Calvert. 1992. 'A Battle-of-the-Sexes Game with Incomplete Information,' *Games and Economic Behavior,* Vol. 4: 347-72.

Banks, Jeffrey S. and Rangarajan K. Sundaram. 1990. 'Repeated Games, Finite Automata, and Complexity,' *Games and Economic Behavior,* Vol. 2: 97-117.

Banks, Jeffrey S. and Joel Sobel. 1987. 'Equilibrium Selection in Signaling Games,' *Econometrica,* 55: 647-61.

Baron, David P. 1993. 'Government Formation and Endogenous Parties,' *American Political Science Review,* 87: 34-47.

Baron, David P. and John A. Ferejohn. 1989. 'Bargaining in Legislatures,' *American Political Science Review,* 83: 1181-206.

Barzel, Yoram. 1989. *Economic Analysis of Property Rights.* Cambridge: Cambridge University Press.

Barzilai, Gad and Itai Sened. 1998. 'How courts establish political status and how they lose it: An institutional perspective of judicial strategies.' Unpublished Manuscript, Tel Aviv University.

Bauer, Raymond A, Ithiel de Sola Pool and Lewis A. Dexter. 1968. *American Business and Public Policy.* New York: Atherton.

Bentham, Jeremy. 1952-4. *Jeremy Bentham's Economic Writings,* edited by Stark. Allen and Unwin, London.

Berlin, Isaiah, Sir. 1958. *Two Concepts of Liberty.* Oxford: Clarendon Press.

Bianco, William T. and Robert H. Bates. 1990. 'Cooperation by Design: Leadership, Structure and Collective Dilemmas,' *American Political Science Review,* 84, 133-149.

Binmore, Ken and Partha Dasgupta (Eds). 1987. *The Economics of Bargaining.* New York: Basil and Blackwell.

Black, Duncan. 1958. *The Theory of Committees and Elections.* Cambridge: Cambridge University Press.

Blau, J.H. 1972. 'A Direct Proof of Arrow's Theorem,' *Econometrica,* 40(1): 61-7.

Bluhm, William T. 1984. *Force or Freedom: The Paradox in Modern Political Thought,* New Haven: Yale University Press.

Box, Pelham H. 1967. *The Origin of the Paraguayan War (1929),* New York: Russel & Russel.

Brams, Steven J. 1980. *Biblical Games: A Strategic Analysis of Stories in the Old Testament.* Cambridge, Mass: The MIT Press.

Brams, Steven J. *Superpower Games: Applying Game Theory to Superpower Conflict.* New Haven: Yale University Press.

Brams, Steven J. 1994. *The Theory of Moves.* New York: Cambridge University Press.

Brams, Steven J. and Alan Taylor. 1996. *Fair Division*. New York: Cambridge University Press.

Buber, Martin. 1966. *I and Thou*. Edinburgh: T.N.T. Clark.

Buchanan, James M. 1975. *The Limits of Liberty*. Chicago: The University of Chicago Press.

Buchanan, James M. 1986. *Liberty, Markets and State*. New York: New York University Press.

Buchanan, James M. 1988. 'The Economic Theory of Politics Reborn,' *Challenge*, March-April.

Buchanan, James M. and Gordon Tullock. 1962. *The Calculus of Consent*. Ann Arbor: University of Michigan Press.

Budge, Ian and Michael Laver. 1985. 'Office Seeking and Policy Pursuit in Coalition Theory,' *Legislative Studies Quarterly*, 11: 485-506.

Bueno De Mesquita, Bruce. 1981. *The War Trap*. New Haven: Yale University Press.

Calvert, Randall L. 1995. 'Rational Actors, Equilibrium and Social Institutions,' in Knight and Sened (Eds) *Explaining Social Institutions*. Ann Arbor: Michigan University Press.

Cho, In-Koo. 1987. 'A Refinement of Sequential Equilibrium,' *Econometrica*, Vol. 55: 1367-89.

Cho, In-Koo and David Kreps. 1987. 'Signaling Games and Stable Equilibria,' *Quarterly Journal of Economics*, 102: 179-221.

Churchman, C. West. 1961. *Predictions and Optimal Decision*. Englewood Cliffs, N.J.: Prentice-Hall.

Coase, Ronald H. 1960. 'The Problem of Social Cost,' *Journal of Law and Economics*, Vol. 3: 1-44.

Coase, Ronald H. 1981. 'The Coase Theorem and the Empty Core: A comment,' *Journal of Law and Economics*, 24: 183-7.

Cohen, Herb. 1980. *You Can Negotiate Anything*. New York: Lyle Stuart.

Cohen, Raymond. 1990. *Culture and Conflict in Egyptian-Israeli Relations*. Bloomington: Indiana University Press.

Cox, Gary W. and Richard D. McKelvey. 1984. 'A Ham Sandwich Theorem for General Measures,' *Social Choice and Welfare*, 1: 75-83.

Crawford, Vincent P. 1987. 'A Theory of Disagreement in Bargaining,' *Econometrica*, Vol. 50(3): 107-37.

Cross, J.G. 1965. 'A Theory of the Bargaining Process,' *American Economic Review*, Vol. 55: 67-94.

Dahl, Robert. 1963. *Modern Political Analysis*. Englewood Cliffs, N.J.: Prentice-Hall.

Dasgupta, Partha. 1974. 'On Some Problems Arising from Professor Rawls' Conception of Distributive Justice,' *Theory and Decision*, Vol. 4: 325.

Demsetz, Harold. 1967. 'Toward A Theory of Property Rights,' *American Economic Review*, Vol. 57: 374-59.

Demsetz, Harold. 1969. 'Information and Efficiency: Another Viewpoint,' *Journal of Law and Economics*, Vol. 12: 1-22.

Demsetz, Harold. 1982. *Economic, Legal, and Political Dimensions of Competition*. Amsterdam: North Holland.

Doron, Gideon. 1986. 'Telling the Big Stories: Policy Response to Analytical Complexities,' *Journal of Policy Analysis and Management*, Vol. 5(4): 798-802.

Doron, Gideon. 1992. 'Rational Choices and the Policy Sciences,' *Policy Studies Review*, Vol. 3-4: 359-69.

Doron, Gideon. 1993. 'Peace or Oil: The Nixon Administration and its Middle East Policy Choices,' in Friedman and William Levantrosser. (Eds), *Cold War Patriot and Stateman*, Westport: Greenwood Press.

Doron, Gideon. 1996. *Strategy of Elections*. Rehovot: Kivunim.

Doron, Gideon. 1998. 'The Politics of Mass Communication in Israel,' *The Annals*, Vol. 555, January: 163-79.

Doron, Gideon and Moshe Maor. 1989. *Barriers to Entry into Israeli Politics*, Tel Aviv: Papyrus (Hebrew).

Doron, Gideon and Itai Sened. 1995. 'The Theory of Political Bargaining,' *Journal of Theoretical Politics*, 7(3): 301-09.

Doron, Gideon and Martin Sherman. 1995. 'A Comprehensive Decision-Making Exposition of Coalition Politics: The Farmer's Perspective of Size,' *Journal of Theoretical Politics*, 7(3): 317-33.

Downs, Anthony. 1957. *An Economic Theory of Democracy*, NewYork: Harper & Row.

Easton, David. 1953. *The Political System*. New York: Alfred A. Knopf.

Edwards, Paul. 1967. 'Hegel, George Wilhelm Friedrich,' in *The Encyclopedia of Philosophy*, 3-4: 435-51.

Eggertsson, Thrainn. 1990. *Economic Behaviour and Institutions*. Cambridge: Cambridge University Press.

Enelow, J. and M. Hinich. 1984. *The Spatial Theory of Voting: An Introduction*. Cambridge: Cambridge University Press.

Ensminger, J. and A. Rutten, 1990. 'The Political Economy of Changing Property Rights: Dismantling a Kenyan Commons,' Political Economy Working Paper No. 146, C PE, Washington University, St. Louis.

Epstein, Lee and Jack Knight. 1997. *Choices Justices Make*. Washington D.C. Congressional Quarterly Press.

Fearon, James D. 1994. 'Domestic Political Audiences and the Escalation of International Disputes,' *American Political Science Review*, Vol. 88(3): 577-93.

Feddersen, Timothy J., Itai Sened, and Stephen G. Wright. 1990. 'Sophisticated Voting and Candidate Entry Under Plurality Rule,' *American Journal of Political Science*. 34: 1005-16.

Fenno, F. Richard. 1966. *The Power of the Purse: Appropriation in Congress*. Boston: Little Brown.

Fenno, Richard. F. 1978. *Home Style: Representatives in Their Districts*. Boston: Little Brown.

Ferejohn, John and James Kuklinski (Eds).1990. *Information and Democratic Process*. Urbana: University of Illinois Press.

Friedman, James W. 1986. *Game Theory with Applications to Economics*. Oxford: Oxford University Press.

Friedman, Milton. 1953. *Essays on Positive Economics*. Chicago: Chicago University Press.

Frohlich, Norman, Joe. A. Oppenheimer and Cheryl L. Eavey. 1987a. 'Choices of Principles of Distributive Justice in Experimental Groups,' *American Journal of Political Science*, Vol. 31: 606-36.

Frohlich, Norman, Joe. A. Oppenheimer and Cheryl L. Eavey. 1987b. 'Laboratory Results on Rawls' Distributive Justice,' *British Journal of Political Science*, 17: 1-21.

Frohlich, Norman, Joe A. Oppenheimer and Oran R. Young. 1971. *Political Leadership and Collective Goods*. Princeton: Princeton University Press.

Frohlich, Norman and Joe A. Oppenheimer. 1974. 'The Carrot and the Stick,' *Public Choice*, Vol. XIX: 43-61.

Fudenberg, Drew and Erik Maskin. 1986. 'The Folk Theorem in Repeated Games with Discounting or with Incomplete Information,' *Econometrica*, 54: 533-54.

Furubotn, Eirik G. and Svetozar Pejovic. 1972. 'Property Rights and Economic Theory: A Survey of Recent Literature,' *The Journal of Economic Literature*, 110(4): 1137-62.

Furubotn, Eirik G. and Rudolf Richter. 1997. *Institutions and Economic Theory: The Contribution of the New Institutional Economics*. Ann Arbor: University of Michigan Press.

Gardner, R. and E. Ostrom. 1991. 'Rules and Games,' *Public Choice*, 70(2): 121-50.

Grofman, Bernard (Eds). 1993. *Information, Participation and Choice*. Ann Arbor: University of Michigan Press.

Groseclose, Tim and James M. Snyder. 1996. 'Buying Supermajorities,' *American Political Science Review*, Vol. 90(2): 303-15.

Hahn, Robert W., and Gordon L. Hester. 1989. 'Marketable Permits: Lessons for Theory and Practice,' *Ecology Law Quarterly*, Vol. 16.

Hammond, Thomas H. and Gary J. Miller. 1987. 'The Core of the Constitution,' *American Political Science Review*, 81: 1156-74.

Hardin, G. 1968. 'The Tragedy of the Commons,' *Science*, 162: 1243-48.

Hardin, Russell. 1971. 'Collective Action as an Agreeable n-Persons' Dilemma,' *Behavioral Science*, 16: 472-81.

Hardin, Russell. 1982. *Collective Action*, Baltimore: Johns Hopkins University Press.

Hayek, Friedrich A. 1945. 'The Use of Knowledge in Society,' *American Economic Review*, Vol. 135: 519-30.

Hayek, Friedrich A. 1967. 'Notes on the Evolution of Systems of Rules of Conduct,' *Studies in Philosophy, Politics, and Economics*. Chicago: Chicago University Press.

Hegel, George Wilhelm Freidrich. 1942(1821). *Hegel's Philosophy of Right*, Translated by T.M. Knox. New York: Oxford University Press.

Hempel, Carl. 1966. *Philosophy of Natural Sciences*. Englewood Cliffs: Prentice-Hall.

Hinich, Melvin J., John O. Ledyard and Peter C. Ordeshook. 1972. 'Nonvoting and the Existence of Equilibrium Under Majority Rule,' *Journal of Economic Theory*, Vol. 4: 144-53.

Hobbes, Thomas. 1968(1651). *Leviathan*. New York: Penguin Classics.

Holt, J.C. 1985. *Magna Carta and Medieval Government*. London: The Hambeldon Press.

Holt, J.C. 1992. *Magna Carta.* Cambridge: Cambridge University Press.

Homans, George. 1950. *The Human Group*. New York: Harcourt Brace & World

Hotelling, Harold.1929. 'Stability in Competition,' *Economic Journal*, Vol. 39:41-57.

Huber, John D. 1996. 'The Vote of Confidence in Parliamentary Systems,' *American Political Science Review*, Vol. 90(2): 269-83.

Hume, David. 1752. *Essays Moral Political and Literary Part II*. London: Cadell.

Hume, David. 1888. *A Treatise of Human Nature*, L.A. Sely-Bigge (Ed). Oxford: The Clarendon Press.

Kant, Imannuel. 1963. 'Perpetual Peace' (1795) *On History*. New York: Bobbs-Merril.

Kant, Imannuel. 1981 (1785). *Grounding for the Metaphysics of Morals.* Indianapolis: Hackett.

Karsh, Efraim and Inari Ruasti. 1991. *Saadam Hussein: A Political Biography,* London: Brassy.

Knight, Jack. 1992. *Institutions and Social Conflict*, Cambridge: Cambridge University Press.

Knight, Jack and Itai Sened (Eds). 1995. *Explaining Social Institutions*. Ann Arbor: Michigan University Press.

Kook, Rebecca. 1995. 'Dilemmas of Ethnic Minorities in Democracies: Palestinians in Israel,' *Politics and Society*, 23(3): 309-36.

Kook, Rebecca. 1992. 'The Politics of Production of Corporate National Identity within Democratic Regimes.' Ph.D. Thesis. Columbia University.

Kollman, K., J.H. Miller and Scott E. Page. 1992. 'Adaptive Parties in Spatial Elections,' *American Political Science Review*, Vol. 86: 929-37.

Kreps, David M. 1997. 'Economics – The Current Position,' *Daedalus*, Vol. 126(1): 59-86.

Kreps, David M. and Robert Wilson. 1982. 'Sequential Equilibria,' *Econometrica*, 50: 1003-37.

Kreps, David M. and Gary Ramey. 1987. 'Structural Consistency, Consistency, and Sequential Rationality,' *Econometrica*, 55: 1331-48.

Krehbiel, Keith. 1992. *Information and Legislative Organization*. Ann Arbor: The University of Michigan Press.

Kuhn, Thomas S. 1970. *The Structure of Scientific Revolutions*. Chicago: University of Chicago Press.

Lakatos, Imre. 1970. 'Falsification and the Methodology of Scientific Research Programmes,' in Lakatos and Musgrave (Eds) *Criticism and the Growth of Knowledge*. Cambridge: Cambridge University Press.

Lakatos, Imre. 1978. *Methodology of Scientific Research Programmes, Philosophical Papers,* Volume I, Edited by J. Worrall and G.P. Currie, Cambridge: Cambridge University Press.

Laver, Michael and Norman Schofield. 1990. *Multi-Party Governments*. Oxford: Oxford University Press.

Laver, Michael and Kenneth A. Shepsle. 1990. 'Coalition and Cabinet Government,' *American Political Science Review,* 84: 873-90.

Laver, Michael and Kenneth A. Shepsle. 1996. *Making and Breaking Governments*. New York: Cambridge University Press.

Ledyard, John O. 1984. 'The Pure Theory of Large Two-Candidate Elections,' *Public Choice*, Vol. 44: 43-7.

Levi, Margaret. 1988. *Of Rule and Revenue*. Berkeley: University of California Press.

Lewis, David. 1969. *Convention: A Philosophical Study*. Cambridge, Harvard University Press.

Libecap, Gary D. 1989. *Contracting for Property Rights*. New York: Cambridge University Press.

Locke, John. 1980(1690). *Second Treatise on Government*, Indianapolis: Hackett.

Luce, Duncan R. and Howard Raiffa. 1967. *Games and Decisions: Introduction and Critical Survey*. New York: Wiley.

MacIntyre, Alasdair. 1988. *Whose Justice? Which Rationality?* Notre Dame: University of Notre Dame Press.

Mayhew, David. 1974. *Congress: The Electoral Connection*. New Haven: Yale University Press.

Maoz, Zeev and Bruce Russett. 1992. 'Alliance, Contiguity, Wealth and Political Stability: Is the Lack of Conflict Among Democracies a Statistical Artifact?' *International Interactions*, Vol. 17: 245-67.

McDonald, John and G.D. Snooks. 1986. *Domesday Economy*. Oxford: Clarendon Press.

McKelvey, Richard D. 1976. 'Intransitivities in Multidimensional Voting Models and Some Implications for Agenda Control,' *Journal of Economic Theory*, 12: 472-82.

McKelvey, Richard D. 1979. 'General Conditions for Global Intransitivities in Formal Voting Models,' *Econometrica*, Vol. 47:1085-112.

McKelvey, Richard D. 1986. 'Covering, Dominance and Institution Free Properties of Social Choice,' *American Journal of Political Science*, Vol. 30: 283-314.

McKelvey, Richard D. and Norman Schofield. 1987. 'Generalized Symmetry Conditions at a Core,' *Econometrica*, Vol. 55: 923-33.

McKelvey, Richard D. and R.E. Wendell. 1976. 'Voting Equilibria in Multidimensional Choice Spaces,' *Mathematics of Operations Research*, 1: 144-58.

Milbarth, Lester W. 1963. *The Washington Lobbyists*. Chicago: Rand McNally.

Mill, James. 1955(1820). *Essay on Government*. Indianapolis: Bobbs-Merrill Co. Inc.

Mill, John Stuart. 1979(1861). *Utilitarianism*. Indianapolis: Hackett.

Mill, John Stuart. 1979(1861). *On Liberty*. Indianapolis: Hackett.

Mill, John Stuart. 1862. *Considerations on Representative Government*. New York: Harper and Brothers.

Mills, C.W. 1956. *The Power Elite*. New York: Oxford University Press.

Mitchell, William C. and C. Munger. 1991. 'Economic Models of Interest Groups,' *American Journal of Political Science*, Vol. 135: 512-46.

Moe, T.M. 1980. *The Organization of Interests*. Chicago: Chicago University Press.

Montessori, Maria. 1932. *Peace and Education,* Geneva: Bureau of Education.

Montesquieu, Charles Louis De Secondant. 1949 (1748). *The Spirit of Law*. Translated by Thomas Nugent. New York: Hafner.

Morgenthau, Hans. 1967. *Politics Among Nations: The Struggle for Power and Peace,* New York: Alfred Knopf.

Morrow, James D. 1986. 'A Spatial Model of International Conflict,' *American Political Science Review,* Vol. 80(4): 1131-50.

Morrow, James D. 1989. 'Capabilities, Uncertainty and Resolve: A Limited Information Model of Crisis Bargaining,' *American Journal of Political Science,* Vol. 33: 941-72.

Morton, R.B. 1987. 'A Group Majority Voting of Model of Public Good Provision,' *Social Choice and Welfare,*Vol. 4: 117-31.

Moyniham, Daniel P. 1970. *Maximum Feasible Misunderstanding*. New York: Free Press.

Mueller, John. 1989. *Retreat from Doomsday, The Obsolescence of Major War*, New York: Basic Books.

Muthoo, A. 1995. 'Bargaining in a Long Term Relationship with Endogenous Termination,' *Journal of Economic Theory*, 66(2): 590-8.

Myerson, Roger. 1978. 'Refinements of the Nash Equilibrium Concept,' *International Journal of Game Theory*, Vol. 7: 73-80.

Nash, John. 1950a. 'The Bargaining Problem,' *Econometrica,* Vol. 18(2): 155-62.

Nash, John. 1950b. 'Equilibrium Points in n-Person Games,' *Proceedings of the National Academy of Science, USA*, Vol. 36(1): 48-9.

Nash, John. 1951. 'Non-Cooperative Games,' *Annals of Mathematics,* 54(2): 286-95.

Nash, John. 1953. 'Two Persons Cooperative Games,' *Econometrica*, Vol. 21: 128-40.

Niemi, Richard and Herbert Weisberg. 1968. 'A Mathematical Solution for the probability of the Paradox of Voting,' *Behavioral Science,* 13: 317-23.

Noll, Roger. 1985. 'Government Regulatory Behavior: A Multidisciplinary Survey and Synthesis,' in R. Noll (Ed) *Regulatory Policy and the Social Sciences*. Berkeley: University of California Press.

North, Douglass C. 1981. *Structure and Change In Economic History*. New York: Norton.

North, Douglass C. 1984. 'Government and the Cost of Exchange in History,' *Journal of Economic History*, 44(2): 255-64.

North, Douglass C. 1986. 'Institutions, Economic Growth and Freedom: An Historical Introduction,' in M.A. Walker (Ed) *Freedom Democracy and Economic Welfare I*, Proceedings of an International Symposium, Vancouver: The Fraser Institute.

North, Douglass C. 1987. 'Institutions, Transaction Costs and Economic Growth,' *Economic Inquiry*, 125(3): 419-28.

North, Douglass C. 1990. *Institutions, Institutional Change and Economic Performance*, Cambridge: Cambridge University Press.

North, Douglass C. 1993. 'Economic Performance Through Time,' presented as the Prize Lecture in Economic Science in Memory of Alfred Nobel.

North, Douglass C. and Andrew R. Rutten. 1987. 'The Northwest Ordinance in Historical Perspective,' in Klingman and Vedder (Eds) *Essays on the Economy of the Old Northwest*. Athens: Ohio University Press.

North, Douglass C. and R.P. Thomas. 1973. *The Rise of the Western World: A New Economic History*. Cambridge: Cambridge University Press.

North, Douglass C. and Barry W. Weingast. 1989. 'The Evolution of Institutions Governing Public Choice in 17th Century England,' *Journal of Economic History*, Vol. 49: 803-32.

Nozick, Robert. 1975. *Anarchy, State and Utopia*. New York: Basic Books.

Ofek, Dganit, Kevin Quinn and Itai Sened 'Voters, Parties and Coalition Formation in Israel: Theory and Evidence,' Washington University, Unpublished Working Paper.

Olson, Mancur, Jr. 1965. *The Logic of Collective Action*. 2nd edn. Cambridge: Harvard University Press.

Olson, Mancur, Jr. 1993. 'Dictatorship, Democracy, and Development,' *American Political Science Review*, Vol. 83(3): 567-76.

Olson, Mary. 1995. 'Regulatory Agency Discretion among Competing Industries: Inside the FDA,' *The Journal of Law, Economics and Organization*, 11(2): 379-405.

Ordeshook, Peter C. 1986. *Game Theory and Political Theory*, Cambridge: Cambridge University Press.

Osborn, Martin J. and Ariel Rubinstein. 1994. *A Course in Game Theory*, Cambridge, Massachusetts: The MIT Press.

Ostrom, Elinor. 1990: *Governing the Commons*, Cambridge: Cambridge University Press.

Ostrom, Elinor. 1986: 'An Agenda for the Study of Institutions,' *Public Choice*, 148: 3-25.

Palfrey, Thomas R. 1984. 'Spatial Equilibrium with Entry,' *Review of Economic Studies*, Vol. 51: 139-56.

Palfrey, Thomas R. and Howard Rosenthal. 1984. 'Participation and the Provision of Discrete Public Goods: A Strategic Analysis,' *Journal of Public Economics*, Vol. 24: 71-93.

Palfrey, Thomas R. and Howard Rosenthal. 1985. 'Voter Participation and Strategic Uncertainty,' *American Political Science Review*, Vol. 79: 62-78.

Palfrey, Thomas R. and Howard Rosenthal. 1988. 'Private Incentives in Social Dilemma: The Effects of Incomplete Information and Altruism,' *Journal of Public Economics*, Vol. 28: 171-93.

Pelletiere, Stephen C. 1992. *The Iran-Iraq War: A Chaos in a Vacuum*. New York: Praeger.

Peltzman, Sam. 1976. 'Towards a More General Theory of Regulation,' *Journal of Law and Economics*, Vol. 35: 133-48.

Peretz, Don and Gideon Doron. 1997. *The Government and Politics of Israel*. Boulder: Westview Press.

Plott, Charles. 1967. 'A Notion of Equilibrium and its Possibility Under Majority Rule,' *American Economic Review*, 57: 787-806.

Plott, Charles R. 1976. 'Axiomatic Social Choice: An Introduction and Overview,' *American Journal of Political Science*, Vol. 20: 511-96.

Poole, Keith and Howard Rosenthal. 1991. 'Patterns of Congressional Voting,' *American Journal of Political Science*, Vol. 35: 228-43.

Popper, Karl R. 1959. *The Logic of Scientific Discovery*, London: Hatchinson.

Potters, Jan and Frans van Winden. 1996. 'Models of Interest Groups: Four Different Approaches,' in N. Schofield (Ed) *Collective Decision-Making: Social Choice and Political Economy*, London: Kluwer Academic Publishers.

Poundstone, William. 1992. *Prisoners' Dilemma*. New York: Doubleday.

Powell, G. Bingham. 1982. *Contemporary Democracies: Participation, Stability and Violence*. Cambridge: Harvard University Press.

Powell, Robert. 1987. 'Crisis Bargaining, Escalation and MAD,' *American Political Science Review*, Vol. 81(3): 717-35.

Powell, Robert. 1988. 'Nuclear Brinkmanship with Two-Sided Incomplete Information,' *American Political Science Review*, Vol. 82(1): 155-78.

Powell, Robert. 1989. 'Nuclear Deterrence Theory and the Strategy of Limited Retaliation,' *American Political Science Review*, Vol. 83(2): 503-519.

Powell, Robert. 1990. *Nuclear Deterrence Theory: The Search of Credibility*. Cambridge: Cambridge University Press.

Powell, Robert. 1993. 'Guns, Butter and Anarchy,' *American Political Science Review*, Vol. 87(1): 115-32.

Powell, Robert. 1996. 'Uncertainty, Shifting Power and Appeasement,' *American Political Science Review*, Vol. 90(4): 749-64.

Pressman, Jeffrey L. and Aaron Wildavsky. 1973. *Implementation*. Berkeley: University of California Press.

Rae, Douglass. 1967. *The Political Consequence of Electoral Law*. New Haven: Yale University Press.

Rappoport, Anatol and Melvin Guyer. 1966. 'A Taxonomy of 2X2 Games,' *General Systems*, Vol. 11: 203-14.

Rasmusen, Eric. 1989. *Games and Information*. Cambridge: Basil Blackwell.

Riker, William H. 1957. 'Events and Situations,' *The Journal of Philosophy*, Vol. LIV: 57-70.

Riker, William H. 1962. *The Theory of Political Coalitions*. New Haven: Yale University Press.

Riker, William H. 1964. *Federalism: Origin, Operation, Significance*. Boston: Little Brown.

Riker, William H. 1964b. 'Some Ambiguities in the notion of Power,' *American Political Science Review*, 58(2): 341-9.

Riker, William H. 1965. *Democracy in the United States*, 2nd edn. New York: The Macmillan Co.

Riker, William H. 1971. 'Public Safety as a Public Good,' in E. Rostow (Ed) *Is Law Dead?* New York: Simon & Shuster.

Riker, William H. 1976. 'Comments on Vincent Ostrom's Paper,' *Public Choice*, Vol. 27: 13-5.

Riker, William H. 1980. 'Implications From the Disequilibrium of Majority Rule For the Study of Institutions,' *American Political Science Review*, Vol. 74: 432-46.

Riker, William H. 1982. *Liberalism Against Populism*. San Francisco: Freeman.

Riker, William H. 1986. *The Art of Political Manipulation*. New Haven: Yale University Press.

Riker, William H. 1988. 'The place of political science in public choice,' *Public Choice*, 57: 247-57.

Riker, William H. 1990. 'Civil Rights and Property Rights,' in E.F. Paul and H. Dickman (Eds) *Liberty, Property, and the Future of Constitutional Development*. Albany: SUNY Press.

Riker, William H. 1995. 'The Experience of Creating Institutions: The Framing of the United States Constitution,' in Knight and Sened (Eds) *Explaining Social Institutions*, Ann Arbor: University of Michigan Press.

Riker, William H. and Peter Ordeshook. 1968. 'The Calculus of Voting,' *American Political Science Review*, 62: 25-42.

Riker, William H. and Peter C. Ordeshook. 1973. *An Introduction to Positive Political Theory*. Englewood Cliffs: Prentice-Hall.

Riker, William H. and Itai Sened. 1991. 'A Political Theory of the Origin of Property Rights: Airport Slots,' *American Journal of Political Science*, Vol. 35: 951-69.

Roth, E. A. 1979. *Axiomatic Models of Bargaining*. New York: Springer Verlag.

Rousseau, Jean-Jacques. 1987 (1757). *The Social Contract*. Indianapolis: Hackett.

Rubinstein, Ariel. 1982. 'Perfect Equilibrium in a Bargaining Problem,' *Econometrica*, Vol. 50(1): 97-109.

Rubinstein, Ariel. 1985. 'A Bargaining Model with Incomplete Information about Time Preferences,' *Econometrica*, 53(5): 1151-72.

Rubinstein, Ariel. 1986. 'Finite Automata Play in Repeated Prisoners' Dilemma,' *Journal of Economic Theory*, Vol. 3: 83-96.

Rubinstein, Ariel. 1991. 'Comments on the Interpretation of Game Theory,' *Econometrica*, 59(4): 909-24.

Salisbury, Robert H. 1969. 'An Exchange Theory of Interest Groups,' *Midwest Journal of Political Science*, Vol. 13: 1-32.

Samuelson, Paul. 1947. *Foundations of Economic Analysis*. Cambridge, MA: Harvard University Press.

Samuelson, Paul. 1954. 'The Pure Theory of Public Expenditure,' *Review of Economics and Statistics*, Vol. 36: 387-90.

Samuelson, Paul. 1955. 'Diagrammatic Exposition of the Theory of Public Expenditure,' *Review of Economics and Statistics*, Vol. 37: 350-6.

Schelling, Thomas C. 1960. *The Strategy of Conflict*. Cambridge: Harvard University Press.

Schelling, Thomas C. 1984. *Choice and Consequences: Perspective of an Errant Economist*. Cambridge, MA: Harvard University Press.

Schofield, Norman. 1978. 'Instability of Simple Dynamic Games,' *Review of Economic Studies*, Vol. 45: 575-94.

Schofield, Norman. 1983. 'Generic Instability of Majority Rule,' *Review of Economic Studies*, Vol. 50: 695-705.

Schofield, Norman. 1984. 'Generic Properties of Simple Bergson-Samuelson Welfare Functions,' *Journal of Mathematical Economics*, Vol. 7: 175-92.

Schofield, Norman. 1984a. 'Social Equilibrium and Cycles on Compact Sets,' *Journal of Economic Theory*, Vol. 33(1): 59-71.

Schofield, Norman. 1984b. 'Classification Theorem for Smooth Social Choice on a Manifold,' *Social Choice and Welfare*, Vol. 1: 187-210.

Schofield, Norman. 1985a. 'Anarchy, Altruism and Cooperation,' *Social Choice and Welfare*, Vol. 2, 207-19.

Schofield, Norman. 1985b. *Social Choice and Democracy*. New York: Springer Verlag.

Schofield, Norman. 1986 'Existence of a 'Structurally Stable' Equilibrium for a non-Collegial Voting Rule,' *Public Choice*, Vol. 51: 267-84.

Schofield, Norman. 1990. 'An Empirical Analysis of the Conditions for Stable Coalition Governments,' presented at the Conference on Political Science in honor of W.H. Riker, University of Rochester, Rochester, New York, October 11-14.

Schofield, Norman. 1993. 'Party Competition in a Spatial Model of Coalition Formation,' in W. Barnett, M.J. Hinich and N. Schofield (Eds) *Institutions, Competition and Representation*. Cambridge: Cambridge University Press.

Schofield, N. 1995. 'Existence of a Smooth Social Choice Functor,' in W. Barnett, H. Moulin, M. Salles and N. Schofield (Eds) *Social Choice, Welfare and Ethics*. Cambridge: Cambridge University Press.

Schofield, Norman. 1996. 'The Heart of a Polity,' in Schofield, N. (Ed.) *Collective Decision Making,* Boston: Kluwer.

Schofield, Norman. 1999. 'The Heart and the Uncovered Set,' *Journal of Economics* 8: 79-113.

Schofield, Norman, Itai Sened and David Nixon. 1998. 'Nash Equilibria in Multiparty Competition with 'Stochastic' Voters,' *Annals of Operations Research*, 84: 3-27.

Schofield, Norman and Itai Sened. 2000. 'Political Equilibrium in Multiparty Democracies,' Unpublished manuscript, Washington University.

Schofield, Norman and Robert Parks. 2000. 'Nash Equilibrium in a Spatial Model of Coalition Bargaining,' *Mathematical Social Science*, 39: 133-147.

Schotter, Andrew. 1981. *The Economic Theory of Social Institutions*, Cambridge: Cambridge University Press.

Schultz, Kenneth A. 1998. 'Domestic Opposition and Signaling in International Crises,' *American Political Science Review,* Vol. 92(4): 829-44.

Selten, Reinhard. 1975. 'Reexamination of the Perfectness Concept for Equilibrium Points in Extensive Games,' *International Journal of Game Theory*, Vol. 4: 25-55.

Sen, Amartya K. 1970. *Collective Choice and Social Welfare*. San Francisco: Holden Day.

Sen, Amartya K. 1974. 'Rawls Versus Bentham,' *Theory and Decision*, 4: 301-10.

Sen, Amartya K. 1982. *Choice, Welfare and Measurement*. Cambridge: MIT Press.

Sen, Amartya K. 1986. *On Ethics and Economics*. New York: Blackwell.

Sened, Itai. 1991. 'Contemporary Theory of Institutions in Perspective,' *Journal of Theoretical Politics*, Vol. 3(4): 379-402.

Sened, Itai. 1995a. 'A Political Theory of the Evolution of Rights,' in J. Knight and I. Sened (Eds) *Explaining Social Institutions*. Ann Arbor: The University of Michigan Press.

Sened, Itai. 1995b. 'Equilibria in Weighted Voting Games With Side-Payments,' *The Journal of Theoretical Politics*, Vol. 7(3): 283-300.

Sened, Itai. 1996. 'A Model of Coalition Formation: Theory and Evidence,' *The Journal of Politics*, Vol. 58(2): 350-72.

Sened, Itai. 1997. *The Political Institution of Private Property*. Cambridge: Cambridge University Press.

Sened, Itai. 1999. 'Uniqueness of a Cheapest Minimum Coalition in Multiparty Parliamentary Systems,' Working Paper, Washington University in St. Louis.

Sened, Itai. 2000. Review of Institutions and Economic Theory: The Contribution of The New Institutional Economics, By Eirik G. Furubotn and Rudolf Richter. *Journal of Economic Literature*, Vol. XXXVIII: 1721-2.

Sened, Itai and William H. Riker. 1996. 'Common Property and Private Property: The Case of Air Slots,' *Journal of Theoretical Politics*, Vol. 8(4): 427-49.

Sharkansky, Ira. 1982. *Public Administration,* San Francisco: W.H. Freeman.

Shepsle, Kenneth A. 1979. 'Institutional Arrangements and Equilibrium in Multi-dimensional Voting Models,' *American Journal of Political Science*, 23: 27-59.

Shepsle, Kenneth A. 1986. 'Institutional Equilibrium and Equilibrium Institutions,' in Herbert F. Weisberg (Ed) *Political Science: The Science of Politics*. New York: Agathon Press.

Shepsle, Kenneth A. 1990. *Models of Multiparty Competition*. Chur: Hardwood Academic Press.

Shepsle, Kenneth A. and Barry R. Weingast. 1981a. 'Structure-Induced Equilibrium and Legislative Choice,' *Public Choice*, Vol. 37: 503-19.

Shepsle, Kenneth A. and Barry R. Weingast. 1981b. 'Political Preferences for the Pork Barrel: A Generalization,' *American Journal of Political Science*, Vol. 25(1): 96-111.

Sherman, Martin. 1998. *Despots, Democrats and Determinants of International Conflict*. London: MacMillan.

Sherman, Martin and Gideon Doron. 1997. 'War and Peace as Rational Choice in the Middle East,' *Journal of Strategic Studies*, Vol. 20(1): 72-102.

Simon, Herbert. 1957. *Models of Man*, New York: John Wiley.

Simon, Herbert. 1982. *Models of Bounded Rationality*. Cambridge: MIT Press.

Simmel, Georg. 1955. *Conflict and the Web of Group-Affiliation*. New York: The Free Press.

Simpson, A.W.B. 1986 (1962). *A History of The Land Law*, Oxford: Oxford University Press.

Skottowe, B. Constable. 1886. *A Short History of Parliament*. London: Swan Sonnenschein, Lowry & Co.

Stigler, George J. 1942. *The Theory of Competitive Price*, New York: McMillan

Stigler, George J. 1971. 'The Economic Theory of Regulation,' *Bell Journal of Economics and Management Science*, 2(3): 3-21.

Strøm, Kaare. 1990. *Minority Government and Majority Rule*. Cambridge: Cambridge University Press.

Sugden, Robert. 1986. *The Economics of Rights, Co-operation and Welfare*. Oxford: Basil Blackwell.

Taylor, Michael. 1987. *The Possibility of Cooperation*, New York: Cambridge University Press.

Tefler, D. 1999. 'Bargaining with Asymmetric Information in Non-Stationary Markets,' *Economic Theory*, 13(3): 577-601.

Tsebelis, George and Jeanette Money. 1997. *Bicameralism*. New York: Cambridge University Press.

Tuftee, Edward R. 1978. *Political Control of the Economy*. Princeton: Princeton University Press.

Ullmann, Edna. 1977. *The Emergence of Norms*, Oxford: The Clarendon Press.

Umbeck, John R. 1981. *A Theory of Property Rights*. Ames: Iowa State University Press.

Von Neumann, John and Oskar Morgenstern. 1944. *The Theory of Games and Economic Behavior*. New York: Wiley.

Weber, Max. 1958. 'Politics as a Vocation,' in H.H. Gareth and W.C. Mills (Eds) *From Max Weber*. New York: Oxford University Press.

Weimer, David L. and Aidan R. Vining. 1989. *Policy Analysis: Concepts and Practice*. Englewood Cliffs, Prentice-Hall.

Wildavsky, Aaron. 1974. *The Politics of Budgetary Process*. 2nd edn. Boston: Little Brown.

Williamson, Oliver. 1986. 'The Economics of Governance: Framework and Implications,' R.N. Langois (Ed) *Economics as a Process: Essays in the New Institutional Economics*. Cambridge: Cambridge University Press.

Wittman, Donald, 1989. 'Why Democracies Produce Efficient Results,' *Journal of Political Economy*, Vol. 97 (6): 1395-424.

Wittman, Donald, 1995. *The Myth of Democratic Failure*. Chicago: The University of Chicago Press.

Index